INSIGHT AND INTUITION
(a guide to psychic unfoldment)

INSIGHT AND INTUITION
(a guide to psychic unfoldment)

JULIE SOSKIN

Published by
Light Publishing

First published in 1996 by
Light Publishing
The College of Psychic Studies
16 Queensberry Place, London, SW7 2EB

Printed 1996
Reprinted 1998

British Library Cataloguing-in-Publication Data

A catalogue record of this book
is available from The British Library
ISBN 0 903336 13 8 (hardback)
ISBN 0 903336 14 6 (paperback)

The aim of LIGHT PUBLISHING and THE COLLEGE OF PSYCHIC STUDIES is to explore all aspects of spiritual and psychic knowledge.

The views expressed in all books published by LIGHT PUBLISHING and THE COLLEGE OF PSYCHIC STUDIES are those of the author, and do not necessarily reflect the views of The College of Psychic Studies.

"We have room for all who realise the importance, in a materialistic age, of expressing a belief that there is something behind matter and that death does not end all. . ." *From a preliminary meeting of the College, November 1883. This was the declared note of the then new College and it remains so to this day.*

Printed and bound in Great Britain by
Whitstable Litho Printers Ltd., Whitstable, Kent.

CONTENTS

INTRODUCTION

What was for me a life-long interest became my profession. Over the years, my work has brought me many strange experiences and encounters, on many different levels, and it has also offered me a tremendous richness of opportunity on a deep, soul level. In focussing on the psychic, the unseen forces, we have automatically to observe ourselves, which takes us consciously into the never-ending process of unfoldment.

The definition of the much-misused word "psychic" is; "of, or pertaining to, phemomena that appear to come from outside the domain of physical law". It comes from the Greek word "psyche", meaning, "of, or pertaining to, soul, mind and spirit". In Greek mythology, it is the personification of the human soul. It is also the name of a Greek goddess, in whose story we may find some illumination.

Psyche was a mortal princess, with whom the god Cupid (Eros to the Romans) fell in love, to the dismay of his mother, Aphrodite (Venus), who was jealous of Psyche's beauty. Aphrodite imposed impossible tasks on the princess, but despite great hardship Psyche managed to perform all of them, and Aphrodite finally relented, giving her the cup of immortality to drink. As she drank, two butterflies' wings manifested from her being.

A winged girl is a relic of the conception of the soul as a bird or insect. This illustrates the Platonic philosophy of love, in its highest sense, as an agent of the progress of the soul. The story reveals that through experience and knowledge we grow, and that through the heart we ultimately metamorphose into immortality, at which time we shall understand the soul's eternal flame.

The story has a happy ending, for not only did Cupid's happiness melt Aphrodite's heart so much that she danced at the wedding, but their first child was a daughter, whom they named Joy.

The word "psychic" is the adjective that relates to the noun "psyche", and as such it is a very appropriate description indeed, for it draws us into the very same transformative process that the princess Psyche discovered.

Psychic awareness is but a by-product of spiritual growth: seek it for itself and you will always be led down cul-de-sacs. However, the discipline entailed in any psychic work is a wonderful furtherance of greater living. Rather than abandoning psychic exercises, let us recognise the pitfalls of psychic work, and continue to use them wholeheartedly, as a perfect aid in the transformational process of the spiritual being.

When used properly, psychic unfoldment can and does enhance the progress of the soul. We know that there are many pitfalls, and that we must at all times be watchful, but every path in life is potentially dangerous, and to stagnate will cause disease. We must have courage. One's true intent is one's greatest beacon for advancement.

When a student first visits me to be interviewed for a psychic development group, they have probably had a feeling of inner precipitation: a feeling that there is more to life than the normal, three-dimensional experience, a feeling that something, or someone, is trying to tell them something that is not yet quite within their grasp.

It is their own inner voice that is speaking to them, but it is impossible to say what, if anything, triggers this. Some students have had psychic experiences, possibly brought on by a great shock or trauma, but often it happens over a long period of time, with a feeling of some distant memory trying to enter the consciousness.

Recently, however, what could be called the awakening process has started to happen quickly, and this leads to problems of how to maintain an anchor and a balance.

During my twelve years of teaching, there has been a steady rise of these experiences, and the demand for classes is now so huge that it is difficult to accommodate all who are interested. A mass awakening is taking place, and it is happening to many people who previously would either have ridiculed this subject or simply dismissed it. An interest in all matters psychic is now very much part of the general awareness. Every week, in any daily newspaper, some affiliated topic is being written about, and no longer with derision. The media, which in the past have treated the subject either as a joke or as some sensational way of scaring people, as in horror films, are now at a loss to know how to report it. We are, however, beginning to see some intelligent journalism on what is perhaps the most important aspect of the end of this millenium.

There are many theories as to why this is happening. Some would say that it is because the power of organised religions has dwindled, and in that there may be some truth, not necessarily because the church has failed, but because humanity has spiritually come of age. People are no longer satisfied with dogma, for they are recognising their spirituality within, as a personal experience of truth. How easy it was just to follow the words of a priest, teacher or elder.

Spiritual maturity means we now have to
THINK FOR OURSELVES.

Psychic awareness is part of spiritual growth, and all of us, whether or not we are conscious of it, are on the spiritual pathway. We are all learning and growing on all levels. Perhaps because the spiritual self has taken a back seat for so long, it now requires a period of concentration in order to catch up.

In my channelled books there is much reference to the changing times, and one cannot now refer to psychic growth without mentioning this aspect. As I understand it, humankind has reached a point of consciousness-expansion which has taken it to the edge of a band of energy. This means, in effect, that we have arrived at a point of break-through to another state of awareness. Critical mass is occurring.

The one at the top of the mountain sees a very different terrain from the one at the bottom or the one halfway up. None of them is aware of what the others can see, but that does not mean that all viewpoints are not equally valid. Humanity is coming into a different space of awareness. We are beginning to contact what, for many, is still unseen. Of course, there are many different levels and frequencies of unseen forces: on the material level, electricity is unseen, but we all accept it as a reality because our light bulbs work. Thus, one way of accepting psychic energy is by actualising the force. Here, however, we may fall into a trap, for in my opinion there is no complete physical way of proving psychic realities. The only incontrovertible evidence lies deep within the inner knowing of the individual. When the ones at the top of the mountain look out over the world, they believe what they see. It is their reality, because that is where they are. When individuals see with their inner eyes, they too, know.

This is not an intellectual thought-process. It is not even a feeling. It is the deep, inner knowing of intuition, and true intuition is rarely wrong. The trick lies in isolating it from the clutter of the outer worlds and of the intellectual mind. The intellect is a wonderful instrument, and can do many amazing things, but it is simply the wrong instrument for contacting the intuition. Indeed, in order to focus on the unseen forces, you must let go of the intellect. This does not, of course, mean abandoning it (you will still need it!), but if one wishes to learn how to focus the intuition, one must learn to quiet the busy, chattering mind. This, then, is the benefit of meditation, and of similar relaxing states.

Recently there has been a popular craze for "magic eye" pictures. At first glance, these seem to be no more than a pattern formed of random images, but by concentrating "through" the pattern we are able to see a three-dimensional picture within the two-dimensional pattern. To obtain a view of this picture, you need to shift your focus. Psychic work is exactly the same, in that it, too, requires a shift of focus. Someone who neither believes in, nor cares about, the presence of the second image, will never see it, because they will not bother to look for it. This is the "Catch 22" situation of trying to prove psychic reality, for unless someone knows it exists, they simply would not train their senses in order to receive it. This knowing comes from the same inner push, the inner awareness that we have just acknowledged.

Developing our psychic faculties, then, is mainly a question of training ourselves to focus. A psychic must, above all else, be observant of all experiences, and the first aspect of development must be to focus on, and to learn about, oneself. No one is perfect, but psychic work is certainly not for the careless mind: indeed, it requires great discipline and dedication. The rewards in knowledge and self growth are plenty, but the road to psychic awareness is paved with difficulties, which is why it is essential to obtain some degree of inner balance from the outset. Unfortunately I have seen too many untrained, or inadequately trained, psychics falter. The idea that it is some gift from Heaven, requiring no assistance from us, is nonsense. Any naturally gifted person, for example an athlete or a pianist, will still need to develop and focus that gift, and the same is true of the psychic faculties. Anyone with fingers can, with enough patience, learn to play a tune on the piano, but very few will become concert pianists. Equally, anyone who is truly interested can develop their psychic skills to some degree, but few will work in the field. This does not matter, though, for the training and discipline involved will enable you to live a happier and more productive life. One of my fellow students once remarked to me, "I know I will never make a medium, but I equally know that this work has made me a better person".

During the writing of this book, the difficulty involved in

selecting material became obvious. The problem was not a shortage of possible contents, but an over-abundance: at least one complete book could have been written on the subject of each chapter. In the process of selection, I have deliberately veered towards the construction of a basic framework for psychic students, and have endeavoured to give a healthy skeleton upon which you can build. It is up to each student to explore particular subjects further if desired, and to this end I have listed books for guidance and reference, most of which are comprehensive.

Please, from day one, realise that psychic unfoldment is not a precise science, and that you must take full responsibility for your own energy. I hope that you will read, understand and enjoy this work with an open heart and mind. It has obviously been written from my own perspective, and if you read things with which you disagree, that is perfectly all right: every teacher to whom you feel drawn will reveal to you something of value. Never feel that there is only one truth and only one teaching, for this leads to fundamentalism and bigotry. The pure energy of the Universal Light Force exists within everything. The way it is received is dependent upon the outer veils of both teacher and pupil.

The rewards are plenty, and the exploration of relatively unknown territories is thrilling. It is a very long road, and one that has no end. It is always exciting, always challenging, always expansive. Enjoy your development. Enjoy your life.

Very much love, JULIE.

(July, 1996).

Dedicated to the memory of my father, who died earlier this year.

With every death there must come birth, for it is the spirit of life that we must cherish.

Its invocation is the clearest bell resounding across space and time.

It propels us out of despair, it reaches out to us from the darkness, and through the veils we catch glimpses of transcendence.

Your unassuming truth spoke to me in my growth, and your graceful humility quietly had its effect.

You had disregard for privilege, and never aspired to position or wealth, admitting logic and intuition as your only mentors.

Your uncompromising, innate truthfulness never faltered. Your curiosity, your quest for answers and your love of knowledge inspired.

You expected nothing, and by example taught me truth. A good soul: not perfect, but, my father, you were perfect for me.

In death we can understand the meaning of life, knowing all we have is that indomitable spark that carries us, as every father carries us home.

Thank you. Julie.

ACKNOWLEDGEMENTS

Most grateful thanks go to my "spellchecks" at home; to Trish, my new-found angel, who helped the text to blossom; and to The College of Psychic Studies, for both publishing this work and providing me with the "grit" to help polish my stone!

Throughout this book, when an individual is referred to, the words "they", "their", "them", and "themselves" have frequently been used in place of the expressions "he or she", "his or her", "him or her", and "himself or herself". The author is aware of the grammatical incorrectness of these substitutions, which have been made in order to avoid the excessively complex sentences otherwise necessitated by the recognition of gender issues.

Chapter 1
OPENINGS

Right action calls for right thinking, and before beginning your psychic unfoldment you must ask yourself a fundamental question. Why do you want to further your development? If it is for entertainment, or because you think your psychic abilities will give you the upper hand in life, you are in for quite a shock, because, like any worthwhile goal, psychic development requires effort and dedication. One of the most common misconceptions in this field is that some teacher or guru, or perhaps an exercise, mantra or teaching, has all the answers, but the only person who ultimately has the answers is you, and therefore it is with you that we must start.

This book has been kept as simple as possible. The meditations and exercises are tried and proven, but they are only guidelines, and of themselves they will not bring you instant redemption or instant knowledge. The urge towards true psychic unfoldment must originate from a genuine desire to expand and unify with the higher forces in the universe, for the good of yourself and for the good of humanity.

You must be prepared to work on yourself, to examine yourself without reservation, and to observe yourself, knowing that you will find many illusions, imbalances, negativities and faults. If you have really committed yourself, the process becomes easier. If, however, you are not prepared to put in the time and effort required for self-illumination, you will not develop much beyond the lower psychic fields, and you might as well put away this book now. If, on the other hand, you decide to take this powerful step, the rewards are plenty, and beneath all the veils of illusion you will find the real you, the Light, the goodness and the truth.

In modern life we spend a lot of time blocking out extraneous sounds, but now we must learn to LISTEN. The art of listening is extremely important. We must learn to listen to ourselves. It is therefore advisable deliberately to set aside a little time each day or each week, for meditation. Even two to five minutes of quality time can be enough.

There are different schools of thought on meditating. Speaking from experience, it feels more natural to meditate when you want to, and not to force yourself, because in forcing yourself you create a tug-of-war within. Eventually, if you will persevere, there will come a time when the whole of your life is a meditation. For most people, however, it starts with a simple early discipline.

What better place to start your focus than with your own breath? Find a quiet spot, close your eyes, and listen to your own breathing, making sure that there is nothing pushed or forced, just the gentle rhythm of your own natural breath. Breathing is something we all do, every moment of every day. To focus upon it allows us to focus on the natural movement of life and the life force. Listening to your breathing, and attuning to your breath, feeling a part of your breath, will take you automatically into your deep, inner silence; the still place within. If you have never meditated before, this may take a little practice, but do not put yourself under any pressure: progress will happen naturally. The simple act of listening to your breathing is putting you into the quiet state, helping you to develop what will become the major "tool of the trade", which is OBSERVATION.

Gently focussing on your inner stillness, become fully aware of it. Feel it and know it, recognising, if you can, that this is the core of your being, the hub of the wheel. Everything else around you may be in turmoil, but this part is always present, always still.

When you really feel that you are in contact with this deep, silent energy, allow your breath to "catch" the stillness, and breathe it outwards into the whole of your body, through every nerve, fibre and cell of your being. Then, as though it were a ripple on a pond, continue to breathe it outwards from your physical body and into your aura, like waves of light from the silent stillness at your centre. Focus on this process until you feel these waves of light a healthy distance away from your body, which is approximately an arm's length. You may wish to hold that stillness by visualising a golden band around the outer areas of your aura. (The aura is formed of the subtle energy fields which emanate from the body. A force field that vibrates according to your thoughts, emotions and physical state, it is discussed comprehensively in Chapter Six). This connection with the breath is valuable for all stages of development, and in the early stages try it every day. It need only take a few minutes, and it is of immense value.

ENERGY FOLLOWS THOUGHT

Everything in the universe is composed of energy, and you are no exception. Over the last ten years or so there has been a glut of books on the market about positive thought. Many of them have real value, especially if you are a person who is in the habit of being gloomy. To be aware of what you say to others is an eye-opener. Listen to yourself speak. How many of your statements are negative ones? For instance, we often prefix our sentences with "I can't", or," I'm afraid" What sort of message is that sending out to the world? By consciously changing our negative words, we begin to look at our reactions, thereby automatically changing our energy and vibration. In time, and through this change of magnetism, our world will alter. Affirmations are also enormously helpful for introducing positive energy into any scenario, especially a health condition.

Positive thought can indeed transform a situation, but its use on its own, without a connection with the core soul self, will not fully integrate the spiritual self. If, however, you contact your innate positive energy as just explained, then you immediately begin to set about the process of illumination.

Consciously opening up to spiritual forces is a major aspect of psychic development, and any psychic development group will give you some instruction on "opening up." When students "open up", they are, in effect, summoning the unison of Light Forces to them in the service of humanity. It is as though you are sending out an arrow of light to the higher realms, and you cannot consciously open up without acknowledging what I shall refer to as the Universal Light Force Energy. You may use other words to describe this energy: Divine or Cosmic Consciousness, the Creating Force, or simply God. It is the energy of which we are all a part, and within each of us it exists as a spark of Light. This Light within is the hub of the wheel described in the exercise. Acknowledging it brings us into greater touch with all other beings.

At this point you will probably automatically want to be of service. This obviously necessitates some healthy degree of balance, which can only come through self awareness. You can learn this, not in some distant dimension or in some heavenly world: it is here in every moment of your waking, conscious life. In opening up, you are effectively saying that you wish to create a person who is aligned to Light, and the first step in alignment is clearance of all negative energies. Unfortunately these negative aspects in your life may have become habitual, and for some strange reason most people are reluctant to create any change. Change is not only inevitable: it is also essential for growth. Once you have touched the inner Light Force within, it sets about illumination, shining outwards, and revealing any inconsistency or imbalance. If you just watch, being observant at all times, correction becomes a natural process of balance through aligned desire.

Think about our planet. Take your mind above the globe for just a moment. Our world is spinning on its axis. It is spinning at 66,000 miles per hour around our sun, which in turn is, with the rest of the solar system, hurtling around the universe at 630,000 miles per hour. With that recognition, it is difficult not to understand that movement is growth. The cosmos is part of a kaleidoscope of energies, the colours moving and blending, connecting and interacting, with each other and with us. Acknowledge the dance of the cosmos, thereby acknowledging your dance of life.

Students should initially aim to observe themselves consciously at least two or three times a week. Do this in a detached manner, particularly when there are interpersonal reactions and irritations. Observe how you feel, and observe how the other party reacts to you. In time you may be able consciously to shift your own reaction, and whilst you are doing so, observe again the other party - the observations will be fascinating. Please remember to observe without judgement or criticism. In the early stages, the intensity of awareness of imbalance can make you feel critical of yourself. Guilt is not only an unnecessary emotion: it can also be very destructive.

We all occasionally find ourselves off-balance, and we all fall prey to illusions. If you are looking, it is likely that you are prepared to face them, and by the process of shining a light on any such situation, it will in time automatically dissolve: just by observing your negativities you will feel uncomfortable with them, and so you will want them removed. Be gentle but firm.

A student's first experience with "opening up" usually comes within a group situation, but working within a group is not essential, as long as you have no reservations or fears. Always project your intentions in a focused way, and ask for the greatest good to work through you. Then you are perfectly safe.

YOUR GREATEST - AND ULTIMATELY YOUR ONLY - PROTECTION IS AN OPEN, LOVING, PURE, HEART.

Having mastered the breathing, and, more importantly, being prepared and able to let go of day-to-day worries, let us now focus on the psychic centres commonly called chakras. There are a great many teachings and books based on these energies: please explore these if you wish. I use them here, not as a magic formula but as a focus. "Chakra" comes from the Sanskrit word meaning "Wheel", or "Disc". It is a spinning vortex of energy created by the connection between the consciousness and the physical body. The chakras are unseen with normal vision, but act rather like internal "floppy discs" that hold the programming of all our conditions. The chakra points do not exist in any specific place in the body, but are referred to in association with different areas, because the vibration of each place has a corresponding vibration of energy. However, the human mind, the conscious mind, the little mind, needs structures. It is an unusual student who is able immediately to by-pass the human thought process, so it is better that we give the mind a point on which to concentrate.

Number One: The Base, or Root, Chakra.
    Located at the base of the spine. This centre is always open: its energy is connected to the earth and to physical survival, and it therefore only closes on death. The flow of energy from this centre extends downwards through the legs and feet, and into the earth, like a tap root. When it is flowing properly, the individual may be considered to be "grounded". Grounding is essential as a foundation for anything we wish to achieve in life, but particularly psychic development. In this work you must aim to keep your feet on the ground at all times. The Base centre's natural colour is red, and its feeling is best described as "I have".

Number Two: The Sacral Centre.
    Located approximately three or four vertebrae up from the base of the spine, level with the top of the reproductive organs. This chakra is also connected with survival, this time through reproduction, creativity and expansion. It is an energy of pure force that can, if properly trained, be extremely beneficial. Its colour is orange, and its feeling is best described as "I desire, I want, or I feel."

Number Three: The Solar Plexus, or Power, Centre.
    Located around the stomach area. This centre is often

described as lower mental or emotional energy. It is yellow in colour, and reacts rather like the digestion it rules, for it is a transformative energy. It is the "I can" energy.

Number Four: The Heart centre.
The point of balance, the middle way. It is love without conditions, total self-acceptance and equilibrium. Its colour is green. Not surprisingly, it is best described as "I love."

Number Five: The Throat Centre.
The centre of communication and sound. This is the first centre that utilises the spiritual qualities of your being. For its activation, you must have made the decision to walk forward into the Light, regardless of the consequences. It's colour is bright sky-blue, and its feeling is described best as "I speak."

Number Six: The Brow, or Ajna, Centre.
The centre of vision. It is known in the West as the Third Eye, although this label is deceptive: strictly speaking, the Third Eye is located behind the brow, in the area of the pineal gland. The Brow centre is therefore the window to the Third Eye. It is activated in the intuitive person. It is sight beyond sight. Its colour is Indigo, and its feeling is best described as "I see."

Number Seven: The Crown Centre.
Our connection with the Divine Light Source. Like the Base centre, it is ever open whilst we live. It is pure thought. It is limitless consciousness, which we really cannot fully comprehend. Its colour is violet, and its feeling is best described as "I Know."

The seven chakras can also relate to phases of man in evolution. For instance, the Base energy is the survival energy that we could ascribe to early primitive man. Having evolved as a race, we are vibrating now between the third (power consciousness) and the fourth (love) rays. These energies can also be equated with individual progression from infancy to old age.

The chakra colours correspond to the colours of the rainbow - the principle energetic vibrations of our Earth-plane existence. As the pure white Divine Universal Light enters the Crown, our body becomes like a prism, reflecting the Light into the different areas as different colours of the spectrum, so that it manifests as violet, mutating to indigo, then blue, and so on, as it passes through the physical.

Since colour is the human brain's translation of energy, the simplest and most effective way of opening up is to breathe energy into each chakra point. The colours directly relate to the type of energy emanating from the centre.

Red is the colour of the volcanic, vibrant, inner Earth: the physical life force.

Orange is the colour of flame, the orange flames being the ones that ignite the fire. The Sacral energy is a force that leaps and rises like a flame, giving energy to other centres when it is flowing properly. It is the "rocket" energy: it gets things moving.

Yellow connects with sunlight, and when we think of the sun we think of openness, warmth, sympathy and compassion.

Green is the perfect colour for the middle centre, for it relates to the natural things that we see all around us. Nature seeks always to balance and equalise, and the Heart centre is our point of equilibrium. Moreover, what could be more natural than Love, which is the Heart's energy?

Moving now to the Throat, the first of the spiritual centres, we look upwards, to the blue of the sky. Through this centre we automatically lift our horizons above the ground in order to look at areas beyond ourselves, beyond the third-dimensional state.

Indigo, often associated with gem-stones and sharp, crystalline light, opens our eyes to the vibrational energies of crystals. These are a powerful communication focus, both on our planet and in other worlds, and through their energy we can "see" other dimensions.

Violet is the highest colour in the spectrum. It is often used to imply wisdom or power, and can be seen, even today, in the robes of kings and priests, although its significance is long-forgotten by most people. The crown is our most powerful chakra: it leads us back into the white Light of the Divine Universal Consciousness.

When you are working with the colours, try to connect fully with them, and to absorb their energy. There are many minor chakras which are also often active, but the seven described above are the focus of all the main aspects of living.

The centres are not located in the organs: for instance, the Heart centre is not located in the actual organ of the heart and if all this is new to you, you may find it easiest to visualise the centres along the spinal column. For instance, your Heart centre can be contacted at the spot level with the heart organ, but in the middle of the spine. Do not worry too much about the precise location of the centres, because in practising the following exercise you will locate them naturally:

Gently focus on each breath, breathing once, twice, or three times into each centre starting at the Base or the Crown. If you find your mind wandering, lead it gently back into these areas.

This exercise is multi-faceted, for it serves as a focus for meditation, and allows contact with psychic energies, but perhaps most importantly it is a healing and balancing exercise. Learning to heal yourself is fundamental to psychic growth, and this simple exercise can set the healing process in motion, even after practising it only once or twice. In concentrating energy into each centre, you will become familiar with the energies, automatically adjusting them by the focus of your breath.

In the early stages of this work, it is a good idea to "close down" after any experiential exercise. In the original Tantric system, each chakra is described as a lotus flower, and each lotus blossom has a different number of petals, starting at the Base with only four, and ending with the "many-petalled" or "one-thousand-petalled" Crown. We can therefore effectively use this image to open and close the centres. If you want to "close down", then, the easiest way to do so is by visualising each of your centres individually as a flower, and seeing the petals gently close. If you prefer, you can use the visualisation of an open window or door closing.

A great deal of discussion surrounds the closing procedure, and much emphasis is placed on the importance of "being closed." Unfortunately in the past much of this was born of ignorance or fear, so let us be very clear on this matter: your energy belongs to you, and to no one else. Please do not give it away. It is your responsibility right from the outset, and the only thing that can harm you is your own fear.

The majority of the population have their three lower chakras open all the time. The Base is the energy of the Earth. It is what allows us to breathe, and to exist physically. The Sacral is the second base centre. It is survival, creativity, and earthly power. The third centre, the Solar Plexus, is the energy of emotional feelings and sympathy. These are all aspects of ourselves which we need all the time, and even after closing down these centres, the moment you feel or respond to anything, they are open again. It is good to know how to close them, for it enables you to be conscious of your own energies, but it is impossible to keep them permanently shut. However, through your own meditational observations you will be in control, and have the ability to adjust your energies when required. For the majority of people, this is the first time they take control of their energy - and therefore their life.

Most students arrive at a time when they are extremely open to outer energies and influences. This could be confusing, and may affect their health, so to experience and practise closing is invaluable, as it allows students to feel their own energies, and to differentiate between them and those of the outer worlds.

Another frequent problem for an untrained psychic is a draining of energy. Some people are like leeches. Without realising it, they draw on the energies of others, and if you ever feel depleted by anyone, it is probably because they are draining yours from your Solar Plexus. If you are observant you will be aware that this is happening. It is most important to block the drainage, and if you become aware of it while it is occurring, a very quick method of protection is to fold your arms over your Solar Plexus. If you are sitting, you could also cross your legs. This will instantaneously close the open doorway of your energy. Alternatively, visualise yourself in a circle of golden light: you can create this at any time if you feel threatened in any way. Actively allowing a loss of energy from your Solar Plexus is not advisable. It is usually done out of sympathy, but in fact it does not help the other person for very long. Never be tempted to use your energy in this way. Why deplete your lower mental and emotional energies when you have access through your Heart to the Universal Light Force, with its unending energy.

As you end any exercise, create your own focused closing procedure as a habit, like brushing your teeth before bed. A good programme for this is to be aware of your connection with the Light Force as a channel. Remember your Crown and Base centre are always open. The Crown being your link to the divine and your Base being your link to the earth. Draw the Universal Light down through your Crown centre into the Brow. Then, as a ritual, visualise it CLEANSING, CLEARING, and if you feel the need, helping to CLOSE the centres down. When you reach the Base, you can visualise its energy as being connected to the Earth. There is no need to be concerned if you are uncomfortable with visualisation, as just "thinking" the process will have the desired results. Energy follows thought, whether through visualisation or simple mental process. Visualisation is only used as a focus, a means to an end.

Over the years many students have commented on certain physical disturbances whilst opening the various chakra points, and the most common disturbance occurs in the Throat. This is nothing to be concerned about, and is largely due to the Throat being the least-used of the centres. When a student begins consciously to open the centres, it is a bit like a creaky, unused door, which needs oiling. After a very short period of time the discomfort will go, and then the disappearance of these disturbances becomes just as puzzling! In general terms, a disturbance indicates an obstruction of energy. With gentle perseverance this will clear, and when it does, the disturbance will disappear. The student will feel nothing, other than a sense of expansion.

Please remember that every individual senses these subtle forces differently. Never measure yourself against any other person. We all develop at our own pace. Because the student is very often more than ready to open when starting these exercises, there may be an initial rush of energy, which usually subsides very quickly. There can be many plateaux in development, and some of these even necessitate shifting one's concentration back to the physical worlds. In the developing process, we have to balance every aspect of the being, including and especially the material and physical. Acknowledge and work only with what is right for you, even if that means differing from others' ideas on the subject.

In no way does the psychic development process contradict any true religious beliefs. Indeed, you do not even have to have any beliefs in order to study. Most people, however, can accept that there is a Force which is greater than the personality self. How one perceives it is unimportant. The energy to which I refer is pure Force, beyond any verbal description. It is this "energy-which-is-beyond-words" that is perhaps the only real truth, for truth changes according to the perspective from which one views it. Insisting that your truth is the only truth is not only foolish: it can lead to fanaticism. When you find a good thing, you want to share it, and that is quite natural, but even someone on a similar wavelength is unlikely to experience energies in exactly the same way as you. The most important thing, therefore, is to follow only those things which ring completely true for you. One of the joys of this work lies in observing different people, from different walks of life and different cultures, joining together in unison. The Universal Light Force manifests itself as Love within the human condition, and to be connected to it is to be connected to Love's creation, which is joy.

EXERCISE

This is a basic opening exercise, which you can adjust to your own specifications when needed.

Find a quiet spot, and be comfortable. Sitting with your arms and legs uncrossed is advisable, because it creates an open flow of energy, and your limbs will not go to sleep. It is also a good idea, at least to begin with, to keep your feet firmly on the floor.

Even at this stage "pure motive" is of paramount importance. Be prepared to let go of your every-day cares. Take two or three deep breaths, consciously releasing any negativity on the out-breaths. LET GO. If you need a visualisation to help you, think of yourself under a crystal clear waterfall, which is massaging you, cleansing you of all your anxieties and troubles. Pay particular attention to stress areas. Make sure that your jaw is relaxed, and that the tongue is not clenched against the roof of the mouth. Feel the flow in your neck, and imagine your shoulder blades opening to let out all the pent-up tension. Release the upper arms, and loosen the hands and feet. The discipline of letting go is paramount for the ability to focus for psychic work. Moreover, it is a wonderful exercise in stress management, furthering your equilibrium and growth.

Close your eyes, and listen to your own breathing: nothing pushed or forced, just the gentle rhythm of your own natural breath. Breathe clearly and steadily, feeling your whole self to be at one with your breath. Carry on concentrating until you feel really comfortable. The simple act of listening to your breath is very powerful: even a couple of minutes will draw you directly into your inner stillness. When you are comfortable, breathe the stillness throughout your body, and out into your auric space; waves of energy like ripples on a pond, expanding and expanding, until you feel and know yourself to be perfectly still and steady within your own energy. If you wish you can visualise a golden band of light on the outer area of your aura, containing your energy while you work.

Continue by sending your thoughts up to the highest possible spiritual Light Force. It does not matter how you perceive this, but please do not limit yourself. Reach up for it, connecting with it as energy, and feeling it drawing downwards, entering your Crown chakra and flowing through into all the others. Feed it through every part of you, being particularly conscious of your connection and unison with your own inner stillness. If necessary, repeat this part of the exercise, ensuring that you reach up to the highest levels. Remember that energy follows thought, so do not limit yours.

Continue by taking your focus gently but firmly into your Heart centre. Spend a few moments breathing into that area, remembering to keep your breath very steady and rhythmic, so that you are giving out just as much energy as you are drawing in. Feel and know the balance in that centre, and become accustomed to it, so that at any time, be it during a meditation or in your every-day life, you will be able to centre yourself. This is energy management.

When you feel ready, carry on by gently taking your focus to each chakra point. To begin with, you might find it easier to visualise the corresponding colour. At your own pace, breathe at least three times into each centre. Allow these breaths to be perfectly normal, nothing forced or pushed. Starting with your Base centre as the vibrant Earth red; into the Sacral, the orange flame; into the Solar Plexus, yellow sunlight energy; into the Heart, Nature's green; through into the Throat, sky blue; into the Brow, deep crystal Indigo; and lastly into the Crown, where the violet hue leads from the physical state into the pure white Light of Spirit. When you reach the Crown centre, connect consciously with your spiritual self, and hold that connection for a while, experiencing, if possible, yourself as a spiritual being of Light.

Using this simple procedure, you can then go on to focus on

your own meditation. Alternatively, you can use it as a concentration of energy, enabling you to focus psychically on what is appropriate for you. Transmit to the Divine Consciousness that you wish for guidance for personal growth, and illumination on anything that is impeding the process. You will probably not receive this information whilst in meditation, but if the desire for truth is genuine, you will receive insight within twenty-four or forty-eight hours. This often happens when you expect it least - perhaps whilst engaged in a simple, mundane activity such as washing, ironing, or driving your car. This is because at such times the mind is usually more open, being free of the limitations and barriers of concentrated mental activity.

During this procedure you can, if you wish, give yourself key words or phrases upon which to meditate. Some useful examples are:

OBSERVATION.

ENERGY FOLLOWS THOUGHT

THE ART OF LISTENING.

UNCONDITIONAL LOVE.

AN OPEN, PURE, LOVING HEART.

When you have finished, remain aware of your connection with the Light Force above you. Once again, draw it down through the top of your head into the Crown centre, and go through the basic ritual energy-cleansing process:

CLEANSE, CLEAR AND CLOSE each centre in the manner previously described. That is, visualise the closing of a flower, door or window. Work downwards through your Brow, Throat, Heart, Solar Plexus and Sacral centres, and when you come to the Base, feel its energy like a tap root, digging deep into the vibrant Earth. Draw some of that energy into your Base chakra, knowing that it will be used if needed in other areas. As you do this, you may feel particularly connected to the physical earth, and therefore to your physical body, so mentally embrace yourself as both a physical and a spiritual being, loving yourself and your life.

KUNDALINI

As your chakras expand and balance, they will allow what is called the Kundalini energy to rise. Kundalini is a serpent-like force which lies asleep at the base of the spine, awaiting unfoldment. When the centres equalise and grow, and therefore have greater capacity for energy, they will touch each other, and each one will then stimulate the spinning of the chakras above and below it. A rush of energy follows, and with this release the serpentine Kundalini force spirals its way upwards. This should be a gradual process, for then the student can come to terms with the surge of energy which takes place. It is a healing force, and, like any other energy, in its right place it is extremely beneficial, but if it is inadvertently awakened too quickly, it is extremely debilitating for the individual, and in dire cases can lead to severe mental imbalance.

Electricity is wonderful for heating and lighting our homes, but it is life-threatening if tampered with by inexperienced hands. The same is true of the subtle energies, which also require a proper channel and focus, which we must train ourselves to provide. The process of development is just that: a process. It will take time. If you try to force it, it becomes confusing and uncomfortable, and you do not save any time - indeed, you may impede your own progress. Festina lenti should be your motto: Hasten slowly.

Books for Reference.
You Can Heal Your Life, by Louise Hay 1984.
Wheels of Life, by Anodea Judith 1990

The Truth about Chakras, by Anodea Judith 1994
The Chakras, by C.W. Leadbeater 1927
Journey through the Chakras, by Klaubernd Vollmar 1987

Chapter 2
_____

AWAKENINGS

Never underestimate how this work can and does change one's life. Once you have opened doorways to different worlds, your view will be different, and the whole trajectory of your life will be altered. Merely the simple process of opening (practised in Chapter One) improves your energy, and is your own affirmation of Right Living. Living in Truth creates an open energetic force, which clears your pathway in life.

In the material world, people are often controlled by division, but however powerful it can be to "divide and rule", in living the Truth you can never be under someone else's control. Some people, of course, may have a vested interest in your relinquishing your personal power to them.

Partners or other family members can initially feel threatened by the changes brought about by a student's development, because inner changes affect our perceptions, which in turn affect our attitude, and there may thus be a shift in the subtle balance of power that exists, in one way or another, within most home environments. However, usually this understandable alarm can be overcome by loving reassurance, which allows them to feel safe again, to accept the changes, and perhaps, gradually, to make appropriate reciprocal adjustments within themselves.

THINK FOR YOURSELF

When a student is drawn into the psychic worlds, they are searching for universal truths, truths found only within. Self-awareness is fundamentally achieved by studying the microcosm (man), so that we can begin to understand the secrets of the macrocosm (the universe). By examining ourselves and our present situation, we will find the universal truths, for everything in the universe echoes, and is echoed by, everything else.

This concept is nothing new: written over the temple at Delphi are the words: "Man, know thyself, and you will know the universe and God." "Know thyself" echoes throughout many philosophies and teachings. The poet Browning says: "Truth is within ourselves, it takes no rise from outward things, whatever you may believe".

Man is asleep, and will only awaken when he knows and understands himself. In awakening to higher consciousness, we become as different from our former selves as is the butterfly from the caterpillar when it emerges from its dark cocoon. To those whose eyes are closed to all but the outer worlds, this is not only a difficult concept, but one against which they may well rebel, for in recognising it, their status quo may be dramatically altered. If a person is not ready to look within, God help those that try to awaken this sleepy veiled soul, for the unrequested messenger is often shot whilst trying to reveal the light of truth.

There is no point, therefore, in trying to convince the closed mind. At best we can only throw "seeds", in the hope that one day the soil may be fertile, and that the seed will then germinate.

Over the past few decades, the use of self awareness, particularly in connection with spirituality, has centred on the idea of abandoning the ego self, that is, the personality self, or little I. The personality self is the individual existence, the image, or identity, as opposed to the Divine Will, or God Consciousness. It is best described as the veil of illusion - the dark coat that covers the true self. Some students believe that it is necessary to fight their ego, but if you fight anything you create a negative energy. It is far better to learn to love your ego, for in doing so you will dissolve the negative aspect, and in time it will align with the divine, or Big I.

Without due care, the excitement of self discovery can turn into zealotry. Believing that no supreme achievement could be obtained if the slightest traces of the self remained, the English magician and occultist Alesteir Crowley urged his followers, each time that they pronounced the hateful word "I", to slash their arms with a razor. He was by no means the first person to advocate physical self abuse for so-called "spiritual" ends: in the hope of either pleasing God or destroying the ego self, many religious institutions have encouraged flagellation and intolerable fasts. Whether any of these extreme activities actually worked is doubtful, and they certainly will not be advocated here!

It is understandable that having recognised the existence of the ego self, the student should wish to rid themselves of it, and in time they will. It is mentioned here because a balanced approach is so essential to what is, after all, not an exacting science. The middle way is recommended at all times.

UNCONDITIONAL LOVE

As we have seen in Chapter One, the heart centre holds the middle and balancing energy, the bridge between the physical, visible world and the spiritual, unseen worlds. In order to find the true spiritual self, we have to cross the bridge of love. This is not some sentimentalised state, for we are talking about love without condition.

Let us look at this expression for a moment. What is the true meaning of "unconditional love"? Loving someone you are connected with emotionally, such as a partner or a relative, is easy, and to give to someone for whom you have great feeling is commendable, but only natural. However, when an individual is working from the Love ray, giving love to everyone becomes natural: everyone becomes worth their time and effort. This is a state which cannot be artificially induced, for we are talking about an energetic state, which creates its own vibration.

The basic natural law of the whole universe is the Law of Cause and Effect, which is active on all levels, so that whatever energy you radiate to the world will be received. One of the commonest illusions is that if you recognise yourself as spirit, and you are trying to be spiritual, you will "be tested," and the "dark forces", like some bogie man, will be out to get you! This understandable concern stems from an inner struggle - that of the ego self versus the soul self. If there is an inner struggle, the resulting inner energy creates an outer one, which leads to this common illusion. Your energy is a magnetic force: LIKE ALWAYS ATTRACTS LIKE. There are no demons or devils manipulating you, other than yourself. Unfortunately, however, there are even some people who are pleased to think that they are worthy of the "devil's" attention! Most people still reveal an ego self at some time, and this will probably continue for many a long year, so give it as little energy as possible and in time it will dissolve by the higher forces. If you look past the ego with anyone, you will always find something good.

Fears have to be faced, and only by doing so do we rob them of their power. If you have no fear, there will be no temptation. It is very easy to fall into what the great mystic Alice Bailey described as "Glamour", where all sorts of nonsense and illusions can occur. Loving observation is of paramount importance at all times.

SELF CLEANSING

The cleansing of the self happens on many different levels. When you touch your inner light, your soul self, you set in motion the reverberation of Light into all aspects of the self, and this allow any imbalance or negativity to surface. No two students are the same, and the attention given to the various different levels depends on the individual. However, it is not uncommon in development to start the conscious emphasis on what could be described as the psychological being. This would include, for instance, childhood occurrences, and how they set in motion the creation of a particular pattern for adulthood.

Some students may feel that they need counselling, and the true feeling of the student must of course be explored, but there is no need to embark upon laborious, soul-searching activities, through long-drawn-out therapy. Indeed, many therapists have recently altered their approach to long-term therapy, for it can create dependency and "excuses".

Ultimately there can be no excuse good enough to stand in the way of enlightenment, for excuses are only the manifestation of fear: shine the light of Truth on them and they will dissolve. The alliance with the soul self will be your greatest counsel and guide. All you really have to do is watch.

LIVING YOUR TRUTH

Because we are formed of magnetic energy plus the sum total of all our experiences, by making contact with our core (the soul aspect of our being), everything that needs to be revealed will be forthcoming. A student often experiences a struggle between what could be defined as the "little I," the personality self, with the "big I," the soul, or God self. In connecting with the soul self it will bring us sooner or late to loving ourselves and in loving yourself you can be at one with the world.

Our physical body is like a vehicle. It takes us on marvellous and interesting journeys, but will eventually become old and worn, at which time we shall have to "trade it in" for a new model. However, we ourselves are pure energy, and NO ENERGY CAN BE DESTROYED. There are no exceptions. Energy can transmute, but it can never be obliterated, and if we truly understand this, it will make our journey of self discovery much easier.

At conception, the soul is attracted to the parents by the pull of its own magnetic energy. Therefore we all obtain exactly the right parents with whom to continue our life-experiences. All our past experiences create an imprint on our being, and a pattern is set. It is this pattern that dictates our reactions. Our childhood was an important influence, but our difficulties probably started long before it began. Like attracts like, and if we have, as usually happens, created a pattern formed of fear, that pattern will remain set until it is broken, which may take many lifetimes. Acknowledging past lives can sometimes be beneficial, but it is by no means essential. If a student is opening to Light, past lives will be remembered automatically.

We can look for old, negative patterns by exploring the past, and this would provide a fascinating journey, but how long is a piece of string? We may all be very old souls, and therefore we may have to go back over twenty lives or more in order to discover the root of any disturbance. We have all been tortured, and we have all been the torturer. We must acknowledge that at some stage we have to abandon the patterns of the past. Patterns can and must be altered, and we can create a new pattern by first of all melting down the old one. This is achieved with the Universal Energy, the Light Force which we understand as LOVE. Only by true love of oneself can this be obtained. Then one is ready to build anew, rather as a potter creates a pot. They may have an idea of the style and outcome of their design, but for a pot to become a reality, they must handle and mould the clay. Just like a potter, we must remould our future by constantly living in in our truth.

There is no formula for the awakening process. No exercise, visualisation, meditation, or any other factor, that will make the slightest difference unless the student wants to learn the truth about themselves. It is no good being frightened to look into the mirror. Everything and everyone around you is your mirror.

BEGINNINGS

Nowadays there are many meditation books and set visuali-sations, all of which will help you to contact your inner self if you are open. There is probably no such thing as a bad visualisation or meditation - if, of course, the intention is to unite with Light. As a first step, one of the easiest self-help methods, especially if the student has never practised any meditational exercises before, is to have an image on which to focus. For this purpose the Tarot cards provide very helpful awakening images, and can be used very productively.

Knowledge of the Tarot is unnecessary: simply choose the pack that appeals to you. Probably the best for these purposes is the "Rider-Waite" pack. These cards were designed by the order of the Golden Dawn in 1910, and are very powerful images.

A Tarot pack is divided into two sections. The fifty-six Minor Arcana are very similar to an ordinary deck of cards, with suits and court cards. The Major Arcana consists of twenty-two cards whose rich imagery depicts stages of the journey of life, its development and its growth. For us, the ideal aspect of these cards is that they can be viewed on different levels, from the physical and material aspects of life, right through into the deeply spiritual realms.

Many of these cards relate directly to imagery within the Bible, and there are definite connections with the Qabbalah, which is essentially the theosophy of the Jews. A secret doctrine handed down by initiates, it is a system of occult or esoteric philosophy. Exact details of the origins of the Tarot are shrouded in mystery. The only known fact is that they emerged in central Europe during the Middle Ages. It is probable that the Rider-Waite images consist of a mixture of occult knowledge from different areas and times. Many schools of thought have contributed to them: Egyptology, Astrology, Gnosticism, and Numerology, as well as the Qabbalah. Although there are now very many different designs, the Rider-Waite designs seem to be the blue print for most modern Tarot packs.

Further study can be pursued through the many books available on the market, but please remember that whatever you might read in any book, the most important messages from the cards are drawn from one's own imagination and intuition.

Here are some brief messages of illumination held within the twenty-two steps, or stages, of self-development depicted in the Major Arcana.

The Fool

He is either depicted as no 0 or no 22, and therein lies a clue to the Fool's mystery. "Many a true word is spoken in jest," and we can certainly equate our Fool with the jester, for the jester was very often the only person at court who dared to tell the truth to the King. The Fool is often the wise man in disguise, and the wisest man knows that he knows nothing. So if you pick the Fool, you have certainly set out on your inner journey. All around you there are signs to guide you. Take care.

The Magician

The power of true magic lies in the knowledge that we have the ability to control our lives. Everything we do and say originates in thought. In the Magician we have the message of positive thought, in terms of "as ye think, so shall ye be." Think clearly, and, if possible, independently. Thought is magic. It can and does influence events. Begin to observe and work with your thoughts.

The High Priestess

A lover of mysticism, she always indicates change. The High Priestess has innate, inner knowledge that is not always shared, maybe because it is not always communicable, and can therefore only manifest through deep intuition. The High Priestess understands much beyond the normal worlds, and she well knows the inconstancy of life through the moon's phases, but she uses these with wisdom. Trust your intuition above all things.

The Empress

This card depicts the archetypal aspects of mature womanhood: the Earth Mother, the bountiful, compassionate, loving Venus energy. Compassion and understanding will be the greatest attributes to help balance and guide. Look at your female aspects: are they balanced without fear?

The Emperor

The Emperor is the archetypal man. Connected with Mars, he is an authoritative character. He indicates strength, courage and will-power. Examine your male and female aspects, for when you draw either the Empress or the Emperor, it probably means that one or other aspect is not fully balanced.

The Hierophant

Also sometimes called The Pope or High Priest, this card is very spiritual. It means wisdom brought about by inspiration, intelligence and discrimination. Listen to your intuition and inner voice, for in that you will find divine inspiration, and with your own inspirational power you can help yourself. The gods are with you.

The Lovers

This Mercurial card has another title, "Children of the Voice." The voice is the echo of the Universal Light Force beginning consciously to manifest within the children of the world. This stage of development is reason, and the balancing of the emotions. Look for that balance within your stillness. This card is often chosen by students who are highly psychic.

The Chariot

Because you have begun to listen to your inner voice, you now begin to be in control of your life. Travelling your own pathway, you have bravely taken up the reins, and although your journey may not be easy, you can, if necessary, steer yourself away from danger. You have to learn to control the forces around you, and this can only be done through your own courage and strength.

Justice

Justice is not about judgement, for true justice lies in understanding and applying the law of the universe, which is absolute - the Law of Cause and Effect. Therefore justice can never be avoided. No one gets away with anything, not because some heavenly being or devil is pointing the finger, but because what is given out is always returned by the natural magnetic energies that work through every living thing.

The Hermit

This stage of development always occurs in a student of Truth, for when we realise that our views are not shared by the masses, this often necessitates a period of withdrawal. You may not live in a cave, but the insular feeling is similar. During such a period, great wisdom is drawn from innate inner wisdom and light. Very often, having found the comfort and strength of the inner being, students are reluctant to return and relate to society again. It must be remembered that knowledge is to be shared, and from your position of strength you can now work with the world.

The Wheel

We are all part of a giant cosmic wheel, of wheels within wheels, turning like clockwork, creating energy. Change, always a part of life, is coming into yours, so embrace the turning wheel. Without movement there is stagnancy, and this breeds dis-ease. Let go of the past, and look to the future, knowing that everything that happens to you is helping your journey.

Strength

This card could also be called "Taming the Beast." Only by balancing the lower animal energies with the higher spirituality do we really obtain strength. No one ever faces anything in life which they are unable to handle. All our hardships allow us to build up spiritual muscle, so embrace your life with all its difficulties, and know them as your friend, not your enemy. If we bother to look, we will find all the inner strength we need at all times.

The Hanged Man

We are told that sacrifice is spiritual, but is this true of yours? Examine whether your sacrifice is really necessary. Ask yourself, am I doing this in the true note of love for my fellow man, or is it an excuse not to get on with my life? In sacrificing something for another, you may be robbing them of a spiritual opportunity. This card also relates to your new-found perspective, for in seeing things differently, you may find yourself set apart from your loved ones. Follow only your truth.

Death

This card asks you to examine what death really means. As we are energy which can never be destroyed, there can be no final death, only change. Death is often considered a failure, but in fact it denotes a journey well completed. Something in your life is not conducive any more: release it in love, and move on. Remember that in death there is birth.

Temperance

This card advocates the middle way in all things. Most people do not allow their natural balance to work. Wisdom and restraint are the messages. It also relates to time, for if we allow it, time is the greatest healer. The flowing, healing waters of time will nourish you, supplementing your deficiencies.

The Devil

The Devil is the direct opposite of the Lovers. Instead of listening to the quiet, still voice within, you are listening only to the voice of fear. Fear has its temptations, which must be resisted at all costs. Face your worst fears. Look the devil directly in the eye, and he will disappear, for he is only the personification of your fear. Be free of the devil's chains, for we can only be controlled by fear. Lose your fear and you have control.

The Tower

This is the lightning flash of illumination of spiritual realisation that is often brought about by great trauma and pain. It is as though the shock of disaster brings us finally to our senses, and we often wake up as a completely different person. This is a time of great upheaval. It often indicates a violent separation from a person, a place, or even, at its highest level, a removal to a completely different way of life and living. It may not be easy, but it is probably the most beneficial experience of your life.

The Star

In all cultures and creeds we have the image of the Star. No one on the spiritual pathway has a quiet life; we have chosen great adventure. To be illuminated we must know ourselves one hundred per cent, and facing such revelation is at times very hard. Life is very exacting, and will give us, in no uncertain terms, the lessons we need. Illumination is the outcome, and hope is always present.

The Moon

This is a double-edged sword, for it indicates great inspiration and illumination. However, the flip side of this coin is delusion and lunacy. No-one likes to admit to having been deceived, and it is even harder to own up to self-deception. Be inspired by the reflection of the suns light upon the moon, and see the truth. You will often see the reflection before you notice the reality. We all make mistakes. Forgive yourself, and walk on.

The Sun

Success requires great effort, and in order to attain it you must be prepared to be single-minded. The message here is to apply yourself constantly. "Backbone" is more important than "wishbone", for wishful thinking will get you nowhere. Right thoughts plus constant application will achieve advancement. Learn the lessons of the past: shift your focus away from the negative aspects in your life, concentrate on what you truly want, and sooner or later you will obtain it. Remember, however, that everything is transitory. Your only real security will be found, not in material things, but in the connection with your inner sun. In communication with your soul light, you realise that you are immortal, and that the flame of life is eternal.

Judgement.

In life we experience many "deaths", and after each of them we are "reborn" to start another stage of our journey. This often occurs after a crisis point from which we assess our circumstances in a new light of understanding. The only true judgement is divine. After great trials you will be compensated for previous losses, and, like the phoenix rising from the ashes, you will emerge triumphant. You realise that without the losses and hardships, illumination would never have occurred.

The World

This card often comes to one who has the world at their feet, but has not as yet registered that fact. If we only knew it, we all have the world at our feet. It represents the gaining of control over the material worldly aspect. The lower and higher energies are then aligned, and truly begin to work in unison. Anything and everything becomes possible. Ironically, this is the point where we realise that all our needs are met, and that we want for nothing.

EXERCISE

Separate the Major from the Minor cards, and shuffle the twenty-two Major cards until they feel warm in your hands. Mentally ask for the card that will indicate your present stage, and will help you the most. Cut the deck into two piles, taking the card from the top of the lower pile. This is the right card for you.

Sit quietly and open up, either in your own way or by using the exercise in Chapter One. As you bring your focus up to the Crown centre, acknowledge yourself as a spiritual being, and take your focus to a point about six to ten inches above your head. This area is often referred to as the eighth centre. Strictly speaking, however, it is not a centre but a gateway, an entry point between the Universal Light Forces and you as a physical vehicle. It may help you to think of a diamond crystal hanging in this place. Visualise the image of the card you have cut, illuminated by the light of the crystal above your head. Slowly draw it downwards into your free and open mind, and at the same time ask for guidance for your own self growth.

Allow your mind to go where it wants. The picture may turn into a story, and the characters and one of the many symbols may come alive. If you find your mind wandering on to every-day matters, unless they are directly connected with the card, discipline yourself to draw your mind gently back to the image, even if that means opening your eyes and physically looking at the card again.

To release old patterns and to move forward, you will obtain the answers, although it does not always happen during the actual meditation. Very often you receive the real answers when you least expect them, perhaps when you are busy doing something mundane such as washing, hoovering, or driving your car. This is because the mind is often free to pass on the information when you are not pressurised.

You can translate your visualisation in much the same way as you would interpret a dream, but in fact it is likely to be self-explanatory.

After five or ten minutes, mentally acknowledge your meditation in your conscious mind, visualise your card in a circle of light, and gently pull this "bubble" into your heart area. In doing this, you are giving yourself the opportunity for self healing.

If you feel you have not obtained enough inspiration, do the exercise again at a later date, choosing either the same or a different card. Some people like to choose a card every day, to give them guidance.

When you have finished, close down in the usual way.

Books for Reference.
Walk On. By Christmas Humphries
Ponder on This. By Alice A. Bailey
The Initiate. By his pupil, Cyril Scott 1920
The Initiate in the New World. By his pupil, Cyril Scott 1927
The Initiate in the Dark Cycle. By his pupil, Cyril Scott 1932
Jung and Tarot, An Archetypal Journey. By Sallie Nichols 1980
The Prediction Book of The Tarot. By Madeline Montalban 1983
The Wisdom of the Tarot. By Elisabeth Haich 1975

Chapter 3

PSYCHIC
UNFOLDMENT

The purpose here is not to convert you, nor to convince you of psychic reality. If you have picked up this book, it is likely that you are in some way aware, or sense the existence of these forces, and are now considering furthering your knowledge. If you need to explore evidential material, look in any good book shop. Many authoritative individuals have written on these subjects, and there are now hundreds, even thousands, of such works. However, whether the existence of psychic energies can be proven in a substantial way is very much open to discussion, and many charlatans have been uncovered through their own zeal to convince us of the existence of unseen forces.

The only real evidence is in your heart and mind. There you know the truth, and there no one can disprove your own evidence. This is not blind faith: it is real, concrete knowing, and that is always one hundred per cent correct. Never stop your questioning, because this will take you into higher realms if you allow it, but there must be a cut-off point in analysis. You would not dissect someone in order to understand your love for them. This would not clarify the reality of your love. In contacting your inner knowing, you will find your reality, and the aim of this book is to help you to achieve that goal.

Although, unfortunately, one probably cannot teach anyone else exactly how to be aware of their psychism, there are many techniques for disciplining the self, thus enabling the psychic focus to be developed: it is all about focus. Just as the "magic eye" picture changes when you re-focus your eyes, by altering your perception you change your reality.

When students are interviewed for psychic development classes, they often say, "I've been told that I am psychic, or a healer." Well, to a greater or lesser degree, everyone is psychic, and everyone is a healer. Just as any person with five fingers can learn to play a tune on the piano, but very few will reach professional standing, so you can learn to exercise your psychic faculties, without necessarily working in this field. Like anything else in life it requires dedication and commitment.

Many "feelings" come from a psychic faculty. For instance, when you go into a strange room, and immediately either get a sense of well-being or a wary feeling; when you go into a house for the first time, and sense that it has been a happy or an unhappy home; when you meet someone for the first time, and immediately know whether you like or dislike them, and whether or not you can trust them. How many times have your first impressions been proved correct? These instincts, which are instantaneous, could be referred to as "animal psychism", because the vehicle that we call our body is animal, and as such we have animal instincts. These instincts include a kind of natural telepathy which is often used whether we are aware of it or not, but when it is properly focused, it is not only useful but in some cases life preserving. These animal senses are far too useful to abandon - much better to observe and use them productively.

In energy terms, we could connect animal psychism to the two lowest centres, which are the base and the sacral. The base centre is the energy that lets us breathe, and be alive in the body. It is physical survival. The second centre which is the sacral energy is connected to the strong creative energy of procreation. The most powerful desire in the cosmos is to reach out and expand. Mankind is no exception to that rule, and it is through connecting with the sacral energy that we observe this, first in a physical sense, and later on through our connection with the Higher Mind. In contacting and employing the energy of these two centres, we can extend our awareness of instinctive psychism.

When we connect with the next centre, the Solar Plexus, we are connecting sympathetically with our own emotions, and by expanding the Solar Plexus energy, we can develop our empathy with others. In its highest state, the solar plexus goes beyond negative emotions, and reaches true compassion. As we connect psychically with the Solar Plexus, we can receive what is commonly referred to as an auric reading.

The solar plexus is the centre that can sap our energy, and sooner or later an untrained psychic will unfortunately become depleted in some way. In extreme cases this can and does lead to illness.

As previously explained, the aura is the emanation of all our energies, mind, body and spirit. It is the energy field around all living things. When observed by sensitives it is described as light, and very often the different frequencies can be seen as colours, which change when the individual changes his or her mood or response. All your thoughts, feelings, desires and fears can be picked up within the auric field. It is like a psychic imprint, which can be attuned to through training and discipline. Every living thing has an aura, so a sensitive could just as easily observe these energy fields around a plant, a tree or an animal.

In this century we have discovered a way to photograph the aura. This is called Kirlian photography, named after the Armenian couple who discovered the process. In Kirlian photographs we see colours which we can endeavour to interpret, through faculties which are built into the human psyche. For instance, in nature, very often red means "danger" and too much red in the aura is dangerous, and often indicates an angry person. It can also mean that there is an abundance of physical energy. Using his or her own faculties, a sensitive will probably see these colours very much more subtly, and translate them intuitively. Later, we shall look more closely at the colour aspects of healing and sensitivity.

You, as a sensitive, do not need a camera to see auric emanations. With a little bit of discipline, psychics can do this with their own equipment, which are the senses that we all have, locked away within unused areas of the mind. The tragedy is that most of the population do not make use of them, which is almost equivalent to walking around blindfolded. We can, with a little training, have access to many "unseen" forces, and use them productively for ourselves and others. With a little effort and perseverance, anyone can train the inner eye to observe auric emanations.

READING THE AURA.

First, a word of warning: Because the untrained or improperly trained psychic cannot differentiate between the desire and the actuality, the whole process can become very hit-and-miss: they may, out of ignorance, misinterpret a perception as a fact, and feed this back to the sitter.

For instance, suppose that a person went to a psychic just after an interview for a job, and that the psychic picked this up correctly. This is fine, but if the sitter is confident of obtaining the job, the untrained psychic could interpret that confidence as a future certainty.

To give an example of this type of error: many years ago, a lady came to see me. She was in a highly troubled state, having been to a fortune teller who had told her that both her daughters would die. There can be no valid purpose in predicting death, and it is against the law in many countries, even if such a prediction subsequently proves to be accurate. In this case it transpired that the lady's greatest fear was the loss of her daughters. The psychic correctly picked this up, but incorrectly interpreted her fears as a fact.

When a psychic has been properly trained, however, there are many very beneficial aspects to reading the aura. To someone who does not know themselves, a good auric reading is like a mirror, and is enormously helpful. It can assist the person to see themselves clearly, and therefore to rebalance themselves if necessary.

It is quite possible that communication and connection with the aura will form your first encounter with psychic energies. There are energies all around every living thing, your body is an energy and we observe this when we open to our psychic perception. In the early stages of development, this connection with unseen energies may need a certain amount of practice, and you are therefore advised to be as relaxed as you possibly can before you start: you need to be balanced and focused, the by-product of this balancing procedure being a general feeling of well-being and joy. You are the instrument, and any instrument needs to be kept in good repair. It is a good idea to go through your opening procedure. In time you will be able to do this within minutes, but to begin with do not hurry. The more centred you are the better.

Energy follows thought, so send your thoughts to the person with whose aura you wish to connect. Never link with someone in this way without their permission. Working in a group, the asset would be that you can work on each other, which in turn acts as a self-awareness exercise: in receiving information that someone has sensed about you, you can begin to observe your own emanation, and why you sometimes get negative responses from others.

The sending of thought is a Yang (male energy) action, and so, having done that, you must balance it by opening yourself to receive the answer, which is a Yin (female energy) action. One of the greatest myths of this work is that only the female energy is used, but nothing could be further from the truth. If one only used female energies, we would be sitting around waiting for ever. We need the focussed, arrow-like, male energy to connect, and the open, welcoming, female energy to receive.

Clear, concise focus is essential, for without the clarity of focus you will only receive nebulous information. The more precise the question, the clearer the reply. However, when a student begins this work, the information received may be very jumbled. Please do not worry about it - it does take time. Just be disciplined and patient.

INTERPRETING INFORMATION

Many people receive information in the form of pictures or symbols. To the novice this can be confusing, as the information comes into the mind very rapidly. Some practice is needed to translate such sensory information into thoughts and words, but with a little effort you will make the adjustment.

Remember that the information is coming through your mind, so it is your mind that must translate. Ask yourself what each symbol means to you, and how it makes you feel. For instance, you might receive an image of a cat. If you, the sensitive, like cats, this could be a positive sign, but if you are frightened of them the image probably means that you are picking up the individual's fears. Within the psychic focus, the mind relays things in a similar way to dreams, so there has to be much practice at deciphering the information very quickly.

The moment you have sent the arrow of energy and made the connection with someone, all your thoughts and feelings must be observed as belonging to them, not you. Most students initially find it difficult to let go of themselves: because the information comes through the student's own mind, it is difficult to perceive the information as being connected with others. Initially there is only the subtlest difference between the feeling of one's own thought process and that of any individual to whom we are linked. Like a telephone conversation, this is a two-way procedure, and at first the energies can be jumbled. We must learn to send the signals and listen for the reply. With just a little practice this will happen surprisingly quickly. In any group, even if none of the students has done this work before, by the end of the first evening all of them will have received some psychic sense and information.

AURIC COLOUR READING

Perhaps the best way to start is to tune in to the energies around an individual, which can be done both mentally and through healing activities. If you are going to connect mentally, do so in the way already described, and observe the response. At first you may be aware of colours around the head. Few sensitives physically see the colour (this may come later), but you will see with your inner eye, which is just as effective.

In a mentally active person you will see a great deal of energy around the head, for like everything else, thoughts are energy. If the energy is grey, or any other dark shade, this indicates negative thoughts. We often speak of energy in terms of colours. For instance, we may speak of "grey" or "dark" thoughts, or of being "browned off." We describe a coward as being yellow, and a depressed individual as being blue. We talk of people being red with anger, green with envy, "in the pink". These descriptions stem from our instinctive awareness of the auric emanations.

You, the receiver, must interpret the colours by your own intuition, but the principal colours do seem to have standard meanings, which one could base on the chakra colours. For instance, red relates to the Base centre, orange to the Sacral, and so on, but there are of course many subtleties within the colour spectrum.

In general terms, the clearer the colour the healthier the energy. You, the sensitive, must ask yourself if the colour is pleasant. This may sound simplistic, but if the energy is balanced, whatever colour you see will appear clear and pleasing.

Red (the energy of the Base chakra) that looks clear and clean is probably indicative of someone with very healthy physical energy, but an example of how negativities effect the energy field is that you may see blood red, which could mean physical depletion, or vermilion, which could denote anger.

The Sacral orange depicted with a nice, flame-like quality is good, normal, creative energy, but if that orange is of a rancid hue, it could denote unhealthy sexual appetites.

Moving up to the yellow of the Solar Plexus: a lovely, pleasing yellow denotes a compassionate person, but a musty yellow could indicate greed and paranoia.

A clear, sharp green is the energy of the Heart (love), but olive green denotes jealousy. Violent green is the colour of a sick person with dangerous preoccupations.

Blue, the Throat energy, is often associated with healing, but you might, for example, find some dark spots within that colour, indicating a lack of self-esteem. If the darker blues are observed around the throat itself, it might mean that the person is self-destructive.

Indigo, associated with the Brow chakra, is not observed around most people, but when it is, it is often the sign of someone using their higher intuitive sense - a priest or priestess energy.

Violet around the head is a positive sign, indicating that the individual is opening to the spiritual realms, but if it is very prominent, or is violent-looking, this unhealthy sign may mean that the person is an escapist who has lost all sense of reality, and is trying to abandon the physical realms.

Remember that the above are just general guides. The most important and the most effective interpretations come from you.

Experiment on others, and then acknowledge their feed-back. Very often you will pick up things that you could not possibly have known in any "normal" way. However, it is not advisable to do this at random, until you are strong within your own centred energy. It is so easy to pick up negative thoughts and feelings from others - one of the commonest experiences in untrained psychics is mood swings which do not originate from any apparent factors. This is because the sensitive is taking on board other people's energies, sometimes with very unpleasant consequences. Learning to attune to their Higher Self, and to the Universal Light Force Energy, is essential to the "trainee" psychic. Some negative experiences can put off the new student for good, but you really have nothing to fear if you approach the whole subject with intelligence and balance.

As you achieve competence in observing the colours within the energy fields, you will probably begin automatically to pick up other aspects of your sitters. Thoughts are easily received, often entering your mind at the speed of light or faster, so be alert. The aura is the individual pattern of energies, the emanation from that person at that moment. You can observe this by an easy experiment. Ask someone to have very pleasant thoughts, and observe the aura, then ask them to think of something unpleasant. The aura will change immediately. What you receive as information is what that person is projecting in that instant. Very little stays in the normal energy fields for any length of time, unless it is perpetuated by the energy of more thoughts or emotions. So anything picked up by the sensitive will be thoughts or emotions felt at that time, or at the very most within the previous two days. Unless further energy is fed to a thought or emotion, it disappears. Beyond an arm's length however, there is more ingrained material.

When you are experimenting with friends or in a group, linking with the aura can be very amusing. For instance, one student in my class was fed back her thoughts on a soap opera she had recently watched! There can be no secrets whilst working in this field. Needless to say, you will not endear yourself to others if you read their minds without their permission. Sometimes, however, receiving "loose" thought-energies becomes unavoidable: you could, for instance, pick up someone's thoughts whilst passing them on the stairs. If that happens, wrap such thoughts into a bubble of light, and let them go, for they do not belong to you. My own teacher once told me a lovely story: she always knew where anyone was at any given time, just by tuning into them. On one occasion, when her adult daughter was late home, she tried to divine her whereabouts, but was firmly told by her Guide energy, "If your daughter wanted you to know where she was, she would tell you!".

Opening one's sixth sense does sometimes present moral dilemmas. As a child I was often puzzled and dismayed when visitors lied to my parents - mostly out of politeness. At first I would expose these falsehoods, but I very soon found that it was not only distressing for the visitor, but for my family also, so I learned to shut up.

Most people feel uncomfortable if they lie and deceive. In energy terms, it creates confusion within the aura. As we know, like attracts like, and so this confused energy will make for confused feed-back from others. Everything is energy, and deception is no exception, so everyone, no matter how insensitive they are, will, on some level, sense the imbalance. There is an innate need in all of us to be open and honest, and this will eventually shine through with everyone. That is why truth will triumph sooner or later. It is not, however, our business as sensitives to be in any way judgemental of someone who we know is lying, for we will not help anyone by being critical.

The help that our sensitive awareness can give to others is immeasurable. It is a creative talent, and like any other talent it needs careful and disciplined handling. Your work as a sensitive should bring joy, both to you and to those who seek your help. If it does not, then there is something wrong, and you should stand back and take stock.

Students very often do not realise that the unfoldment process works in stages. You cannot develop one aspect of the self without balancing others. So it is often the case that a student will attend a development group, and after a while seemingly come to a plateau. This generally means that there are other aspects of that student's life that must be examined. Therefore a break in development is required while that individual looks into other areas, whether they be emotional, mental or physical issues. Whatever it is, an adjustment and balancing of these areas is essential to the growth of the individual.

Imbalances of all descriptions can be observed in the aura, including the physical aspect of the person. As with anything else, practice can make you very competent in specialised areas. There are some psychics, for instance, who have trained their ability to align so precisely with the physical state that they can see inside the body.

It is relatively easy for a disciplined psychic to spot a recently operated area. Any physical damage tears at the aura, and this is easily observed. Please be very careful in the relaying of such information. You can cause great alarm to someone by telling them that they have a physical imbalance. The imbalance may, after all, be slight - something that will adjust itself without treatment.

In general terms, a psychic reading should not involve physical diagnosis. This should be left to the professionals in this field, i.e. trained doctors. Remember that psychism is not a precise science, and that one can often pick things up incorrectly. Never allow yourself to become so self-assured that you fail to admit that you could be wrong, because even the most experienced psychics can occasionally make mistakes.

If someone, in good faith, comes to you for advice, you are duty bound to give them the truth, however remember in the early stages psychic perception is low and therefore the student will veer towards negative information, so make certain that you open yourself to the higher intuitive fields before you tackle the difficult dilemmas of negative impressions. If you sense something of a highly personal nature, ask for guidance on how to present it in a way that will neither offend nor hurt. Over the years, I have found that even enormously difficult subjects can be broached with sensitivity and love, thereby giving the person hope and comfort. Never fudge the truth, but give it in a loving manner.

EXERCISE

This particular exercise has been chosen because it helps clear negative energy, for to do this work we must be as clear an instrument as possible.

Start your meditation in the usual way, paying particular

attention to the chakras. Breathe at least three times into each of them, psychically acknowledging the different energy of each one. If any are less or more energetic, go back and gently breathe into those areas. There is never any need to force the energy: a gently purposeful breath will achieve what is required.

When you have finished, decide on which centre you wish to concentrate. Let this be a purely intuitive choice. When you have decided, visualise in front of you a door of the same colour as your chosen chakra. For example, if you have chosen the Sacral centre the door will be orange. If you selected the heart, the door will be green. In your mind's eye, open the door and go in, observing what is inside. Look around. You may find that you are not in a room at all. This does not matter, but if you are in a room, pay particular attention to what is on the walls and what is the subject of any picture. Are there any cupboards? If there are, what is inside them? What colour is your room? Is there any one else in there? If there are any images or senses that you do not understand, mentally ask what they mean. You will receive the answer. Call upon Guidance - it is always at hand if you ask.

After five or six minutes, leave the room, closing the door behind you. Immediately enclose the image within a bubble of light, and either see it float out of sight, or breathe it into your heart centre, where it will dissolve. Feel the balance of your own energies through your heart, and then close in the usual way.

As with any other visualisation, you can interpret this in the same way as a dream. Relate your interpretation to the particular energy of the centre chosen. For instance, the Solar Plexus will almost certainly be about your emotions.

The size of the room is relevant: the more spacious it is, the easier you feel about yourself. The picture, if there was one, is often an image of you. The contents of the cupboards are illustrations of anything left undone in your life. A bundle of letters, for instance, might mean unfinished business with the author of those letters. If your cupboard was bare, this is a healthy sign, for it means that you have left nothing undone.

This exercise is like a self-examination, and by surrounding it with light at the end you are giving yourself the opportunity to let go of negativities. Gradually this will translate into the conscious mind, and come into actuality in your day-to-day existence, helping to create more balance.

Books for Reference
The New Clairvoyance by Rev. Mario Schoenmaker 1986
Mind Magic by.Betty Shine 1991
The Colour Therapy Workbook by Theo Gimbel 1993

Chapter 4

ENERGIES

Everything - is energy: not just living things such as animals and plants, but also inanimate objects. It is only our limited visual perspective that sees things as solid, for in reality they are vibrating clusters of atoms. If we shift our perspective, we can receive not only different perceptions but also greater insight into the universe.

The whole solar system coalesced from a cloud of gas and dust-particles, which came together to create the planets and the sun. The entire known universe started with the Big Bang, and everything that has subsequently sprung from it is made from the same energetic material. Everything in the cosmos, ourselves included, is inextricably inter-linked.

No one questions our ability to talk to someone on the other side of the world by using a mobile telephone. These telephones transmit energies in the form of radio waves, instantaneously connecting people over vast distances. Similarly, light waves bounce into our eyes, where they are transformed into electrical energy and instantaneously transmitted to the brain, where they are interpreted. Through the eyes, ears, nose, tongue and sense of touch, the body instantly deciphers any energy upon which we choose to focus.

We know that many creatures use the earth's magnetic energy for survival purposes. For instance, birds use it to navigate, turtles use it to guide them back to their birth place, and sharks are able to select the weaker creatures within a group by observing the electro-magnetic fields (auras) around them. The hammerhead shark evolved into that shape in order to enhance its electro-magnetic sensors, and the array of such sensors around the bill of the duck-billed platypus assists it to sense the presence of creatures beneath the mud.

You, too, can easily expand your senses to encompass the unseen energies. As mentioned earlier, all you need to do is to move your focus, just as you do with the "magic eye" pictures, only in this case you shift your inner focus. To someone who cannot accept psychic realities, this may seem impossible, but whether or not they realise it, everyone is constantly using their inner senses.

Do not take my word for it; try it for yourself. The next time you walk into a house for the first time, or meet a new person, deliberately shift your attention, consciously open your mind, and sense what is around you. All types of energy can be identified in this way?.

Psychometry, which is the sensing of energy around an inanimate object is popular with development groups, and demonstrates this very well. Take an object that only the owner has used or worn. Hold it in your hand very gently, open your mind, and see what you receive. It is important that you be able to verify any information, so to begin with, only work on an object belonging to someone you know. Probably you will pick up the immediate thoughts and emotions of the owner. These will consist of what the owner has been thinking and feeling, usually within the previous twenty-four or forty-eight hours. Just like the aura, objects will hold information for a very short period of time: unless energy perpetuates an emotion or thought, it will automatically dissolve. You are unlikely to gather from an object something that happened to the owner five years ago, unless they are still energising it in some way.

This exercise is immediate, and you do not have to be

connected with some advanced high frequency. It is almost a gut, or animal level, psychism, which makes use of the Solar Plexus energy. If you are going to do this exercise, do not labour for the receipt of information. Pick up the object, hold it lightly, and focus your inner senses upon it. From that very second until such time as you break your focus, everything that comes into your mind will be about the object and the person who owns it. As with any psychic work, it is not advisable to tune into an object or person without their permission.

This is a good exercise for beginning to discipline your psychic perceptions. It can be great fun, and should not be taken too seriously. It often reveals amusing thoughts and feelings, and its main purpose is to show the pupil how easy it is to connect with the energy around an object. Probably no great revelation will occur, for it is the equivalent of practising scales on the piano.

There are energy imprints on everything, and sometimes they have such a violent or destructive quality that they radiate through time and space, instead of dissolving in the normal way. They can sometimes even continue for several centuries. There are very many famous hauntings that you could put under the heading of memory imprints. Each of these cases could be likened to a scratch on a record, which causes the needle to play the same passage over and over again. One famous example of this occurs in York in the basement of an old building, where the ghosts of Roman soldiers are often seen marching through caves. No doubt you have also heard of some "lady in white" haunting a room or building. In these cases, the violent emotions of that person have sent a kind of shock wave out into the atmosphere, and it will go on playing for ever unless it is checked.

The flat where my husband and I first lived contained one of these imprints: each night, just after midnight, we would hear a succession of sounds. They were always the same, and always took the same amount of time. We would hear the screeching of car brakes, followed by the panicky sound of the front door slamming, and very hurried footsteps on the stairs.

On several occasions in the same house, I heard the sound of a child singing, and on one occasion I looked around to see the ghost of a small, Latin-looking child. She was oblivious to me, and as children often do, she was happily playing and singing to herself. Some weeks after this, at a social gathering, I met a man who, upon hearing where I lived, exclaimed that he knew the house very well, as it had once belonged to his boss. He went on to say that one of the tenant families there had suffered a dreadful tragedy when their little girl died. The family was Italian!

There are some things in life that are so strange that when recounting them you wonder if you will be believed, but I relay this now, as it directly relates to the "scratched record" sounds in our flat: Finally, after putting up with it for quite some time, my husband had had enough. One night, he shot out of bed just as the footsteps were coming up the stairs, and this time whatever or whoever it was, was confronted. It stopped dead, and never returned. We both felt what we were experiencing was the panic of the little girl's father on finding out that his daughter was dead. Such was the intensity of his reaction that it lingered in the atmosphere until it was transformed, in this case by our recognition.

There are now so many documented stories of this kind of occurrence that it surprising that some people still refuse to open their minds. The energy I have just described is a different kind of haunting from that of the spirit of a departed soul on which we will later speak, but both in a sense have imprinted themselves upon the atmosphere.

Our atmosphere is very absorbent, making all our out going energies stay in the "air", where they can be plucked and later used. Our thoughts, for instance, can have a great impact on what happens. The previously mentioned universal principle of "What goes out must come back" is in some instances enhanced by emotional energy: an evil thought (often called the "evil eye") directed at someone can, if the "target" is vulnerable, have dire consequences. In some countries, eye-to-eye contact is discouraged, the feeling being that the eye is the doorway to the soul, and that if you look at another person you may give your soul away. This kind of "magic" usually evaporates when tried out on less emotionally based people, yet even though we in the West think ourselves above this kind of thing, many business transactions are executed in the same sort of way. Emotionally based energy flying into the atmosphere, coupled with directed thought emanations, creating the desired outcome, which is exactly the same as the energy used in a magic ritual.

MAGIC

Magic, not to be confused with conjuring tricks, or sleight-of-hand, is easily achieved. It is merely the transmission of focussed thought, fuelled by emotional force, or it could equally be emotional focus backed up by powerful thought. On their own these energies are not so strong, but in combination they will create either havoc or harmony. This is the energy of so-called black or white magic, and to a lesser degree virtually everyone will have some form of it in their lives. We all, at times, have very strong feelings, and it is clear, therefore, that psychic students, who are deliberately opening themselves to unseen energies, must very quickly learn to become balanced. Be on your guard, because what we send out always returns to us.

You may hear someone say, "Why was that person so awful to me, when I have done nothing to them?". "Equally, of course, someone may remark upon an unexpectedly kind action, perhaps from a total stranger". The answer is that at some time they did do something awful, or something kind, to someone, for an action is not necessarily returned to us by its original recipient. This is because every action is energy, and we are all connected with every other living things in the cosmos.

If you begin to observe how the energy frequencies work in this way, you will begin to understand the whole energy process. This is best achieved by observing occurrences in your own life.

An action and its corresponding reaction do not always occur within the same lifetime, but there are certainly occasions when it is possible, if one is alert, to recognise the repayment of some past deed, be it a positive or a negative one".

In the early stages, students are tested, not by the finger of God coming from the sky, but by themselves. They will instinctively push themselves, knowing that they must be strong and resolute, and not influenced by others. This is why so many successful mediums and psychics are self-sufficient. Strong in their own being, they often realise that they have very little need for the sort of emotional security that others demand. All this work helps build spiritual muscle. Every step of the way there are pitfalls, but they all combine to create an enormously potent force and strength for the individual. This process can, and often does, take many years, but a lesson properly learned is never forgotten, and will serve for the rest of one's life.

People assume that white magic is harmless, but how can one judge? Healing is actually a form of white magic, and all compassionate souls want to heal the world; but do we have the right? If you send healing without being asked, you may be denying the recipient a very important strengthening exercise. This could be likened to forcing an unwanted gift upon someone, because some will have deliberately chosen to suffer, in order to learn and grow.

Sometimes, unfortunately, we can fall foul of trying to control others by our healing or prayers. All healing and psychic work must be given unconditionally, which is not so easy, for in order to give unconditionally, we ourselves need to be in an unconditional state.

Black magic uses exactly the same elements, but doing so with conscious evil intent. The desire to control people crosses the line between the two. Examine your motives at all times, and continuously ask yourself what is the real reason for your undertaking this work. No one is perfect, but we can create a good, healthy, balanced energy as a base for our efforts. In most people the creation of this balance will fluctuate, but gradually it will seep into even the densest parts of our being, and eventually we will be able to live our whole lives in unconditional love, the love that demands nothing in return. For most of us this state is a very long way down the track, but do not despair when your self-observations reveal to you your own imbalances. Guilt and regret are harmful emotions, so simply acknowledge, learn, and let go.

DEVAS

Not only are there energies everywhere within and around every living being: if we continue to open to the unseen forces, we will also discover many unseen dimensions. The closest of these, existing parallel to our own third-dimensional world, are the Devic forces. Most people do not acknowledge these energies consciously, but within this range there is an array of beings, from little sprite energies up to the mighty energy of the Archangels.

All these energies work alongside the human animal state. They help repair and heal all physical things. We all have what is called an etheric body, which is most commonly defined as the etheric blue-print. This contains all the genetic information of our physical bodies. It has a very subtle energy that even some healers hardly recognise. However, any healer will have automatically attracted a Devic helper, who will be working along side them, either with or without their knowledge, and it is with the etheric energy that these are most aligned.

To make contact with the Devas, find a quiet spot, preferably out in the country. Walk slowly along, with your senses fully open. Be as quiet and still within as you can manage, and gradually you will become aware of these beings all around. You may make some connection with the spirits around the trees and plants, for everything, even a blade of grass, has an etheric counterpart.

It is impossible to list all the energies, and even if it were possible to communicate with all of those on Earth, there are many more outside our planet. However, although all energies vibrate at a different frequency, everything comes from the same Source, and with a little effort, attunement can be made to any energy. Many of the frequencies are beyond our immediate range, but by attuning ourselves to some of the numerous unseen forces, we can extend our range of perceptions. To paraphrase William Shakespeare, there are many things in Heaven and on Earth that are beyond our imaginings, although at this time we are opening to them more than ever before.

The indisputable law of the universe is: NO ENERGY CAN BE DESTROYED. You and I are energy. Everything is energy. We all transmute energy constantly, but our energy can never be obliterated, and when we finally acknowledge this fact within our deepest consciousness, we lose all fear, which is the most important energetic transmutation that could ever take place. Without fear we become free from conditionings, free from outer control, and for the first time we can take up the reins of our own lives.

When you reach this point, you will realise that so many things in the past were done out of fear, and that your whole way of thinking needs to be revised - abandoned, even. The diminishment of fear means that we are becoming conscious of our own power. This is not power over others, for someone without fear would not wish power over others. It is the power of connection to the true energy of your being; the spirit of yourself; the inner Soul Force; the power of Love, that power which is the polar opposite of fear.

Attuning to different energies does not of itself lead us into that freedom, but the more diligently we work upon the different aspects of our lives, the less afraid we become. Thus the unfoldment process continues to unveil all our illusions, bringing us finally back into peace.

EXERCISE

As well as the psychometry exercise, you may wish to try your hand at sensing energies. In the following exercise, which is aimed primarily at self healing, you are acknowledging and adjusting your own energies. Open up all your chakra centres as already described, and continue by acknowledging which centres are less or more powerful. Firstly draw your attention and focus to the lesser ones. Simply breathe gently and purposefully into each centre. Feel and sense the centres expanding, making sure that they all feel good and vibrant, and be open to any intuitive information. You can, if you wish, go through the centres in this way every day. If you have any physical imbalances, this exercise is very effective if done whilst lying flat on your back on the floor.

There are many helpful forms of visualisations and exercises. The one described below is often referred to as "cutting the ties." This is a marvellous way of dissolving any negative feelings, and it works particularly well if you have had trouble with a parent or child. You can even participate in this exercise if that person is dead, for in death the emotional hold can still be strong.

When you feel completely comfortable after your usual opening, expanding exercise, visualise yourself in a clear bubble of white light. For several moments just be comfortable and happy within your bubble. Then, outside the bubble, place an image of the person with whom you are having difficulties. It might be your mother, father, child, husband or wife, lover, friend, or even your boss.

The exercise must be practised without emotion. If you are deeply embroiled in a tussle with someone this may be difficult, but do persevere. Even if you can only hold it for a few seconds, it will begin to break the negativity. It may be easier to imagine the person as a photograph. If, however, you do feel yourself getting anxious or emotional, even if the emotions are loving ones, stop the exercise and try again later.

Having concentrated on the image outside your bubble, visualise that image within its own bubble of light, quite separate from your own. When that is firmly in place, mentally draw a figure of eight: once, twice or three times, encompassing and separating the two bubbles. Watch then as the figure eight splits and the two bubbles separate, and the one with the other person in it floats gently on the breeze, just like a child's bubble, and finally, gently, floats away.

If you wish, you can simplify the whole procedure by just creating one bubble around the other person, and simply visualising it floating away in light. Please remember at all times to be devoid of emotion. The whole exercise need only take a few minutes: you can, with practice, hold your concentration for that length of time. It is a most effective exercise, and one that has been given to a large number of students over the years. The positive feed back from these students alone would fill a book.

Many years ago, when my husband and I had our first child, we lived in a first floor flat, and downstairs lived unpleasant and noisy neighbours. On innumerable occasions we would be awoken in the depths of the night by the deafening sounds of their stereo, and the banging of doors. This disruption affected many other residents of the road. Several other neighbours complained, and called the police, but to no avail.

The stress and tension for me, with a young baby and no peace of mind, became such that for the first and only time in my life I came close to hating this family, and it was a most uncomfortable feeling. It became obvious to me that this awful pattern would need to be broken in some way, and that the situation would have to be healed. At that time, I had just begun sitting in a development group, where we practised absent healing, which involves the sending of healing light to those who are ill, or who need upliftment in some way. I had read no books on healing or visualisation, but I instinctively knew that I had to encircle my neighbours with light.

As you might imagine, at first this was enormously difficult to do without feeling negative towards them. After a few attempts, however, I managed to hold them in light for ten seconds. It then became easier, and the exercise was repeated once or twice more. (It was, however, in those first few seconds that the tie was broken). Whether the neighbours actually made less noise, or whether I simply noticed it less, I cannot say, but within approximately three or four weeks they had ceased to bother me, and within three months they moved away!

It is very important in undertaking this exercise not to have any pre- conceived ideas of the outcome: all healing must be unconditional. It may not have the expected results, but if performed as described, you will cease to be affected by the person or situation that has given you grief, thus making way for another veil to be lifted.

Books for reference

Cutting the Ties that Bind, by Phyllis Krystal 1982
Exploring the Fourth Dimension by John D. Ralphs 1992

Chapter 5

HEALING

Healing is an enormous subject, and one that would fill many books. The main reason for its inclusion in a book that deals principally with psychic unfoldment is that anyone working with psychic energies should be doing so in the hope of fostering wholeness and harmony in themselves and others. You are therefore urged to make use of healing energies: any level of psychic reading should be a healing experience, and indeed your own development is a process of self healing.

Contacting the energies used in healing adds to the spectrum of our experiences with the unseen forces. Because the healing flow can be physically felt by most people, it can increase the student's confidence during the early days of their psychic development, thereby encouraging them to attune to their own psychic faculties. Even more significant is the fact that in welcoming the healing forces we come into contact with the Divine Rays, a contact that spurs us into opening up as clear and effective channels. Experience and knowledge of healing energies, and how they operate, can therefore greatly assist you, the psychic, to serve others.

As we have already seen, all things are energy. Spiritual healing requires no faith, nor does it even require the recipient's knowledge that healing is being administered. It is a direction of clear, positive Light Force energy, that same energy that runs through everything in the universe. It can never be depleted or exhausted, because it has no beginning and no end. It is constant, so if you administer healing properly you can never be drained: indeed, healers very often feel an increase in their own energy after giving a healing session.

Most students start their healing work by channelling the universal light force energy through their hands. If you have never sensed energy before, a simple way of doing so is to hold your hands straight out in front of you, clenching your fists over and over until they begin to ache. Let your arms drop to your sides, and then gently lift your hands so that the palms face each other. Now slowly draw your hands together. The connection with this energy is very subtle, so do it gently. You should find that you reach a point of resistance, where you can feel the emanation of the energy that you have just created in your hands. The sensing of this energy is similar to the feeling that you will experience whilst healing. Different people sense it in different ways: some people feel it as warmth, some have a tingling in their fingers, and there are some who experience it as a cool breeze.

In giving healing, we are balancing the energies of the body, mind and spirit. Spiritual healing links with the spirit, and brings about an alignment between it and the other levels. It is therefore effective for the treatment not only of physical problems, but also of emotional and mental imbalances.

Healing can, and does, sometimes work miraculously, although one would be unwise to expect miracles. Disease (disease) is an outward sign of inner imbalance. Each person's imbalance is unique, so although you may be able to help someone presenting with, for example, eczema, that does not mean that you will automatically be able to help every eczema sufferer who comes to you. Conversely, of course, a lack of response in, for example, an arthritis sufferer, will not necessarily signal your inability to help anyone else with that illness.

In the past, people usually only went to a healer as a last resort, and unfortunately this is still often the case. Although the situation is now changing at an astonishingly rapid rate, people tend to go first through the orthodox channels, and if, for whatever reason, are unable to get satisfaction, a patient may have come to a point of no return before consulting a healer, and a cure will then be difficult to achieve. If someone is terminally ill, their body may have deteriorated too far to be brought around; or maybe it is simply their time to leave this "mortal coil". Whatever the outcome, it is not our place to theorise about the whys and wherefores.

If someone has healing when a problem first reveals itself, it can be enormously helpful, either on its own or as a splendid adjunct to orthodox, or any other, healing methods. There is no manipulation, no administering of drugs, and there does not even have to be any direct physical contact. There is no possible side effect, because all the healer is doing is encouraging the patient's own healing processes. Within our bodies we have all the ingredients required for healing ourselves, and by gently adjusting the body into balance, spiritual healing helps it to contact these mechanisms. Sometimes the results appear magical, but in reality the process is the most natural thing in the world. It is just as normal as anything else in nature, for, like nature, our bodies have the ability to realign themselves.

One of my first confirmations of healing was in my very first development group. In this group, at the start of every evening, we used to send out absent or distant healing, which means sending healing to anyone who is unable to be present. As I had never practised this before, and could not really think of anyone who was ill, I put my mother-in-law's name into the healing force, as she was going through a very difficult emotional patch. I thought no more about it until the following Sunday, when she suddenly announced that on the previous Thursday, at a quarter to eight, she had slumped down into her chair. She said that as she did so, a wave of feeling came over her, and she suddenly knew that everything would be all right. Our meetings took place on Thursdays, and always started at 7.30 p.m., so the healing would have been taking place at about 7.45. At that time, my mother-in-law knew nothing of my interest in these subjects, and I had told no one of the healing exercise.

One might ask: How did this occur? What energy can go through the atmosphere? The answer is a perfectly logical one.

We take for granted that when we dial a number on our mobile 'phone we will be connected with someone else, perhaps hundreds of miles away. We also take for granted the radio and television waves that travel through the atmosphere, for through a telephone, a radio, a television set, we can experience concrete manifestations of these waves - these unseen forces.

Healing is the greatest manifestation of all: anyone who has experienced it needs no proof of their subsequent sense of well-being. No word may have been spoken, but the feeling of the Light Force that manifests itself as unconditional love is tangible and absolute. One criticism levelled at healing, and many other holistic therapies by orthodox doctors is that it is folkloristic and old fashioned. Are we, then, to deny the existence of an energy that does so much good, simply because it has been in use for thousands of years? This would, surely, be the equivalent of our walking around blindfolded, on the grounds that human beings have always had eyes, and that it is therefore high time that they learned to see by other means.

Mercifully, many orthodox doctors are beginning seriously to investigate spiritual healing, and in 1995 one of many pilot studies was carried out. It took place over a period of six months, and involved the monitoring, by doctors, of sixty elderly patients to whom healing was being regularly administered. The project, entitled "Alternative Help for the Older Person", was a great success, and the ensuing report has now been distributed to over 600 areas world-wide. Dr. Sidney Jones, who was initially sceptical, was subsequently quoted on television as saying, "At first I couldn't understand it, and therefore I rather dismissed it, but I am now forced to believe that there is a phenomenon here that is worth taking seriously. If we had a drug that did that much good, it would be very much in demand.". This scheme is one among many current serious investigations of complementary healing.

Every healer, be they medical doctor, alternative therapist or spiritual healer, should have the well-being of their patients as their prime objective. One should always bear in mind that what is right for one patient may not be right for another, and that a spiritual healer is not qualified to give any sort of medical opinion.

It is important that patients themselves be aware of their own bodies, and of what healing method is best suited to them. They can achieve this by getting in touch with their inner self, although unfortunately not many people are yet sufficiently confident to do this.

There are many types of treatment available, and patients must avail themselves of the one which suits them best. It may be orthodox treatment, or a complementary holistic therapy, or perhaps a combination of both. Consulting a healer may help them to sense what they need, although in many cases spiritual healing alone is sufficient to correct the problem.

The healing force works from the inner core energy outwards, thus balancing the whole being. Although of course it is both customary and desirable for a patient to have sought a diagnosis from a doctor, the healer does not even need to know what is wrong. All that is necessary is for them to make themselves available to the healing flow, and to be an instrument of Light. However, anyone who works with these subtle forces becomes very sensitive to the different frequencies. They will almost certainly know intuitively where to direct the flow, and will in time learn to adjust the more subtle energies around and within the patient's body.

Never allow yourself to feel inadequate whilst giving healing. On one occasion, one of my healing students suddenly dropped her hands during a healing exercise, walking away from the partner on whom she was practising. When asked what was wrong, she replied, "I can't do this, I'm not good enough!" The purity of the energy often reveals our own imbalances, but if we all waited until we were perfect, no good would ever be done. Any healing given with an open heart and loving intent is worthwhile.

DEATH AND DYING

If a patient does not recover, do not take it as a failure on your part: from time to time most healers encounter a death among their patients. Unfortunately, for most people in our society, death is a taboo subject, but it should not be viewed in this way, for it is simply the end of a journey.

It is ironic that enormous effort goes into the preparations for a birth, but that there is little or no preparation for death, which remains shrouded in fear. Death is one of the major issues for healers today: more elderly and terminally ill patients than ever before are seeking their help.

The whole subject must be addressed with intelligence and sensitivity. If we can understand that we are energy, and that energy can never be destroyed, we will also understand that death is nothing more than a transformation, a doorway into another experience. Just as we would prepare ourselves for any journey, let us think seriously about preparation for death - the most important journey of our lives. In giving healing to terminally ill patients, you can offer them the opportunity to move out of their present existence with dignity and inner peace, and in some cases you will witness tremendous joy in the process.

The most important place to start as a healer is with yourself - be in touch with your body. It is a physical instrument, and, like any instrument, it needs servicing and maintenance. A common misconception among those doing spiritual work is that their own health will be automatically taken care of, but in fact this is always the responsibility of the individual. In addition to a wholesome diet and sufficient sleep, some form of exercise is essential to good health. What ever type suits you is the best one for you. As a suggestion, walking, yoga and dance are excellent, for these put us it touch with a sense of life and living. It is not essential to exercise every day, but ideally we should do it at least two or three times a week.

BREAKING OLD PATTERNS

If we think in terms of everything being energy, we can better understand the whole subject of healing. We know that everyone emanates their own energy, in the form of the aura. This energy field around the body is living and vibrant. It contains all the inner patterns, emotional, mental and physical.

These patterns are formed by past experiences. A bad experience in childhood will create a negative pattern, and if this is perpetuated by the individual in adult life, there comes a point where it "sets". If it is not recognised and thoroughly dealt with by the individual, then it will be taken into the next life, and the next and the next, until finally the soul acknowledges and clears it.

If we were born into the sort of family situation that is likely to cause bad childhood experiences of one sort or another, it is extremely likely that the negativity was established in the last life, or maybe the one before, or the one before that. There seems, however, to be little point in spending long hours in meditation and/or therapy, trying to discover the long-past whys and wherefores. The situation could be likened to an endless piece of string, in that we could go on pulling at it for eternity in our search for the origin of a negative pattern. It is far better to focus on the dissolution of that negativity here and now.

We are the sum total of all our experiences, and this amalgam emanates a vibration. The vibration creates a magnetic force, and the force dictates what experiences we shall attract on all levels. We can break the patterns of the past, and direct our own future, by dealing with the vibration of today. This is, the only way of changing old patterns. Knowing their origins does not of itself alter them.

Being in touch with the inner soul light creates the fire that melts the old, worn-out patterns, and our way of living creates the new one. Ultimately, each individual has to reshape themselves, and healing can be the most effective way of helping someone get in touch with their "fire."

There are many different ways of administering spiritual healing. One of the most effective is not by directly touching the body, but by pouring healing energy through the patient's aura. Auras radiate through the atmosphere in waves, each one giving off a different vibrational energy, and when you become sufficiently sensitive, you will be able to feel these waves, which form layers around the body.

The first wave, the one closest to the body, holds the current patterns of the physical state. It is called the physical etheric. The next layer contains the emotional frequency. Further out is the band that holds what is commonly called the lower mental, and next is the astral band. The astral is usually felt within, or just an arm's length away from, the physical body. Most of the disturbances that a healer encounters with a patient are to be found within these wave bands. When you go beyond the astral, you come to more subtle energies, which relate to the spiritual aspects of the individual, and are not so commonly acknowledged.

The first layer beyond the astral is the etheric template, which holds all past conditionings, including those of past lives. It also holds the memory of how the body should be in its perfect form, and by pouring healing energy into this area, we can restructure the inner physical condition. Physical cellular regrowth then occurs within the inner etheric layer, and the outer one feeds this through the subtle bodies. By the time you start to sense the etheric template, you will almost certainly be working outside the patient's arm's length.

Beyond the etheric template is the Buddhic, or Nirvanic, layer: the higher mind, the level of personal-individual absorption into the highest Self.

Lastly we come to the Divine link, the causal body. Loosely speaking, this is the Soul Self, the frequency on which cosmic connections are made, but only by those human beings who have attained freedom from the individualized monad, that is those who have attained enlightenment and self-realisation, and are therefore completely unattached to anything material.

There is a direct relationship between these vibrational levels and the whole evolutionary process of mankind. Primal man was of the physical emanation, which is purely survival-based. Next, mankind reached into the creative, or procreative, state, this can be affiliated with the second centre the sacral, but within the wave band of the aura, it is experienced as a vibrational energy or ray. Coming up into the next ray, we find the lower mind, and it is at this stage of development that mankind evolves into thinking Man. The Fourth wave or ray is for most people their current vibration. This is the Heart ray, the bridge between lower and higher experience. The gateway to this is unconditional love. The Fifth Ray is the one to which the vast majority of the masses are now aspiring. This is important, because by touching this frequency we at last gain access to the spiritual world.

The Buddhic and causal levels are beyond most people's experience, but for healing purposes they can still, in certain circumstances, be used to align the patient to the cosmic rays. This can only be done by a healer who is also vibrating to these levels, and it is not necessary work for most patients.

It obviously takes a bit of practice to become adept at perceiving the energy fields. Think of your senses as both a receiver and, later, a transmitter of frequencies. You as the healer need to learn to attune to these various frequencies, but this is not as hard as it sounds, because once you have located a frequency, it will become easier for you to return to it at will. It is a bit like learning a tune: once you have memorised it, you will always remember how it goes. Allow your natural sensitivity to be your guide. Healing is such a natural process that the less your brain is involved the better.

It is important not to measure yourself against others. Never feel either inferior or superior, for we are all on our way to enlightenment, albeit via a multiplicity of paths, and we all have more to learn. Like attracts like, and each healer will attract patients on a similar "wave-band" to his or her own. If ever you feel uncomfortable about treating someone who comes to you for healing, do not do it. Intuit who can better serve them. We cannot be all things to all people.

When anyone near us is feeling unwell or depressed, our most natural instinct is to go and hold them. When we do this, we are surrounding their aura with positive sympathy. This is healing. When we cut or hurt ourselves, the first thing we do is to hold our hands over the damaged area. This is healing. When we hold our arms open to someone we are greeting, or someone who is crying, this is also healing. In any healing exercise, therefore, it is important to allow your natural instincts to help you. However, it is not good to get emotionally involved with your patient. If that happens, you will find that you will give out from within your own energy, mainly from the Solar Plexus centre. This can create a depletion of energy which can, if unchecked, be most unpleasant, and can in extreme cases lead to a healer's total breakdown.

We have all experienced being in the same room as someone who is draining us. As they seemingly feel better and better, we feel more and more depleted. As I have said in an earlier chapter, such people rarely realise that they are sucking energy from others, so it is important that we as healers and psychics protect ourselves by being in control of our own energies at all times. In any case, this sort of drainage rarely does the recipient any long term good, as it is simply an exchange of energy between two human beings. Nothing is permanently solved by allowing it to take place. Sometimes it happens without our knowledge, but if you become aware of being drained, either mentally pull a golden band around your solar plexus, or physically fold your arms over that area, thus shutting off your personal "drainage valve".

EXERCISES.

You do not need a particular place in which to heal. Just do it where you feel most comfortable. Usually the patient sits on a stool, or a chair with a low back, so that the healer can move around the patient, and have easy access to the spine, which is an important place of focus for many healing techniques.

Giving healing is rather like having a conversation with someone's energy field. Always start by being in a balanced state yourself, for you are the instrument, and every instrument needs to be clean, and in good running order. Before any healing it is a good idea to have practised some kind of focussed meditation. This need not take long, and it will enable you to work better.

Start by lightly touching your patient's shoulders. This forms a link between you and them, and also lets them know that you are beginning your work. When you have finished, touch the shoulders again. This will give you a chance to break the connection, and will signal to your patient that you have finished. This need be the beginning and end to physical touch. The less you do so the better.

You may wish to start healing with the following exercise, which is useful in all circumstances. It helps to calm the patient, and makes contact with their "spirit level", which is their point of equilibrium. Obviously a persons spirit or soul does not exist in a particular place within the body, however in the area described we can find the core internal physical force which can connect to the core or soul force of spirit.

Stand to one side of the patient. Holding your hands with palms facing their chest and back, physically or mentally touch the area of the top of the thymus, which is just above the Heart centre. You will find this on the sternum (breast bone) and on the back, just below the base of the neck. Having touched these spots, immediately move your hands slowly outwards from the back and front of the body.

You will feel the sensation of expanding energy pushing your hands away, a feeling not dissimilar to that experienced during the exercise mentioned earlier in this chapter. When you feel that you have made contact with the patient's energy, begin to draw it gently out into the main auric field (the normal physical energy radiation discussed earlier), which is out into, and slightly beyond, the astral. So your hands should now be approximately an arm's length away from the patient's body.

In one movement, draw the energy around to form a semicircle of energy around one side of the patient, then move round and do the same on the other side. You have now created, within the patient's auric field, a circle of light from their own core spirit. This is almost exactly what you achieve for yourself when you do the opening exercise given in Chapter One.

Stand behind your patient, with your arms "embracing" the energy. You will experience a feeling similar to that of holding a rubber ball. Allow your hands to become like sponges, and gently absorb some of the energy into each palm. Then gently place your hands over - not covering - your patient's Crown centre. Release this energy into the crown, from where it will be fed into other areas.

This exercise aligns the patient with their own inner calm, their still place, their equilibrium. This in turn helps them to contact their soul self, allowing them to be in a very relaxed state, so that the healing can flow more productively. For almost any patient this exercise can immediately create a calmness that is very healing. It is excellent for all ailments, especially those of emotional origin.

There are all sorts of methods of healing, and with experience you must intuit which is best for you and your patient. A simple one to start with involves simply sensing the Chakra energies:

Stand sideways-on to your patient, with both hands facing inwards. Starting at the Crown, bring your hands close to each centre, in front and behind the patient. If you prefer, you may gently touch the centres. It does not matter which hand you use in front, although generally you will find, if you are right-handed, that you will want to use the right hand in front, and vice versa if you are left-handed.

As you allow the energy emanating from each centre to push away your hand, sense what feelings you are receiving. Move from centre to centre, remembering after contacting each one to clear your hands of any residual energy. One often sees healers rubbing their hands together at this stage, or even giving an ostentatious clap. This is not necessary, as the process can even be done mentally. A slight brushing of the fingers will suffice.

Healers obtain information in varying ways: you may, for instance, be able to communicate with the colour rays of the centres, and thereby gauge the state of each chakra; you may obtain clairvoyant information concerning the patient; you may simply receive a sense of which chakras are stronger and which are weaker. However, as a general rule it is advisable simply to act as a channel of energy: you do not actually need any particular information for the flow of the Love Force to do its work. Sometimes, though, a clear message may be dropped into your mind, a message which it is impossible to ignore. As always, use your intuition to judge whether or not this can be used to help the patient, and once again - remember to allow any healing process to be totally unconditional.

When you have sensed each centre, go back to any chakra that you feel needs some more work, and feed healing energy into it. You administer this by simply opening your mind to the Universal Light Forces, because energy follows thought. You can channel this energy into a chakra from within an arm's length. Later, however, as you become conversant with the more subtle energies, you may wish to work further away from the body, using the method already described to feed energy through the etheric template.

Take it slowly. It takes time to build up one's repertoire. The very best healing is intuitive, and is developed through trust and confidence. In the early stages you may wish to have a structured regime of starting at a certain place and going through each chakra, but after a while you will probably be drawn immediately to the appropriate areas.

Some people feel very attuned to colour vibration. Using colour can be achieved simply by visualising the appropriate colours being transmitted into the area on which you are working. You may wish to give your patient a simple visualisation connected with colour, so that they can begin to take responsibility for their own healing.

When you have finished giving healing, touch each of the patient's centres, cleansing, clearing, and, if you feel it to be necessary, closing the five middle centres. Always the leave the Crown open to the Source, and the Base open to the Earth energies. Some people like to finish off by enfolding the patient in Light. To do this, visualise, or draw with your hands, a circle of Light around them. Golden or white light is the most effective protection, as it creates a positive energy field that gives the patient some respite through balance, harmony and truth.

The use of crystals is sometimes helpful. Their molecular structure causes them to vibrate at specific frequencies, each type of crystal thereby creating a different response when used within the energy field. We need only observe the widespread use of quartz as an accurate time keeper to realise they have a unique vibratory quality. This is a wide and fascinating subject, some books on the subject are recommended below. However if you make use of the crystals undoubted powers of focus, it is essential to remember that they hold negativity as well as positivity and after use must therefore be cleansed. This is a simple procedure, either visualise light running through your crystal or hold them under clear running water.

Sound is a powerful tool in healing, and is not for the novice. Every chakra vibrates to its own note, and by getting in touch with the correct vibration we can gently feed that area with its own sound. If you are thinking of working in this way, practise with your own bodily vibrations first, and make sure that you are thoroughly conversant with the sensing process. The use of sound is quite dramatic for most patients, and for someone who is very unbalanced it could adjust the energies too violently, so proceed with great caution.

To help align your own centres with sound, a simple exercise is to focus the sound into each centre, starting with the Base. Intuitively "hear" the sound you want to make - usually the lower centres have lower notes. As you sing each note, really feel the vibration of the sound in the relevant centre.

Concentrating on the Base chakra, make a strong note out of the sound "OO". Make this at least two or three times, then move up to the Sacral chakra, and sing the vibration into the area with the sound "OR". (It can be the same note, or a different one. Use your intuition).

Work your way up the chakras, making sounds as follows: Solar plexus, "AH"; Heart, a very open "ARE"; Throat, "A" (as in apple); Brow, "E" and Crown, "E-OO"". This simple exercise is incredibly effective in balancing energy, but never use it on anyone else until you are secure in the accuracy of your own intuition.

A simpler form of the above exercise is to lie on the floor, gently connecting with your breathing, then taking your attention to the centre that feels most unbalanced. Listen for the right sound. Make that sound, and allow the vibration to fill the centre in question. This will very effectively dissolve any offending energy.

To get in touch with the physical body, it is always better to lie on the floor. Simply going through the centres, feeding each one the relevant colour or sound, is extremely powerful, and whilst doing this you can also intuit what your body needs in a physical sense.

If you allow it to work for you, food is a form of medicine. Intuitively you may feel that your body needs a certain type, or even a certain colour, of food, such as green vegetables. Scientist now tell us that the disease fighting substances being discovered in fruits and vegetables are what gives them their different colours. Many of the pigments are antioxidants substances able to disarm unstable free radicals that pit the insides of blood vessels and even damage the DNA that controls how cells grow. The leafy green keeps nitrates in cooked meats from hooking up with amino acids to form cancer. This then gives new meaning to "You must eat your greens!" Like their Ray colours, yellow and red foods are often energising. Red holds a powerful pigment called lycopene and is one of the most powerful antioxidants yet tested. Tomatoes supply as much as 90 percent of our lycopene. Beet pigments may help suppress the growth of bacteria. The pale yellow of potatoes and cauliflower comes from pigments called anthoxanthines (Greek for yellow flower) these function as antioxidants, and the deeper yellow of peppers comes from betacarotenes. Corn gets its colour from another antioxidant, lutein, which has a role in preventing one of the leading causes of blindness. The yellow pigment found in the spice turmeric is thought to help the body's resistance to cancer.

Orange has the pigment betacarotene, this is said to aid the lowering of cholesterol. Green is created by chlorophyll, the substance which collects and stores the energy from the sun. When this is broken down through digestion it becomes a potent defence against cancer. Blue purple - the colour of blueberries is dyed with the pigment anthocyanine (blue flower in Greek) These are also antioxidants which can neutralize several common carcinogens and also dilate blood vessels helping to lower the risk of heart disease and strokes by keeping arteries open and flowing. Experts suspect that the anthocyanines in grapes may be one reason a glass of red wine at dinner helps lower the risk of heart attack.

So when you look around the supermarket next, allow your intuition to guide you to the colour and substance you need for your own health. Nature by many means, including colour, always guides us if we choose to observe.

Your prime objective in any healing work is to help your patients to help themselves. Dependency is not good for you or them, and you must never allow it to develop. If someone is coming to you too regularly, it probably means that they are not making sufficient progress, and not taking charge of their own healing. It may help to give them little exercises to do on their own.

If after a while they make no further progress, suggest that they leave it for a bit, or pass them on to someone else. In many cases, to become fully cured may mean that they have to reassess and alter their whole way of life. Some people will not be ready to face this, and if that is the case there is nothing you can do, for everyone has free will.

Please take the time to make contact with all the energies in your body, which is a wondrous vehicle. It will house you for many years, and give you rich experiences of all kinds. It is truly beautiful. Look after it and it will look after you.

All aspects of yourself - physical, mental, emotional and spiritual - need your care. It is a very simple truth that all healers become healers primarily to help heal themselves, and in learning to heal themselves they will automatically heal others.

Books for Reference

Frontiers of Health, by Dr. Christine R. Page 1992
Spiritual Healing - Miracle or Mirage? by Alan Young 1981
Hands of Light, by Barbara Ann Brennan. 1987.
Quantum Healing by Deepak Chopra M.D. 1989
Ageless Body, Timeless Mind by Deepak Chopra M.D. 1993
Crystal Healing by Edmund Harold. 1990
Love is in the Earth by Melody 1991.

Chapter 6
_____

READING THE
ENERGY FIELDS

The most common initial experience of people who are developing psychic vision is the perception of the energy field around someone's body. Commonly referred to as the aura, it is frequently seen as "lights", and is often first observed in a public place, when one least expects it. This can, at first, be quite worrying, but there is nothing to be concerned about: it is simply a change of focus.

The first experience of seeing someone's energy field usually occurs through the "inner eyes" as opposed to the physical ones, but sooner or later the student will be able to adjust their senses to allow physical perception also.

On Kirlian photographs the aura shows as blobs of colour, but this is somewhat deceptive, as the energies are constantly moving. The auric emanations are like waves of energy vibrating around the individual, and the colour of someone's aura can change in an instant, depending on their thoughts, emotions and feelings.

At first the student is likely to perceive the energies simply as basic colours, and read the aura accordingly, but they will very quickly start to discern subtle variations. Let us take a comprehensive look at the colours. One must bear in mind that different people relate to colour in different ways, so apply your own intuition, always remembering the rule that the purer the colour, the more positive the energy.

Red

In its pure state, red is the colour of earthy, physical energy. If there is plenty of red in the aura, this person is very physically active, and very strong. However, if the red has dark patches, or you see the colour being thrown off the body as sparks of energy, this would almost certainly indicate anger. Crimson might mean a high sex drive, and scarlet may denote ego.

A pink shade, especially a rose pink, often shows unselfishness and sensitivity. If pink surrounds the person, it can denote very spiritual healing taking place, and it is almost certainly the aura of someone who is spiritually aware, and practising healing in some capacity.

Orange

This is a colour of forcefulness. A predominance of pure orange shows someone who has great purpose, and tremendous creativity. It is the flame that will help create warmth in whatever direction it is spread. As the individual develops spiritually, this "flame energy" will help lift them into the higher frequencies. When the colour is not pure, or if it has dark or black energy within it, the natural flow has imploded, and this could mean self-indulgence, and a person wrapped up in their own emotions. A reddish orange is indicative of someone who is devious. If the orange is being thrown off the body, it denotes sexual desires run riot, and could even mean sexual disease or corruption.

Yellow

A bright, clear yellow encircling the body means balanced emotions and clear thought. It also shows compassion in its purest form. Muddy or dark yellow denotes a fearful person who is also resentful. They may be lazy, and consequently believe that the world owes them a living.

Gold is a deeply spiritual colour, and tells us that the person is mystical and spiritually advanced: a highly developed intuition is also likely. Gold is not normally seen in people's energy fields, and it is interesting to note that it is a colour favoured by artists in depicting saintly or godly beings.

Green

Green is the colour of nature. A clear, grass-green colour reveals equilibrium, and healing qualities. This is someone who is selfless and adaptable. They radiate tranquillity, and this affects those around them in a beneficial way. A soft, pastel shade of green highlights the spiritual aspects of the colour, and indicates a healer who is connected to the devic worlds. On the other hand, green with any darkness in it indicates selfishness and envy, particularly if it is thrown off the body as sparks of energy. Anyone with this kind of aura is highly unpleasant to be near, and almost everyone will automatically want to move away from them. Muddy, olive green denotes greed and deceit, and can also reveal a depressed person.

Blue

This is an expansive colour, and usually belongs to someone with an independent spirit, who has discovered a way of communicating with divine energies. Often it denotes a devotional or religious nature. These people are incorruptible, as they are strong within their inner knowledge. A soft blue is also a healing colour, and if it surrounds the aura, it means that either the person is a healer, or that they are receiving healing. Any darkness in a pure blue colour indicates dogmatism and stubborn qualities.

Indigo

A sharp, clear indigo is the colour of the priest or priestess; someone who certainly uses their inner eye, and thus takes an overview of life. It is the colour of spiritual attainment. A seeker of Divine truths, this person is not easy to live with in the mundane world. It is unusual to see this colour intersected by any darkness, but if you do, it would mean that the person was over-intent on their own perfection. This would cause depression, and a feeling that they are not good enough, or that they never do enough.

Purple/violet

This reveals someone of very high spiritual attainment. The colour of kings, it is the last shade in the spectrum before it blends back into the pure white Light of Spirit. When this colour is darkened, it does not indicate negativity, but a person only slightly removed from total connection with the Godhead.

Grey/Black

These colours tell us of some kind of negativity. For instance, if you see a lot of darkness over the head, this could indicate negative thoughts. If you see it around the solar plexus or lower body, this is someone with very negative emotions, and the darker or blacker the aura, the more negative the being. If very dark grey, or black, enfolds the body, this is someone prepared to implement their dark thoughts of revenge and deceit.

Brown

This indicates a materially orientated person, which could be a positive sign, showing good business acumen and organisational skills. A dark, muddy brown, however, almost certainly means a person who is overly engrossed in material accumulation. There is a need to get what they want immediately, and they are consequently very selfish.

Silver/grey

This is someone who is erratic, and who probably has a "quicksilver" temper. It is a colour associated with the Earth spirits. These beings have a very different mentality from that of human beings, and consequently their energies are rarely conducive to our own. Their energy is harmless, and even protective, within its natural environment, but not around human beings, where it could lead to mental illness. Silver indicates someone out of their element. It can reveal ignorance, nebulous thoughts, and a person who lives a life of illusion.

White

This tells us of a fully enlightened Being, and for that reason it is very rarely observed. A body wholly surrounded in white would indicate a Divinely spiritual Being. There are usually only a few of these souls incarnate at any one time. It is sometimes possible to see a white image within the aura; this indicates divine inspiration coming from a spiritual source.

Observing the energy field as colours can be very helpful. As a self awareness process, colour interpretation could be compared with handing someone a mirror, particularly someone who does not know themselves very well. It is also good to be fully aware of one's own aura and what it is doing, and of course to be able to adjust it as and when appropriate (see the exercise at the end of this chapter).

You will best be able to ease into these new perceptions when you are relaxed. Do not try too hard; it is a natural process, and sometimes concentrating with a fixed notion will actually stop the shift. Start by focussing on something simple, like a plant. Place it in front of a bare wall, look hard at it for a moment, then gently relax your focus. You should begin to see a vibrant light emanating from the plant. Alternatively, go for a walk in a quiet spot, sit down and look up at a tree, and try the same exercise. You may then see not only a light, but perhaps also the shimmering energy of the living tree. In time, and with practice, you may be even able to communicate with the spirit of the tree. Acquiring this new way of seeing can take a little time, so do not be discouraged if you do not achieve it on your first attempt.

Consciously awaken your senses all the time. Every time you walk into a room, especially if it is a room which you have never entered before, be alert to, and use, your awakening senses. What are your extra-sensory antenna receiving? Begin to recognise the vibrancy and the swirling movements of energy around everything. Observe a friend or a family member in this way, and you may gain a completely different view of them.

After you have familiarised yourself with the auric emanations, open yourself to the possibility of receiving thoughts and feelings. Open your mind to impressions. You will receive all sorts of images, which are likely to be what the person has been recently thinking or feeling. You may see an image of them going about their business, and where, and with whom, they have been.

The auric energies connected with the lower worlds, that is, the ordinary three-dimensional activities, emotions, thoughts and physical senses, are all to be observed around the body. Each of them has a different frequency, but they all can be attuned to with a little practice.

Even on these lower frequencies, however, it can take a very long time to achieve any degree of accuracy. Contrary to popular belief, there are very few people who can attune in a focussed manner without training, and even those very few would benefit enormously from the discipline of group work. It can take years of practice before one even begins to be confident of the energy and focus that one is receiving. Practise as much as you can, always ensuring that you are doing so with a willing person.

As an auric reader you will be acting as a mirror: remember that mirrors do not judge, they simply reflect. Judging someone's way of being is not your job, and it can be dangerous. Consequently any personal comments made during an auric reading must be given with the clear indication that they are simply your own impressions. Please also remember that you may come across some very vulnerable people, who would gladly hand over to you their responsibility for themselves. In no circumstances must you allow this, for it is not good for them or for you.

THOUGHT FORMS (ELEMENTALS)

As you become more proficient, you may begin to see thought

forms. This is a complex subject, and one that merits our attention.

It can be extremely difficult to establish what thought forms are, and even very experienced mediums often mistake them for people in the spirit world. Generally speaking, thought forms look like cardboard cut-outs, but if there is some emotion involved, it gives life to the image, which may then be interpreted as a spirit or an astral being.

When someone projects a thought or a feeling, it is imprinted upon the atmosphere. On its own it will not live very long, but desire and thought together can create a live form, sometimes referred to as an elemental. With projection, elementals can take on their own life, and like any other living forms, they can have an independent existence. In most cases, however, thoughts and feelings are so transitory that the elemental literally dies through lack of feeding. Particularly in its early life, an elemental needs a great deal of effort and response. However, if negative emotion and/or thought is given to it, it can become rather a nuisance for the person concerned. In extreme cases, where lots of negative energy is used, the thought form can become a dark entity that can literally haunt its parent.

There are two main kinds of thought form. Someone with a largely emotional make up will create a desire-based elemental. This is described as desire/thought. When the individual works more on a mental level, their thought forms will be thought-based, therefore called thought/desire. The elementals of thought/desire are very much more potent, and last much longer.

Everything always returns to its place of origin. The law of cause and effect is in constant operation, and thought forms are not exempt from it. Unfortunately, the energy of the desire/thought elemental can implode, and in very negative cases it can be absorbed into the etheric double. This means that the elemental stays within the subconscious of the "donor", and may in the worst cases lead to addictions.

Thought forms dictate our whole present existence, for the elemental beings are present in both the psychic and physical worlds. They even dictate the very cells in our bodies over many lifetimes. In short, we experience the effects of our own creations. The only way to dissolve harmful elementals is through alignment with the Unconditional Love Ray. This can be achieved through prayer, meditation and healing.

The elementals of thought/desire are much stronger, because these energies have been given substance by some degree of concentration. If these are also aligned with will, the energy becomes very strong indeed. Thankfully few people know how to align these, and even fewer would give the considerable time required for its administration. If this were to be practised from a hateful or negative energy, it would be black magic. On a smaller scale, this is what some nationalities refer to as the "evil eye".

There is a safety aspect, however, because if someone is highly charged negatively, they are also likely to be emotional, and unfocused desire will weaken the process. Desire, no matter how strong, will not by itself be able to create a living form. It needs thought. It must be strongly emphasised here that no real purpose can be achieved by sending bad thoughts, for sooner or later they will always return to the sender.

Any one with clairvoyant eyes will see these elemental beings, but each individual will see them in the shape to which they can best relate. A hateful, spiteful thought form can therefore be perceived as a snake by one person and a wolf by another. More often they are perceived as dark or black energy within the auric fields. This energy can also be seen as a silhouette, or dark shadow, standing over the person. This is where it becomes very difficult to differentiate between the thought form and the astral dark force (the astral energies are discussed later in this book). Consequently we could refer to them in the same way, for the continuing process of thought given to the elemental will create a new, and even more powerful, being, which in essence is not very different from an astral being.

When it has reached this stage, the exorcism of either a self-inflicted thought form or an astral entity is similar. A healer will have to pour light on to the subject in some way, but if the individual is still feeding it with energy, it will not go. In dire cases, the thought form either follows the person into spirit, or upon death will find a new host, which is very often someone with close emotional connections to the original person.

An elemental will disappear when it has finished its task, unless it is fed by further thoughts or desires, so it is essential to be aware of all your emanations. As a seeker of knowledge and truth, aligned to the Light energies, you must take full and absolute responsibility for all your actions, thoughts and desires. When you expand your vibrations, you develop a greater ability to give weight and substance to these types of energy, and as a result they multiply.

It is therefore not uncommon at this stage for the developing psychic to encounter many synchronicities. These are directly brought about by the emanation of thoughts and desires entering into a now clearer atmosphere. There are fewer veils and layers to penetrate, and as a result, thoughts become very powerful, and can manifest as reality within twenty-four hours. Obviously, therefore, the importance of open observation at all times is paramount to your well-being.

Elementals are produced even in the sleep state, and indeed it is there that they can be even more active, because you can produce more desires when you are free of day-to-day activities. A prayer to the Light Forces, particularly the angels, just before going to sleep, is helpful, but as always we must take full responsibility for ourselves. Before entering sleep, a little gentle but enlightening observation of your day may help you to focus on, and therefore eradicate, any potentially dangerous thought patterns, thus ensuring a sound night's sleep and no further come back of your thoughts and actions.

This brings us to a very important aspect of this work for potential healers and psychics. We have absolutely no right to give healing or help without permission. We must at all times wait to be asked, and if we are not asked, we must under no conditions give healing, for in these cases is it born out of our judgement, and is not necessarily for the good of the person involved. Of course some people do not know what healing is and therefore could not ask directly for it, however, if they approach you for help that can be considered as a request for healing. When we give our help and healing it must always be for no ulterior motives. It is the universal light force energy that manifests itself as love within the human condition, and we must give it with the same degree of loving attention.

Such is the powerful force of this work and the energy involved, it is very easy to believe that we can cure or heal anything. It is an unpalatable fact to recognise that if someone or something is disturbing you, the mind will excuse this by interpreting this as someone in need, whereas in reality it could well be from our own judgement. In the guise of healing, our own thoughts and judgements are projected, very often without the healer being aware or conscious of what they are really sending. If that is the case it is certainly not unconditional, it is plainly born out of ego and fear, and a need to make others comply with what we perceive as being correct. No one has the right to try to change another human being, whatever the supposed good intentions. There is no excuse. It does not matter if the person is obnoxious, or even if they are in pain. It is their choice, and that must be accepted. Acceptance is the major step towards unconditional love, and only through obtaining it do we begin to dissolve the negativity. Remember the saying, "the road to hell is paved with good intentions."

There are many pitfalls in this work, and it is no wonder that many mystics, and religious and spiritual people throughout the ages have been against the use of the unseen forces. You are quite safe, however, if you are prepared continuously to work on yourself with total commitment to truth, whatever that may reveal. Be vigilant, for the little mind will always give us excuses, especially if it absolves us from any wrong-doing.

It is an unfortunate fact that through the ages, psychic work has been used for unscrupulous control over others. In most cases this was born, not of a deliberate attempt on the part of the psychic, but of that most dangerous enemy, illusion. Ask yourself, therefore, if you want to delude yourself. If you can wholly and honestly say no, carry on. If, however, there is even the slightest hesitation, it is better to stop now, and spend some time on contemplative and meditational work before you come back to the psychic worlds.

We live our material life within the limitations of the third dimension because that is where we are currently focussed, but for many reasons, mankind is now beginning to shift that focus, and to see beyond the barriers of his own limitations. This can be an alarming prospect, because when barriers come down, there is nothing left to hide behind. Inner connection is therefore essential, not just for psychic development, but for maintaining our balance in a changing world.

As we raise our eyes to higher frequencies, and see things beyond "normal" sight, we may doubt our new vision, because we are conditioned by our own limitations to see only those things that appear to be solid. The truth is that there are no limitations: it is we who created the barriers, and we who possess the ability to destroy them.

EXERCISE

As always, be as relaxed as possible, and go through the opening procedure if you feel the need. Take your thoughts (and therefore your energy) above your head, to the gateway where the Divine Energy enters your being. Cast your mind gently but firmly over all your thoughts and feelings during the last twenty-four or forty-eight hours, particularly those that disturbed you. BE HONEST WITH YOURSELF.

Take an over-view of those thoughts, and if you gave them any unnecessary negative energy, acknowledge the fact. With firm deliberation, visualise your actions, thoughts and emotions, and pour Light over them. Ask the Divine Energy to help you to achieve a freer spirit tomorrow, and if during the day you find that you have sent negative thoughts, focus your mind to send positive ones to the same place.

When reviewing your thoughts, it is no good feeling sorry or guilty, because these reactions are counter-productive. Analysis is not productive either, but you may need to know why you reacted in a negative fashion, so examine each episode, but without responses, particularly emotional ones: this exercise is intended to draw your energy away from the lower worlds, not to make things worse. If you find yourself giving in to self-indulgent responses, stop the exercise and come back to it later.

When you have done this exercise, focus on your own aura. Are you picking up any negative in-coming thoughts or emotions? It is not necessary to know from whom these emanate. In fact, unless you are one hundred percent benevolent and forgiving, that information may cause you to feel resentful. Simply acknowledge that there are some negative thoughts, and from your heart pour the Light Force Energy into and through your aura.

You can do the above exercise in bed, before you go to sleep. It is a good idea to get into the habit of unconditionally examining yourself at night, to clear anything that you may have picked up during the day. If you do so, make sure you do not fall asleep during the exercise, because the focus of the mind will dissipate in sleep, and the emotional body can become dominant. If you do the exercise at any other time, make a point of doing some healthy physical exercise afterwards. Such activities are a good adjunct to the dissolution of thoughts and emotions.

Finish your exercise by drawing the pure Light of the cosmos down through your gateway, into your crown, and pour it through all the chakras, making sure that your connection with the Earth is clear and vibrant. Close the centres if you wish.

Eventually you will be able to observe your life as it unfolds, at which point your whole existence will become a meditation.

Books for Reference.
Vibrational Medicine, by Richard Gerber M.D. 1988
The Magus of Strovolos - The Extraordinary World of a Spiritual Healer,
by Kyriacos C. Markides 1985
The New Clairvoyance, by Rev. Mario Schoenmaker 1986

Chapter 7
<hr>

EARTH
ENERGIES

Anyone who tunes in to the various outside energies could be likened to a radio set being tuned in to different wave-bands. One may view the chakras as transducers: the Base centre receiving long waves, the Crown receiving short waves, and the Heart, the balancing central energy, receiving medium waves! Very high frequencies could be compared with the etheric energies, and ultra-high frequencies with the Outer Cosmic forces. As a receiver, the clearer you become the better. In time you will, through your attunement, become a transmitter also.

As we have seen, the Base centre frequency is that of the physical worlds; the Sacral, that of reproduction and creativity; the Solar Plexus, that of the lower mind and emotions; and the Heart frequency is within the Love range.

The Heart centre is the bridging frequency between the lower and higher energies. It is the bridge that stands in the neutral zone, across which we must pass if we are to rise to higher consciousness for our own higher discovery. For us as individuals to vibrate on this frequency, we must be working from the point of unconditional love.

The word "unconditional" is used so often, and in so many contexts, that its full meaning can become diminished and somewhat obscured. We, however, must examine its meaning in minute detail, and maintain a constant awareness of whether or not we are unconditional in all aspects of our behaviour.

Have you been living your life without conditions? The answer is probably "no". To be brave enough to examine what this means is commendable, for in many ways it entails confronting and breaching barriers such as those created by our upbringing, and by the pressure of society's rules and codes of conduct. It is a hard commitment, but one that is essential to your growth.

You do not have to be a saint, or a perfectly balanced being, in order to attune to the Heart, but you do need to know alignment with the Universal Light Force. When you have achieved this in meditation, even if only once, you will know how it feels, and will therefore desire to remain balanced outside of your meditational state.

In time, you will be able to bring the Heart energy into your normal world, and this balance will enable you to make connection with the Earth spirits. The frequencies on which these beings exist are so refined, and so dissimilar to our own normal state, that Heart energy balance is required for any human being to become a clear instrument of attunement.

Working with your own energies, achieving a level of balance and harmony within, and practising attunement to the auric energies and how they function, you are now able to start tuning into the finer vibrations. Up until now, the energies that we have dealt with have been within the normal range: in fact, your communication with them was constant and instinctive, even before you began to focus on them psychically.

When we go beyond those normal human currents, we are coming to aspects of the living world that remain largely unknown to the vast majority of people, although many of them have been written and spoken of throughout the ages. The Earth spirits are numbered amongst these.

What do we mean when we speak of spirit? In general terms we are, of course, referring to the essence or core, but the word "spirit" can also be used to describe a psychic entity.

Earth spirits are usually first acknowledged as being the spirit of a place: when you are out quietly walking in the countryside, or sitting in your garden, you may feel their presence. Most people equate this feeling with the peace of the moment, or with their love of the plants and trees, and this is not a false impression, for access to these energies lies within the Heart range. There exists, however, a parallel dimension that houses the spiritual forces that work alongside us, aiding our physical state.

There are two major aspects of Earth work, the first of which is attunement to the earth beneath our feet. Like electricity, our energies need to be "earthed." At the beginning of a meditation, for instance, we take a deep breath and let go, releasing all our tensions, anxieties and fears. This we achieve by sending them into the Earth. Many opening exercises give express images of cleansing waters or light, rinsing and relaxing us, allowing any negativities to flow into the Earth. For these purposes the Earth then becomes a neutral zone.

We can tune in to other energies within our planet. Different lands, for instance, have different tonal frequencies. In occult law, there are five main vibrational energies in our Earth. You can experiment with this by lying on the ground and listening intuitively to the sound beneath your body. Start to hum the sound that you hear. Feel the humming vibration running through your body, and listen again, to make sure that it matches the sound beneath you. Obtaining that note is very powerful, and can act as an expanding physical healing.

Do the same thing when you travel to other lands, and you will notice the different energies. It is actually possible to do this without physically travelling, for just by mentally connecting with a country, you will be able to achieve attunement with its note.

Among students of esoteric doctrines, there has long been a widely-held belief that this variety of vibrations is the reason for the existence of the various racial types, and of the separate religions. Moreover, this school of thought holds that the original purpose of each religion was to help a different racial type, by providing the appropriate attunement for each one.

Such matters are, of course, open to discussion, but there can be little doubt that the message of each Divine Master who has incarnated on this planet has to a large extent been subsequently distorted by men wishing to instil fear in others. This was done in order to gain power over the populace, and to set them against those of differing beliefs.

Religions were never meant to instil fear, nor to divide: quite the opposite, in fact. Each land and each race and each religion is part of the scale of existence. There is no such thing as a more powerful or a more worthy note or vibration. Each has its purpose and its place, and by learning to communicate with all of them, we can learn truly to love our planet, and thereby to love everything and everyone upon it.

The second major aspect of earth work is attunement to the spirits of the earth. These come in all sorts of shapes and sizes, and they have been written, sung and talked about throughout history. Elves, fairies, gnomes, nymphs and leprechauns are all familiar words, yet although Shakespeare, amongst others, wrote about them, and artists throughout the ages have acknowledged their presence, their existence is still denied by most.

So what are these elusive species? Connected to every living thing there is a spirit. Every blade of grass, every flower and every tree. These earth energies are part of the usually hidden world that co-exists with our physical one. It is believed that the main purpose of fairies is to absorb the life force emitted by the sun, the psycho-electrical field called "prana", or "chi", and to distribute it to the solid physical worlds. In so doing, they become the essential connection between the sun's energy and the soil's minerals. The different races of fairies have different roles: some work above the ground, and some below, some work for the expansion of cell growth, and some with the mineral, vegetable and animal worlds.

The substance of the Earth spirits is essentially etheric, the finest aspect of physical material. You can see them through attunement to the etheric, or through the energy of the astral. The state of their being is so sensitive and fluid that it can be changed by thought and feeling. Generally we may see them as being composed of pulsating spheres of light with bright nucleii, but when they materialise on the etheric level, they can be interchangeable in shape. Often their shape is determined by their imitating elements of plants and animals, or by their using the thought patterns of human beings. The forms of these beings are many and varied, but they are always perceived as Light Beings, and are usually small in size.

Fairies can change their shape at will, and with this chameleon-like talent they are mischievous and playful. Such is the fineness of their energy that their colours are usually very subtle. They have a fluidity of energy and emanation, and we therefore very often perceive them with wings and flowing limbs. These images are caused by the fine etheric rays of which they are formed.

Under various titles, these elusive beings are present in all cultures. In Gaelic they are called "Sidhe", which means "people of the hills". The native American Indians call them "Nan-A-Push", which means "the little people of the forest". There are spirits everywhere, and they are usually strongly connected to the place where they are seen. We even have different spirits connected to the different elements. Salamanders are the fire spirits, Sylphs are of the air, Nymphs are found in water, and the Gnomes are part of the Earth.

The word "Gnome" is interesting, for it is associated both with the Greek expression for "sound judgement" and the Latin expression for "earth dweller." It also means a misshapen sprite, who, according to the Rosicrucians, were supposed to inhabit the interior of the Earth, and to be the guardians of mines and quarries. The Swiss alchemist Paracelsus describes them as being able to move through earth like fish through water.

In fact there are many different names for nature spirits of all descriptions. We have, for example, the Valkyries of Norse mythology, and the Lamias in Africa, and there are; nymphs, fauns, brownies, trolls, mermaids, leprechauns, the phoenix, sylphs, elves, satyrs and fairies, to name but a few. So many people have reported sightings: are they all in a collective dream state? And if the Earth spirits are indeed figments of over-active imaginations, has not humanity taken great pains to invent such a multiplicity of names for these non-existent beings?

Psychically there is a knowledge that these beings in some way assist the process of the living world. However, theirs is not an easy energy for human beings to work with, and few do. Their very nature is often mischievous, and sometimes disturbing. They can certainly play tricks on we poor mortals, and they take very few of us into their confidence.

Probably the most aloof of all are the Gnomes. The Gnomic energy is so dissimilar to our own that it is almost impossible for most people to align with them. They are very distrustful of humans beings, not surprisingly when you consider that it is their job to guard and help the Earth, for which most of us have scant regard. Most people, on inadvertently wandering into an area where Gnomes reside, experience an uneasy feeling, and a need to get out as soon as possible. Sometimes there is a feeling of literally being ejected from their territory. They rarely do any real harm, but they can disturb and annoy, and they do derive pleasure from the process.

There is danger in making too close a connection with the fairy worlds, for because of its etheric state it can affect people rather like a drug, and they may find it difficult to return to the normal human state. The fairies' evolution is parallel to our own, but rarely do the two interrelate. Sometimes, however, for no particular purpose, a soul has crossed the divide. There are many tales in folklore about the kidnapping of humans for the fairies' own ends.

I have met a handful of people whom I knew to be devic in nature, and experiencing their first incarnation in our dimension. For these folk, life is very hard. You can usually tell them by their appearance, which is always elemental in nature. Mostly they are pale skinned, and they often have some kind of eating disorder, as in the etheric state of their last incarnation they needed no food. Strangely enough, they rarely live in the wild, but favour cities, partly because they can be more anonymous there, and partly because they need constant human energy around them, quite literally to keep them in this world. They prefer their own company, and rarely have many friends. Apparently lonely, they are, however, quite self-reliant, and if they have the inclination, they make exceptional healers. This can be an uneasy experience, however, for the nature spirits and ourselves make for strange bedfellows.

As psychics we must at some time look into these worlds, but within the confines of a development group this is not easy. Make a point of going into quiet places like the woods, or by the sea. Watch the flames of a fire, or sit near rocks. Open up to these energies, and if you are lucky, the spirits will give you a glimpse of their hidden world. Enchanting and delightful though it is, please remain balanced and grounded at all times.

Contact with these species can have its problems. In olden times, people blamed many and varied things on the fairy folk, such as mysterious deaths of animals, and illnesses such as rheumatism and consumption. Cramps and bruising were particularly ascribed to the fairies, who were supposed to pinch people out of annoyance. They were also blamed for plant blights, and even for hair being tangled. They were thought to steal small objects, and were often accused over things that went missing.

Elaborate protection was in olden days advised against fairy intervention. These included turning clothes inside out, and the use of bells, bread, salt and daisy chains, as well as prayer and the Cross. My advice, if you are being troubled by these beings, is always to be truthful, and to have an open, loving heart. You can only be a threat to them if you are mean and uncaring, and once they can see you are neither of these things, they will leave you alone. They believe themselves to be highly superior to us, and we are usually beneath their contempt. They play with us like mischievous children, meaning very little harm, but that childish behaviour can go beyond the pale, so be ever on your guard.

Many of the deeds ascribed to the fairy world are in fact those of etheric spirits, but some could be attributed to thought-form elementals, and to what extent these two overlap is unclear. Each experience must be taken on its own merit, and judged accordingly.

When one hears and reads some of the innumerable tales of the fairy folk, they, like the elementals, sound remarkable. We saw in the last chapter that it is possible to create a being from the etheric thought energy, and in this chapter we have learned that the fairies can change their shape by accessing the thoughts of human beings. When we stop to consider, we begin to realise just how many diverse elements and energies there are in the world.

EXERCISE

Although it can be done indoors our outdoors, this simple exercise is perhaps more pleasantly and easily practised outside, especially in the quiet countryside. Never communicate with the Earth spirits if you experience any kind of fear. If you are in any doubt, leave this exercise for another time.

Allow yourself to feel comfortable and relaxed, and go through the usual opening procedure if you wish. Take your focus very strongly into your heart, which is both your aerial and your transmitter, and the centre where you find your balance. When your heart really feels warm, open and loving, clearly focus your energy into the Base chakra.

Connect with the Earth's physical energy through the soles of your feet, where there are many minor chakras. Dig into the earth as an energetic force. Feel and know the balance between the Base and the Heart centres. Finding this balance may take one or two attempts, but when you have found it, you can "dial in" to any of the frequencies up to the level of the Heart.

Energy follows thought, so attune to any energy you wish. If you are out in the open, you can do this by looking at a tree or a plant, taking your focus slightly to the side of it, and then shifting your focus, thereby allowing the shift of frequencies in your mind. Be very quiet and still.

Sometimes, if you are open, the fairies will come to you automatically. If you really are loving the plants, grass and trees around you, they will be attracted to you anyway. When you see them watching, they may not seem to notice you, and if they do they will probably be highly surprised and amused that you can see them, for they are not accustomed to communication with mortals. You can gain access to the sea spirits in the same way: their energy echoes on the spindrift.

Some of the devic energies are beyond the range of the Heart, but this does not matter, because later you will be able to attune to the higher frequencies from your point of balance.

No exercise that takes you into different worlds is easy. Some people can automatically communicate with these forces, but they are few and far between; most of us have to exercise and persevere. The rewards are worth the effort, for you will find yourself in a dimension full of enchantment and wonder, and if we really choose to listen to these etheric but hardy folk, we will learn much about our own world that hitherto we never knew .

Every physical living thing has a spirit counterpart. If you pick some flowers, or even buy cut flowers from a florist, you can, by communicating with the spirit of the flower, enable it to live much longer than one would normally expect. This is because by communicating with the plants and trees, we give them the very etheric energy that they need in order to thrive.

Equally, you can link with the spirits of the blights and pests in your garden. Do this by communicating to the group soul of that particular insect, and strike a deal with them: give them a certain number of flowers, and ask them to leave the bulk of your crop alone. In this way you can have a pest free garden!

Some spirits of insects are difficult to contact, but even these will very often leave you alone when asked. For instance, if you are plagued by ants in your house, communicate with their spirit, and draw a line over which they must not enter. Tell them that the garden is theirs, but that they must leave your home alone. Many native peoples communicate with the Earth and all living things in this way. We know that the native American Indian shamans can attune to a particular creature, and work in co-operation with it for all sorts of mutually beneficial reasons.

All of the above aspects bring us into greater touch with the many, many energies of our planet. Through these simple exercises, we can learn to co-operate with the Earth and with all the energies that dwell there. By being open, we can gain a wealth of experience of healing and joy, for even if we only bother to learn about one other energy, we will be able to heal and understand ourselves better.

When you finish your exercises, in addition to closing yourself, visualise the Earth in a golden bubble of light. Then do the same for yourself, and rejoice in being a part of this wonderful planet.

Books for Reference
Faeries, by Brian Froud and Alan Lee 1979
The Book of Imaginary Beings, by Jorge Luis Borges 1969
Fairies at work and at play, by Geoffrey Hodson. 1925

Chapter 8

ASTRAL
WORLDS

Up to this point, we have largely been looking at areas to which most people can relate through personal experience in their day-to-day existence. This is because we have been dealing with energies contacted through the attunement of the lower three dimensional frequencies, which we all use at some time. When we begin to deal with the astral worlds, however, we are going beyond the normal state, for we are faced with a different dimension. We are dealing with an energy that is all around us, but is unseen by the vast majority of the population.

The astral worlds comprise a state of existence often referred to as the fourth dimension, which runs parallel to our own. We in the third dimension depend for our existence upon this other world, which is the bridge between the normal physical states and the spiritual worlds. In chakra terms, it resonates with the heart, for like the heart, it is the bridge that connects the higher and lower energies.

The astral holds many different frequencies. It may well be the place referred to in the Bible: "In My Father's house there are many mansions".

DREAMS

One way of connecting with the astral worlds is through sleep, when most people's astral body rises out of the physical body by a few inches; a shift that can be clearly seen by psychics. Sometimes, however, the astral body travels independently of the physical, and this experience is referred to as astral travelling. It can be achieved in a semi-waking state, but it mostly occurs during sleep, and such journeys are often remembered as dreams.

When visiting the astral worlds in sleep, one can get some idea of what the spirit world is about, for it is a place where energy very swiftly follows thought. In astral dreams we can think of a place and be there immediately, and any object or situation that we think about will instantly manifest.

A common factor of all astral dreams is that they feel so real that upon waking there is often a disturbing feeling that something has actually happened. In one sense it has, for it is in this state that we can communicate with the astral beings, including, of course, those who have departed from physical realms; in other words, those who have died. People often say that when they connect with a departed friend or relative in the astral sleep state, they can touch, smell and feel that person's presence to such a degree that he or she seems to be alive.

For comparative purposes, there are different kinds of dream that are worth mentioning here. Firstly there is what could be called the "computer type", which are the ones that recall what has occurred during the previous day. The mind is slotting events and experiences into place, so that they are all neat and tidy, rather as a computer sorts out its programmes.

The second type of dream, probably the most common, is that in which the subconscious is trying to tell us something that our conscious mind is unable, for some reason, to accept. These are the dreams that contain symbols and archetypes that can be interpreted. There are many books that will help you to do this, but each mind is different, and it is best to analyse your symbols for yourself. Almost certainly they will be speaking to you about some concern you have, or pointing out a matter that you must address. Symbols and archetypes are also received while one is working on the auric level, and they can be interpreted in just the same way, as can the imagery that you receive in your meditations and visualisations.

This second type of dream is significant, and particularly so in the case of students developing their psychic senses, because in the process of awakening you will be drawing up into your conscious mind those things that need to be revealed to you. It is therefore a good idea to have a pad and paper by your bed when you go to sleep, so that upon waking you can write them down and analyse them. Some people like to keep a dream diary, and for a time this may be useful. Your dreams, if you use them, can be helpful in connecting you with your inner worlds.

Some dreams are predictive, and one of the commonest dream experiences for an untrained psychic is to receive negative predictions. These may be connected with the dreamer, but equally they might be concerned with global disasters. Such an experience can be very worrying, for the individual may believe that they have been given this dream to warn others, and feel themselves to be in an almost impossible position. However, dreams of this type do not come as a warning; they are caused because time dissolves in the astral state, and we are therefore often able to see a little way ahead. One rarely receives information about disasters that are a long time in the future; they usually occur within two days to a week of the dream.

In the case of a global disaster, the shock waves from the reactions of others explode through time, and very open individuals receive the images. If this happens to you, and you think that you should warn someone, write a letter or make a 'phone call as appropriate, but probably the best thing to do is unconditionally to wrap the image in Light, and send it to the angels, or ask for the Greatest Good to help. Afterwards dissolve it from your mind, and even if it subsequently happens, do not be alarmed, as it is not your responsibility.

Dreams can be valuable. They cross the divide, and allow us to equate our worlds, and consequently to be more at peace with ourselves. Do not be concerned if you are one of those who rarely seem to dream. All it means is that the connection between your higher and your little mind is inactive. The fact that you do not remember does not mean that you never dream. The third type of dream is an described as the astral dream above.

MEDIUMSHIP

There are numerous aspects to working within this field, the most common of which is communication with people who have died. The astral is the area where the vast majority of souls go after death, before they go on into different states. When psychics link into this particular frequency, they are referred to as "mediums", for they literally become mediums of communication between the two worlds.

We know that the physical body eventually decays and disintegrates, but that we ourselves are not the physical body. Our essence, our higher mind, our soul, lives on without the physical state, for that is merely a vehicle for our journey in this dimension. Psychically we can observe the separation of the spirit from the body at the time of death. This process is sometimes described as the breaking of the silver cord, that is, of the etheric string that links us to the physical body. There is a reference to it in the Holy Bible (Ecclesiastes XII. 6), where death is spoken of as the time when, amongst other phenomena, "the silver cord be loosed".

Much has been written about what happens next, but my own experience has led me to conclude that the mind or soul is greeted by a Light Being, very often accompanied by a loved one already in the spirit world; a husband or wife, mother or father, or someone that the individual has loved and trusted. These beings take the newcomer by the hand, and lead them over into the astral worlds.

The whole experience can be startling for the recently-departed person. We tend to believe that sudden death is the best way to leave the physical body, a conclusion born of compassion, of not wanting our loved ones to suffer any unnecessary pain. So when we hear of a sudden death, we may say, "Well, at least they had no pain", or, "At least it was quick".

Actually, the spiritual point of view is quite the opposite. There are many documented cases of spirits turning up at their homes, not knowing they are dead, particularly in cases of accidents. There is a theory, with which I concur, that everyone is warned in their sleep of impending death of a close relative or friend. It may not be remembered consciously, but on a deeper level it will be known.

The best form of passing, from the spiritual point of view, is a gradual transition from the physical body to the astral. This happens quite naturally in old age, when people tend to spend much of their time in sleep. Even going into death from a coma is better than a sudden wrench, for in the coma state the individual will have dipped their toes in the water, so to speak, and be ready to take that step into the spirit realms.

No one ever passes over without the help of a guide, but what happens next depends a great deal upon the the level of intelligence, and the magnetic force, of the individual's energy. It is my understanding that no two people have exactly the same experience, although generally they will then be shown to a place wherein they come to terms with, and then exorcise, all the struggles of their life, and where they will become acclimatised to their new state.

It seems that if a person has fixed ideas on what will greet them when they die, then that is what they will experience. For instance, if someone has very fixed religious beliefs, they will most probably be greeted by the deity of their religion, so a Christian will be greeted by the Christian deity, a Moslem by the Moslem deity, and so on.

The attraction of like energies being an absolute law, each soul will be drawn to the energy and experience most conducive to them: on the astral there are places of learning of all kinds.

If, for instance, someone has an innate musical talent, they may go to a place in the astral realms where musicians reside and compose. Great artistic creations are often born from this plane of existence, and sometimes these are fed into the consciousness of people in incarnation on Earth. This is how child prodigies occur: they are souls that have developed their very fine talents on the astral plane, and brought them back here when they reincarnated.

It is here that the spirits of the "dead" reside, which is why it is often referred to as the spirit world, but there are also indigenous spirits there. These are usually the devas of the astral, better known as angels. These angelic beings are present in all cultures, and are considered by many to be a guardian force. Like the earth spirits of the last chapter, these beings work constantly to hold together the energetic layers between the physical and spiritual worlds. They are consequently paramount to our existence for so many reasons, not least as a healing force. Such is their importance, particularly for psychics and healers, that a whole chapter of this book is devoted to them.

THE LOWER ASTRAL

There are so many layers and levels of the astral planes that it is quite impossible to write about them all in this book. For our purposes, however, let us start with what is commonly called the lower astral, an area of the fourth dimension that is not very pleasant. When a psychic is opening to the astral worlds, one common experience is to see strange, distorted eyes and faces staring at them, usually when they are in the relaxed stage between waking and sleeping.

These blank faces, which peer at you as though you were a strange animal in a zoo, are nothing to worry about. They cannot harm you, but when you first come across them they may appear sinister. It is as though you have inadvertently stumbled into a room where you are unknown, and do not belong. This is limbo, the place of lost or waiting souls.

Everyone who goes into spirit is greeted by a Light Being, but nothing is ever done against the free will of the individual. There are many souls born in the middle ages who are now in the lower astral. They were convinced in life by their elders and that when they died, they must always be alert for the dark angels, and that they must sleep until they were awoken for Judgement Day. They were also convinced that during that sleep, many dark angels would masquerade as good ones, and that they must at all costs be ignored. Consequently there are thousands, perhaps millions, of such souls, all waiting to be awoken by the trumpets of Judgement Day. Every being that tries to guide them over to the higher planes is driven away, on suspicion of being a dark angel. If you inadvertently find yourself in this part of the astral worlds, send Light to these beings, and gently draw yourself through.

There are many competent mediums and healers who have taken on this rescue work for the express purpose of releasing these poor souls from their own cage. This, like any other form of psychic work, must be administered completely unconditionally, with the aid of a Light Being, and in these cases the angels afford the best help.

It is on this level that you will also connect with those souls that haunt a building or person. It is the lowest level of the astral, and is still close to the earth plane. To be that close to the physical planes when you have departed the body is not healthy, for once you have passed over, it is important to move quickly into the Higher Astral. To be left in this in- between world is like having one foot on a boat and one foot on land: it is extremely uncomfortable. The sad thing is that many of these souls are there out of ignorance, or through the control of their elders and teachers for their own ends.

Sometimes one can inadvertently move into this in-between state in sleep. If you do, you will find that it is considered an intrusion, and very often you will be told that you are not wanted, and sent packing. At other times you might find that a soul clings to you like a limpet or a lost dog. If this happens, remember that it cannot harm you. Gently communicate that it is time it moved on, and call for the help of the angels. If the soul is ready, it will want to move on, and will allow the angel to guide it through. If not it will stay in this waiting place until eventually it will be ready to move on.

In a case of haunting, it is important for the medium to make direct contact with the wandering soul. In most cases they are just lost, or they have some emotional attachment to the person or place which they frequent. Communicate with them, and gently guide them over, again with the help of the angels. Please remember that you must never do this kind of work if you are in doubt or fear.

Once you have gained a degree of competence, you will never find yourself in this lower energy, unless of course you wish to do some rescue work there. Remember that nothing can harm you in this world, and that nothing has power over you unless you react in fear. This is a very important point, for fear is always your only real enemy.

It would be foolish to deny the presence of the darker forces in the astral worlds. They do exist, and they can cause havoc when experienced, but they can do nothing without your co-operation, and you only give that when you emanate the negative vibration of fear. Anyone with a fearful disposition should go nowhere near the astral plane, which is, for so many reasons, fraught with difficulties. This is why, during the development process, we put so much time and energy into clearing, aligning and balancing the individual.

One of the most important aspects for a teacher to consider carefully when interviewing someone as a potential psychic student is not how naturally psychic they are, but how emotionally mature. For a teacher to encourage an emotionally unstable student to do psychic work, particularly work on the astral, is equivalent to giving a hand-grenade to a baby. One often hears of cases where someone has a very bad experience during development, and this is usually the cause. The darker forces can only work with dark energy, which is fear-based energy. This is the reason why we place so much emphasis on developing a clear Heart energy, which is imperative if we are to work in the astral.

When you rise beyond the lower astral, you immediately come to areas where you meet most of the souls who, after death, are spending a sojourn in this plane of existence before moving out into other planes. It is impossible to say how long someone will stay, as it is totally dependent upon their own level of vibration. The possibilities are myriad.

It is worth remembering that the spirit does not have a physical body, so that when a connection with a departed soul is made, it either has to project an image for the medium so that he or she can relay this to the sitter, or it creates out of astral energy a body that is to its own liking.

Some souls are not comfortable without a body, and so from the moment of death they retain the astral body of their earthly lives, which means that they remain easily recognisable as the individuals they once were. However, when a "body-less" soul projects an image, or creates an astral body, the medium may receive either a distorted image or one that looks very much younger, than the body that died. This is not uncommon, and it can make identification quite difficult. For evidential purposes, then, it is better not to rely on the physical appearance of the spirit. Try to receive the essence of the person's nature, and ask for some personal detail that is of significance to both the sitter and the soul in spirit. Accurate, clearly-given survival evidence can bring floods of relief and joy to a sitter, especially a bereaved one, and may well mark their first step towards acknowledgement of the unseen realms.

The process of mediumship is a balancing act. In most cases mediums must raise their vibration to that of the astral worlds, whilst souls in spirit must lower their vibration. An analogy can be seen in a helicopter's rotors. When they are moving at top speed you cannot see them at all, and it is only when they slow down that they touch the vibratory note of vision.

When a connection is first made with a soul in spirit, this often brings it back into the denser experiences of its human life, and quite possibly the experiences of its last few days on this Earth. This could well be a most unpleasant experience for it, and one which should not be dwelt upon, either by the medium or by the soul. Sometimes, because it can be painful and emotionally disturbing for them, souls will flatly refuse to remember their death, but mediums do often receive such images. If this happens, relay them quickly, and move on to happier times, for it can be traumatic for both parties.

There are many opinions about whether it is ethically correct to communicate with the dead. Some religions not only discourage it, but ban it as a sin. This is probably meant as a safety net, for it is not work to be taken lightly. To ignore it as part of the psychic experience would be foolish, but it is worth remembering that in terms of different energies, this range of psychic connection is only one facet of a huge diamond.

There are specialists in all fields of psychic work, and this one is no exception, but it is not the most important aspect of the work. Treat it seriously, but do not let it take over. The dead have moved on, and it is right that we leave them in peace. If you have a sitter who has become too dependent on communication with a particular spirit, and you feel that this is becoming a problem for them, encourage them to let go, for it is not healthy to be reliant on anyone in spirit, and as with so many aspects of this work, it is easy to become obsessed. When this happens, it comes under the heading of "glamour" which is not true spiritual work. It is a joy to be a "telephonist" for the spirit world, but you have an important life of your own to lead on this Earth plane, so enjoy the contact, but do not become too attached.

GUIDES AND GUARDIAN ANGELS

If you are going to work in the astral worlds, even if it is only for a short time in a development group, you will always be joined by a guardian force. You already have your own angelic being, who has probably been with you since birth, but when you start communicating with the astral realms you need a certain kind of guide. Most guides are just that: energies that have drawn near to the earth dimension in order to assist us.

When a medium sees a guide, they will have to give it a structure in order to relay it to the conscious mind. Therefore the medium "gives" the guide a body. It is clear, therefore, that two mediums could perceive the same guide energy as two completely different images. This does not mean that one is right and the other wrong, for it is merely each medium's way of personalising the guide. In some cases, however, there is a very definite entity that has followed a medium for a long time, possibly even through past lives. In such a case, any number of mediums would perceive it in the same way.

It is preferable not to come too close to identifying a guide. You as a medium will grow, and just as a child starting in kindergarten needs one set of teachers and later on needs others, so it is in the spiritual realms. As you grow, your guides will almost certainly change over the years, so if you are too attached to one guiding personality, you may not choose to move on when necessary. Every case must be treated individually, however, and on rare occasions there have been contracts between guides and mediums to work together through most, if not all, of the medium's life, usually for some teaching purpose.

In all cases, the guide is only a little ahead of you in energy. Very often they are connected to one or other of the cultures that had strong links with the astral worlds. The most recent culture to have this connection is that of the native Americans, so it is not surprising that many people are aware of their guides as native Americans. Ancient Chinese and Egyptian energies are also conducive to the astral worlds, and psychic artists often portray a guide as a member of one of these three groups. You may not be particularly aware of the image of your guide, but rather have a warm feeling of an energy or person whom you can trust, alongside or behind you.

At the early stages of development it is frequently the case that a "loved one" in spirit acts, for a short time only, as your guide. This will continue until you find your own balance, and you are then "handed over", to a more experienced guide. One of the arguments put forward for having strong contacts with a specific guide is that you can never be fooled if they are present. Unfortunately this is not the case, as it is the easiest thing for a lower astral energy to masquerade as a higher Being, and they do this with great relish. The content of their communication will quickly tell you if this is happening, but even the most competent mediums can sometimes be fooled.

This is one of many areas of this work where people often seem to lose their intelligence. It does not matter what name a guide is giving, or from whence it originated. The question you must always ask is, "Is this information ringing the bell of truth within my heart?" If it is, then listen to it. If it is not, do not be swayed by the name of the guide. Listen to the song, not the singer, and if it is not right for you, leave it alone. Always think for yourself. Never give your control away to anyone, no matter what name they give, or whether they come from Earth or from some marvellous-sounding place in the cosmos. There is no benevolent being in the whole of the cosmos that would make you do anything against your will. Free will is the law. Do not give yours away.

There is a form of mediumship whereby mediums allow entities to use their body. This is called trance mediumship, which is a very specialised form of work, and is only for the very few.

A fact that is little known is that trance mediums need to be extremely strong physically, because taking on the vibrations of a different entity disturbs the bodily frequencies. The very tough trance mediums live a long life, but some are simply not equipped for this specialist task, and unfortunately these tend to die prematurely, usually from some kind of depleting blood disorder like leukaemia.

Even if you are strong, and able to take on this rarefied type of work, it can take as long as seven years for the body to adapt. In the past, mediums were used in this way to enable a higher form of information to be transmitted, but for many reasons this is no longer necessary, and the same information can be received without the painful physical adjustment. An old argument in favour of trance work was that less of the medium's ego personality was present, and that a more spiritual level of information might therefore be received. However, even in full trance there is always something of the medium present, and there are other ways of dropping the personality without completely giving away control. There are indeed so many illusions, dangers and glamours involved in this form of work that unless you are one hundred percent confident, and have a fully experienced teacher, it is often better to steer clear altogether.

In certain situations, often following a shock or trauma of some kind, the veil between the dimensions, which is usually held firmly in place, disappears, and we receive an unexpected glimpse of the etheric states. It is not uncommon, for instance, for a woman in childbirth suddenly to become psychic, or for some emergency or danger to awaken an individual to different states of awareness. It is as though the veil is torn down by a desperate need for reassurance, or by naked, violent panic.

This can also come about through the abuse of drugs or alcohol. In the sixties, many people experimented with mind-expanding drugs, seeking to attain spiritual expansion through altered states. Areas that had traditionally been the exclusive domain of gurus, mystics and seers were suddenly invaded by the populace.

This venture was extremely foolhardy. It is true that drugs can, to a degree, lift the inter-dimensional veil, but not sufficiently to gain automatic access to the higher worlds. If the experimenter is not vibrating on the higher frequencies, the experience will at best be short-lived, and at worst it will take them into the dark areas of the astral. There, the dark forces can latch on to them, and literally take over their life. The person might, for example, start to believe that they hear the voice of God, but this quickly turns out to be a case of possession, sometimes so strong that it can take at least seven to ten years to erase.

Many of the genuine possession cases dealt with in healing clinics have their origins in the misuse of drugs and alcohol. As ever, like attracts like, and as most people who take such substances are doing so with the express desire of escaping this third-dimensional world, that negativity attracts the fear energies from the other worlds. In extreme cases, this leads to madness and suicide.

Some good comes from everything, however, and now a whole generation or more has knowledge of the possibility of a different state of being. You do not need chemical substances to achieve it, however. If you are prepared to put in a little work, you will be privy to things far beyond anything that can be experienced under the influence of drugs.

Unlike the type mentioned above, most cases of apparent possession are actually nothing of the kind. If you are working in this field, particularly if you are a healer, it is likely that you will come across at least one or two nasty dark forces that for one reason or another have attached themselves to an individual. Most suspected cases prove to be nothing more than dark thought forms, but every now and again you come across the real thing. If you suspect this to be the case, never tackle it alone, unless you are absolutely positive that you can be of use. If you feel any doubt or fear, the wisest course is to admit defeat, and to send the patient to someone who specialises in this field, for fear feeds the darker forces as effectively as petrol feeds fire. This type of work can appear glamourous for people with a mission to fight what they believe to be the devil! But there is absolutely nothing glamourous in this work, it requires steely focus and balance. This work must be done quietly and with no fuss, it is not for the untrained or incompetent.

If you decide that you are competent to take on such a case, the first thing that you must impress upon your patient is that they need not be having this experience, because strangely enough, some people grow accustomed to - or even come to rely on - their entity, and do not really want to let it go. You must urge them to do so, for without their commitment, no matter what healing your angels apply, the entity will not permanently leave.

When there is a commitment to progress, the angels are most helpful. Call upon the most relevant energy (see exercise, chapter nine) to assist you in freeing your patient from this appalling situation. In any kind of possession treatment, you are advised to have at least one other person with you. A group of four or five dedicated healers, along with an established angelic band in spirit, will draw out and transmute the dark forces. Dark entities can drain you, and cause you great strain, so all agents involved in removing them must be fully-willing participants. It is not work for the faint-hearted.

Over a period of time, an array of Light Beings may have drawn close to you, to assist you in your work. If you are doing the work of exorcism, you will doubtless have a small band of spirit helpers on the higher planes, and at least one of these will be an angel, since angelic energy is needed for speedy correction of the etheric disturbance caused by possession. Another group of angels will help to move the entity on into Light. No energy can be destroyed, but it can be transmuted, and the angels are great alchemists.

The astral realms are a bridge between the lower physical and higher consciousness forces. They are often used as a form of communication between the two, and they act rather like a news film, revealing what is happening in other times and places. There are great areas of learning, and in the higher realms they contain the great minds.

One particular group of higher vibrations has become very active in recent years, and these I affectionately refer to as "The Professors." When any soul reaches out in consciousness, it arrives at a point where it literally calls out to be given help to expand and grow, and this is always connected with a deep desire to serve humanity. The call is perceived in the higher spheres of the astral realms as an arrow-like firework of Light, and the first thing that happens then is that the Higher Teachers draw close to that individual, and watch over them to see if their desire is genuine: most of them are, for all of us have as our truest desire the need to expand into Light. Once this has been established, the Higher Teachers set about training the individual, and helping them to open to higher concepts.

At the outset, because the human mind is so busy, very often the only way to implement this work is through the sleep state. Since most of this information is beyond the normal intellectual range, the individual will probably not remember much, if any, of what is received, for the knowledge imparted is largely conceptual. However, it is not uncommon for the student, upon waking, to have a strong sense of having been in a place of learning, with wise men and women. The faces of those beings are never seen, because the Master Teachers are way beyond the personality state, and therefore do not have bodies. Upon waking, a common personification of this energy is that they were humanoid and hooded, and sometimes they are recalled as a white, spiritual energy. In this way, the pupil is guided into a new consciousness, and may subsequently find themselves discussing something of which they previously had no knowledge, speaking with authority, while having no idea from whence the knowledge came.

When someone is being guided in this way, they often feel their normal guide draw away, and when this occurs, it will be replaced by a group guide energy: again, this group energy will have no face. They have infinite patience, but are very firm, for theirs is the last personal connection before the individual comes into greater consciousness and full spiritual control.

Guides are like good parents, who, seeing their children grown and strong, encourage them to make a life of their own, even sometimes giving them a bit of a push. Thus it is with the individual who has spiritually come of age, and needs to use their own inner strength. They will be in touch with their own soul force, beginning to receive their own information with no third party involved, and coming towards total unity with the Divine Spirit.

For reasons that will be discussed later, these group guide energies are extremely active at the present time. Their purpose is to help us in our individual transformation, and in global terms to help the whole of humanity.

EXERCISE

Open up in the usual way, making sure you positively affirm that only the "highest, greatest good" work through you. Focus your energy on your Heart centre, breathing into it for a few minutes. Make sure that your breath is regular, so that you breathe in as much air as you breathe out. Practising this expands your ability to give and receive love. Open your mind also, and welcome a guide energy, asking for the most appropriate one for this exercise. It may be an energy that you have worked with before, or it may be a guide that will be with you just for this exercise: it does not matter.

Having established communication, allow the guide to take you by the hand and guide you into the astral realms. Be drawn up and up, a long way up, and when you feel safe, look around you and observe the astral worlds. After a few minutes you will see ahead of you a doorway: go through it with your guide.

Again, look around within this place, If there is anything that you do not understand, ask your guide for clarification. After another few minutes, ask to be taken to the Great Halls of Learning. Move up then into the Higher Astral worlds, and go into those Great Halls, absorbing the information and energy therein. When you are ready, take your guide by the hand again, and let it take you gently back to where you are physically sitting. Thank your guide, release your contact with it, and focus once more on breathing into your Heart chakra.

At the end of this session, go through the chakras, paying particular attention to the Base centre. Really dig it into the earth, like a tap root, down into the vibrant inner energy of the Earth, gently drawing that energy up into the Base, from where it will feed to other areas as and when this is necessary. Feel your body, and send it love as you gently open your eyes and return your consciousness into day-to-day living.

Books for Reference
Spirit Guides, by Iris Belhayes. 1985
Mediumship Made Simple, by Ivy Northage. 1986

Chapter 9

ANGELS, GUIDES
AND DEMONS

At the very moment when you consciously decided to follow the spiritual path, regardless of what that expression might mean to you, you attracted the attention of the Light Beings. These exist in many shapes and forms: in the words of the poet John Milton, "Millions of spiritual creatures walk the Earth unseen, both when we wake and when we sleep." Having come this far in your psychic development, you are by now certain to have around you at least one or two personal guides or helpers on the spirit planes, and now that your psychic eyes are opening, you are perhaps beginning to see them. One mistake made by many students is to want to see these Beings with the naked eye, but that desire will take you down very long roads, most of which will end in illusion.

Few human beings see the spirit people with their physical eyes, although within your inner eye they may be seen in abundance. Similarly you will hear with your inner ears, that is within your mind. You are not being unfaithful to God if you question the inner voices. You must question them.

In their eagerness to experience some miraculous physical manifestation of psychic energies, many seemingly logical and intelligent people dispense with common sense when they arrive at this point, and too many fall foul of voices in the head. The most important and effective means of avoiding problems, and of assisting the inner hearing process, is to work on yourself, and to listen to your heart, where you will find the truth. For true intuition is a knowing. Not a thought, not a feeling and not even a sense, but a deep abiding knowledge. This will speak into your head as "I know." If there is emotional content or mental reason, this is not "knowing". Knowing is a automatic sense of what is correct at any given time. It does not predict in advance, it just knows when the time is right.

Perhaps the most common of all known guides, and certainly the ones most spoken and written about, are the angels, which resonate with the ray of unconditional love, the vibration of the heart. We access them either within the etheric rays, where they do most of their healing work, or through the astral planes, depending on the frequency to which they belong. There are many different angels, ranging from the very small, fairy-like cupids and the individual guardian angels so loved by children, to the mighty energy of the highest angelic forces that hold the Heavens in place. They are the eternal messengers, bringing the Light Force Energy of the Godhead into physical reality.

Angels often appear when death is near, and there are well documented instances of sightings on fields of battle, where they wait to assist soldiers over to spirit, lifting them from the violent atmosphere of war. During the desperate conflicts of World War I, they were glimpsed in such areas as the Somme, and perhaps the most widely known sighting was of what came to be known as the Angel of Mons. A vast Angelic Being, towering over the chaos below, it was reported at the time as having been seen by hundreds of soldiers on both sides.

GUARDIAN ANGELS

Guardian angels form a part of many belief systems, and appear in the literature of many cultures. These Beings are on the spiritual plane, and they watch over us, healing and helping. They are like spiritual "tailors", continuously repairing our etheric body, and as such they are often depicted as being very close to us, within our aura. They also guard us while we sleep, ensuring that we are not bothered by lower astral beings. It is worth remembering, however, that they follow the golden law of free will: like all other Light Beings, they would never go against our desires. In other words, we are always responsible for our own actions, whether they be positive or negative.

One of the most important things to do when you are working psychically is to acquire the habit of asking for help. This is not a sign of weakness, but of intelligent utilisation of the energies and information that abound within the cosmos. Whatever you may need from the spiritual planes, your own guides can connect you with the appropriate energy. If you are being troubled in sleep, by bad dreams or oppressive negative feelings for instance, call upon the appropriate helpers, the Guardian Angels. If you are not sure what you need, always call upon the Greatest, Highest Good. As in most areas of life, you will get most satisfaction if you go straight to the top!

Throughout history, the existence of angels has been acknowledged, not only by Christians, but by many other religions, most notably the Moslem and Jewish faiths. Perhaps their popular appeal reached its peak in the Middle Ages, when in Central Europe reverence for them reached epic proportions. This continued until the time of the great plagues, after which their popularity went into sharp decline.

Apparently the angel Gabriel dictated the Koran to the prophet Mohammed. It was an angel that stopped Abraham from sacrificing his son, a moment that could be considered as the beginning of the Jewish religion. Christians know well the story of the angelic Annunciation to Mary concerning her forthcoming child. The angel Moroni supposedly appeared to Joseph Smith in 1823, an event that led to the writings that became the book of Mormon, and to the founding, in 1830, of the Mormon Sect.

Some of the oldest known artifacts are of winged Beings. In 4000 B.C., on the site of a Sumerian king, an angel is flying overhead whilst the king is praying. In the Greek pantheon, the wings of Hermes and the winged Eros represented the spirit that carried messages between the gods of Olympus and the lesser gods of Earth. Indeed, the angels' purpose, to all who are aware of them, is as emissaries of the gods. The mythological god Apollo was perceived by the Greeks and the Romans as an angelic being, of whom it was said, "Nothing false or impure might be brought near him, for he was a cleansing and enlightening power". This is a good description of the energy emanating from all angelic Beings.

Angels appear in both the Old and New Testaments of the Bible. Mystics and poets have written about them. They are in our psyche, and they seem to be partnered with mortals, whether or not we consciously acknowledge them. While doing the exercise in the previous chapter, you would have experienced some of the very many aspects of the astral planes, and perhaps you met some of the angelic Light Beings.

There is a common belief that the angels form a spiritual hierarchy. This is epitomised in the Old Testament by Jacob's ladder, via which angels travel up and down to levels of Heaven determined by their own type. In "The Celestial Hierarchies", Dionysius the Areopagite, a sixth-century Greek writer, expanded upon this concept when he spoke of the Nine Orders of Heavenly Angels: Seraphim, Cherubim, Thrones, Dominions, Virtues, Powers, Principalities, Archangels and Angels. The highest angels carry out planetary and cosmic missions, while the lower orders help manage the affairs of earth. The Cherubim and the Thrones have the most wisdom, and are the closest to the Divine Source.

In the First Hierarchy, the Seraphim are described as the flames of love. Their task is to transmute the darkness, which they do as a song of creation and celebration. Theirs is a vibration of love, and a creative, resonating field of life. These Beings are in direct communion with God, and as such are Beings of pure Light and thought. The name Seraphim means healer, doctor, surgeon and Higher Being. The serpent image of this angelic order symbolizes rejuvenation, and its logo, the Caduceus, is still used today as the symbol of the medical profession. This image originally appeared as a wand in the hand of the universal god Hermes, who is believed to be one of the Seraphs.

The Cherubim emanate the energy of love, which is the manifestation of the flow of Light Force, This Hebrew word means both "one who intercedes" and "knowledge". The concept of our own friendly cherubs originated here, but these High Powers are not truly represented by the sweet images with which we are so familiar: theirs is the energy of Divine Knowledge and Wisdom.

The Thrones administer the higher justice, holding the balance of all Universal Laws. Dante described this highest Order as the place of "pure love, pure mind, pure will and pure spirit". In Jewish lore they are described as the Great Wheel, or the Many-eyed Ones. The Thrones are said to reside in the third or fourth Heaven. Interestingly, from their description they might have been been confused with modern ideas and visions regarding extra-terrestrials (E.T.s), and some E.T. sightings have given rise to theories that they are indeed angels. It might quite logically be argued that angels could be the original extra-terrestials, for they are surely beyond the Earth!

The second Hierarchy consists of the Dominions, who govern us, the Virtues, who devise strategy, and the Powers, who carry out the Divine plans, and protect against all evil influences. It is also said of the Virtues that they preside over the movement of all the celestial bodies, including the galaxies, the suns, the stars and all the planets, and that their high powers help to hold the threads of the cosmos together. They strive to balance the polarities of matter and spirit. The Powers seem to act as holders of the energy between the different layers of the cosmos, keeping each energy in its rightful place. Dionyius says that it was the Powers who resisted the efforts of demons to take over the world.

The lowest angelic Hierarchy consists of the Principalities, the Archangels and the Angels. These watch over all the nations, the world leaders and the great global movements, and they also have the rather perilous task of being the protectors of religion.

To whichever hierarchical level they belong, the angels are constantly working with us to heal and help us on our spiritual path. Perhaps the ones with whom we have had most contact, other than our own personal guardian angels, are the Archangels. These are seven in number, the best-known being Michael, Gabriel, Raphael and Uriel. There seems to be no doubt that they are messengers, and they are considered to be the most important intermediaries between God and the human race.

In common with their general title, most of the angels' names end in "el", and the derivation of the singular EL is interesting. It is an ancient word, with a long and complex etymological history, which has a common origin with many other ancient words in other languages. Among its many meanings are: brightness, shining, radiant one, the shining one.

Theologians throughout history have tried to intellectualise the angelic force. In the thirteenth century, Thomas Aquinas devoted an entire treatise to angels in his "Summa Theologica". "Every angel" he wrote, "is of a different species, and each species is higher or lower than the other. Angels do not reason as men do, from premise to conclusion, but from the knowledge of a known principle, and this straightaway perceives all its consequent conclusion with no discursive process at all." Their knowledge is intuitive and immediate. It is interesting to note that this description fits perfectly into the mental processes of intuition, and the consciousness of the coming age.

Aquinas believed that the existence of angels was perfectly logical: "The perfect universe must have a precise and orderly arrangement of all things that were created, and an orderly universe cannot have any voids, therefore from logical necessity, it must include angels." This echoes many other great writers and thinkers, who throughout the ages have suggested the existence of a ladder of energies and life forms, from God, the highest, downwards. In energy terms, as a result of the discoveries of modern physics, some scientists are just beginning to arrive at the same sort of conclusion.

DARK ANGELS AND DEMONS

One cannot fully discuss this subject without mentioning the dark angels. These beings seem to be connected with the Fall, which Christians regard as the beginning of time: that is, the original separation from the Source, or God. Dark angels were said to form the shadow side of God. This was the side which communicated with mortals, the bright side being too powerful for humans beings to tolerate. Through the ages, the description of this shadow side developed first into the Word, the Voice or the Touch, and then into a separate entity, with its own free will. With this separation, the negative side assumed dominance.

Lucifer was the name given to the infamous fallen angel, but that word simply means "Light Being". Lucifer in one tradition was a guardian of the planet Venus. Apparently God asked his higher angels who would be willing to work with earth and help humanity by offering constant challengers and temptation. Lucifer volunteered but because of the nature of his work, that is revealing the light through darkness, unfortunately he received bad press and latterly became known as the devil, instead of as his true nature which is the great awakener. Over a period of time, the name Satan gradually came into use, taken from a Hebrew word which meant "adversary". Then from the third century BC onwards, "Satan" gradually became "the devil", and was developed as a separate entity in apocryphal literature. To Christians he became the very embodiment of evil.

Descriptions of the Fall tell us that the angels were the original Beings separated from the Source. God breathed both angels and humans out into the cosmos to weave the fabric of experience. The angels then abandoned free will, because they desired utterly to be part of the Will of God: and so they were directed not to take on physical form, but to work alongside mortals. Their element is just beyond physical matter, and, as we have already seen, it is usually referred to as the etheric. They work only with Divine Will, the unconditional love ray.

However, some of the original angels decided that they did want free will, and through that freedom they chose to leave the Divine Unity. Gradually they drifted away from the Source. Those who fell away took on human bodies, and those who drifted the furthest became demons. Here again, the derivation of the word is illuminating. In Latin, "Deus" means "God", and the Greek "daimonion" means "a genius", "a god-like form", "a thing of divine nature". It seems that the current view of devils and demons came later in history, perhaps via Judaism and Christianity, when energies became personified.

The existence of the Devil as an entity is open to discussion. To me, the devil is fear and temptation, and I do not doubt that one's personal "demons" come not from any "devil", but from one's own mind, born out of the dark thought forms described in Chapter Six. The creation of the devil as an individual is most likely to have originated principally out of an ecclesiastical desire to control the populace through fear.

It seems that the dark angels are representative of the chaos that allows us knowledge of ourselves, for how can we reach an understanding of good if we are unaware of evil? Thus Lucifer, the bringer of Light, was later to become Satan. Satan initially appears to be a monster, until through innumerable experiences of pain and suffering, throughout countless lifetimes, we gain strength and wisdom. We shall then return to the Power and the Light, and only then will Satan reveal himself once more as Lucifer, the Light Being, our teacher and guide. For in love and acceptance we realise that there is no difference; that everything is part of the original spark of God.

In his book "The Secret of Time and Satan: Restoring Lucifer, Bringer of Light, to his Former Glory", the nineteenth century English mystic, Edward Carpenter, gives us this allegory:

".....so at last I saw Satan appear before me (magnificent, fully formed....feet first, with shining limbs). He glanced down from among the bushes..... "Come out!" he said, with a taunt. "Art thou afraid of me?". And I answered him not, but sprang upon him and smote him.

"And he smote me a thousand times, and lashed and scorched and slew me as with hands of flame: and I was glad, for my body lay there dead; and I sprang upon him again with another body......And with another, and another, and again another; and the bodies which I took on yielded before him....but I flung them aside; and the pains which I endured on one body were the powers which I wielded in the next, and I grew in strength till at last I stood equal in might - exultant in pride and joy...then he ceased, and said, "I love thee."

"And lo! his form changed, and he leaned backwards, and drew me upon him. And he bore me up into the air, and floated me over the topmost trees and oceans, and around the curve of the earth under the moon.....Till we stood again in Paradise."

When we study the writings regarding angels throughout history, we can perhaps equate their transformation with the Great Breath: it is as though God breathed us all out at the time of the Separation, and now we are beginning to return.

Numerous writers down the ages have written about, and been aware of, the presence of angels as helpers in their work. Certainly most great artists attribute their inspiration to some kind of heavenly assistance, perhaps best described by George Russel when he says: "This divine daimon touches the burning point of consciousness, and brings beauty and harmony into expression"; and: "Words often would rush swiftly from some hidden depths of consciousness with which the working brain had but little to do." Most modern channellers would certainly echo these words.

Angels are our teachers, guides and friends, and they cannot be corrupted, since as Light Beings they are a part of Divine Will, and so act as the voice of our conscience. Their presence is easily felt, as their etheric energy is all around us. All we need is an open heart, for the angelic ray is the ray of the heart. Like all other guides, they only come to us when called.

D.H. Lawrence speaks of this in his poem "Song of a Man Who Has Come Through", which closes with the lines: "What is knocking at the door in the night? Is it somebody who wants to do us harm? No, no, it is the three strange angels. Admit them, admit them."

If we understand them to be messengers, a question that we must ask ourselves is this: Why are they so popular now, and what message do they have for us today?

EXERCISES

Exercise 1.

Open up your energies in the usual way, and take your focus into your heart, spending a few minutes breathing into it with equal breaths.

Now make a conscious connection to a unison point of Light. This can be accessed by connecting to the gateway six to ten inches above our heads and within this space visualise a large diamond crystal hanging above your head. Draw down into this crystal the pure Light of the Source, the Universal Light Force. Hear the vibration, and watch as the Light enters the crystal, and vibrates out into the atmosphere as the seven colours of the rainbow.

Breathe these colours into the top of your head through the Crown centre, through into all areas of the head, especially in the area of the third eye, which is toward the back of the head, behind the Brow centre. If you like, you can tune in to the sound of the vibration by making a clear, resonant note, at the same time breathing the sound into the Crown also. Next, lift your awareness to the spirit of the gateway point, being very conscious of having an open, free, loving heart. Welcome the angels into your heart, and for a few minutes enjoy the contact with your own angelic Being.

Ask it to show you some of the different angelic vibrations. Let it take you by the hand, and lead you up the ladder of consciousness, Observe and ask what you are receiving. After a few minutes, when you are ready, allow your angel to help you return. Still with an open, loving heart, let your angel wrap its wings around you. Feel it stroke you with its etheric energies, repairing and healing any damage. This will feel as though you were being gently caressed within a warm, cosy duvet. No angel requires our thanks, but we as humans need to give it, so at the end of the exercise, thank your angel, and end your meditation in your usual way.

Exercise 2.

This is an exercise that you can do as a healing for others. It is especially beneficial when someone has been bereaved or otherwise traumatised, or has suffered the kind of physical shock experienced during surgery.

Make your own connection, and start, as in any other healing activity, by touching the shoulders of your patient or partner. Begin healing in the usual way.

After a while, drop your arms to your sides, and step back, sightly away from your patient's aura. Finding your own energy balance, lift your arms to an open position, and welcome the angels in to assist. Allow their energy to superimpose itself upon your etheric, and gently walk back into the patient's energy field.

Let the angels take over: as you do so, you will find that your hand makes a stroking action around, and quite close to, your patient's physical body. This stroking action will probably move gradually from the head area, right the way down to the feet. It is a wonderful experience, both for the patient and the healer.

When you have finished, thank your angels, and you will find that they will leave gracefully and without ceremony, for theirs is a love without judgement or cause. They never ask "is that person worthy?". They only see the necessity for the healing, wait to be asked, and apply it regardless. In making contact with these

Beings, our lives are the richer, and we can better understand the true meaning and value of unconditional love.

Exercise 3

The seven main Archangels have a particularly strong connection with us, to uplift and guide. Invoke the energy that you feel may best heal and serve. Energy follows thought, so all you have to do when you are in a relaxed meditative state is to invoke the appropriate angel, using thought and/or imagery. There are many named angels, but the following list is intended as a guide.

Michael.

Heaven's Defender. He battles against evil. He was supposed to be the giver of the Ten Commandments, and is often called for at death. He regenerates the body, and is the Prince of Light. It is foretold in the Book of Daniel that when the world is really in danger, Michael will once again appear.

Before the birth of the legend of St George, he was the slayer of the dragon whose connections are with the Earth. Many ancient sites are the focal point of dragon power. These are called Michael Mounts, and one of the ley-lines running across England is known as the Michael Line. Michael seems to have a particular connection with England.

Gabriel.

The only female angel energy, the meaning of her name is both splendid and ironic: it means "governor", or "power". She is the angel of truth, and sits on the left side of God. The bringer of good news, particularly of births. It is said that she worked with the genes of early mankind, and that Adam and Eve were her first experiments. The literal translation of Luke's words, when he describes the Annunciation, is that Gabriel "came in unto her, placing something within her." Perhaps hers is the energy to invoke in cases of infertility?

Raphael.

Another of the healing angels, he has been depicted by artists such as Botticelli, Titian, and Rembrant. He is the protector of travellers, and he is Guardian of The Tree of Life in Eden. He is also a healer of the Earth, and an angel of the sun. He is always positive, and has a sunny disposition. As he has also been described as "a guide in hell", his energy is obviously one to ask for if negative forces trouble you.

Uriel.

Angel of repentance, and of music and poetry. He interprets prophecies. His is a very fiery character, and he has often been associated with absolute righteousness. He watches over thunder and terror, and is considered to be the angel with the sharpest eyes. He is associated with the month of September, which contains the sign of Virgo, the perfectionist. He believes in order, and apparently on the Day of Judgement will destroy the bars of the gates of Hades, of which he is the door-keeper. Milton described his as "the sharpest sighted spirit of all in Heaven" and as he was supposed to be the angel who showed up to remind Moses for not circumcising his own son, he has very sharp sight indeed! In praying to Uriel, remember that he is the Fire of God, and will undoubtedly "tell it like it is".

Raquel.

He is a friend of God, and watches over behaviour. Angel of Earth, and Guardian of the Second Heaven, perhaps prayer directed to him should be about Justice.

Saraquel (or Sariel).

The healer who taught Moses, he is also considered to be the angel of death. Sometimes depicted as one of the fallen angels, he redeems himself in the war between the Sons of Light and Darkness as one of the fighting units of the Sons of Light. If you have transgressed, perhaps your prayers could be directed to Sariel

Metatron.

The angel of many eyes. A heavenly scribe, he watches and records everything. Metatron is for many people the greatest angel. He teaches us that the whole purpose of life is to re-unite the female and male energies into one whole: angels are often considered to hold both these energies together, being androgynous. The name could be derived from the latin Metator, which means guide or measurer, and could also be where we get the word mentor. His energy therefore must be of a helper or teacher.

There are many others, including the Essenes, and Remiel, who is the Angel of Hope and true Visions.

When you finish any exercise, either go through the usual cleanse, clear and closing procedure, or simply focus on your own balance. The heart centre is the best focal point for this.

Feel and know yourself as a spiritual and physical being. Surround yourself with love.

A Child's Prayer to a Guardian Angel.

Angel of God, my guardian dear,
To whom His love commits me here,
Ever this day be at my side.
To light, to guard, to rule and guide.
                              Amen

Books for Reference
Angels, An Endangered Species, by Malcolm Godwin 1990
The Many Faces of Angels, by Harvey Humann. 1986
Ask your Angels by A.Daniel, T. Wyllie and A. Ramer 1992
The Sun and the Serpent by Hamish Miller and Paul Broadhurst
    1989.

Chapter 10
_____

TRANCE

History provides us with numerous examples of communication with "the gods" through altered states of consciousness. The seer at Delphi, who was known as the Oracle of Apollo, and who had priestess status, would divine the future in a full trance state. Some parts of the Old Testament contain chapters that are apparently delivered in trance.

So what is trance, and how does it work? Technically speaking trance is a state in which the person has passed into another state of being, or altered state. A state of insensibility to external surroundings with suspension of some of the vital functions, as in a hypnotic state. This could easily describe channelling, but trance in mediumship is usually considered to be another entity speaking through the medium, in other words a kind of possession.

In what is called a "light trance", the participant can have a degree of awareness of what is happening around them. Someone in a "full trance" has no knowledge at all of what is transpiring, to the extent that if a needle is stuck into them, not only do feel no pain, but often they do not bleed until they are back into a normal state.

Information that is received in the trance state is open to conjecture. One theory is that the voices of the gods must have emanated from the individual recipient's central nervous system, exploiting the right hemisphere, leaving the left free for the emergence of consciousness: the language of men supposedly involving only one hemisphere in order to leave the other to God.

There are different types of trance. The most obvious one occurs during meditation, when an individual can move through varying degrees of trance, but one could sometimes be considered to be in a form of light trance whilst doing the most mundane things. It is not uncommon, for instance, for someone to drive home, and to find on arrival that they do not remember the journey. If someone is very used to driving, it is as though the mind goes into "automatic pilot", a degree of light trance, especially on a familiar route. Equally, when someone's energy is completely focussed on a particular activity, a type of trance state can occur. One can observe this in athletes and dancers: when they are fully centred in their actions, they are operating in a trance-like state.

Some young Western people dance the night away, oblivious to the outside world, fixed in their self-induced ecstasy state. This is probably exciting, but it is also very dangerous, particularly where drugs and alcohol are used. This ecstatic state loosens the veils between the worlds, and the consciousness slips into the lower astral, where, as discussed in earlier chapters there are grave dangers.

In modern mediumship, we talk about a state of trance when an entity in the spirit or astral world takes control, and speaks through the medium. Communication with entities in spirit does not always necessitate a full trance state. The medium can give up their body to an entity, which would necessitate full trance, or they may hear the words of the entity, and relay them in a light trance. Full trance is not work for the inexperienced. This is for many reasons, one of which is that it is very easy for a lower entity, pretending to be someone else, to speak through an untrained medium. This is where the Shamans have the advantage, for they have built up, over many generations, a powerful link with their ancestors, whom they know and trust. It is worth noting, however, that even the Shamans can be hoodwinked occasionally.

SHAMANISM

Various tribal peoples around the world use some form of Shamanism, a word that was originally applied to the semi-religious practices of certain Siberian tribes. The Shamans are tribal mediums, and are not to be confused with medicine men and women, sometimes referred to as witch doctors, who consult the spirits as advisors on health problems, and as an aid to divination.

Shamans in trance were thought to have left their bodies to visit the spirit world, and it was noted by missionaries at the turn of the century that they seemed to rely on a "technique of ecstasy", involving a close relationship with the spirits. They made use of full trance to communicate with the spirits of the tribe, an activity that included contact with their ancestors.

It is not hard to imagine the reaction of the missionaries to these activities. They were, of course, convinced that trance was the work of the devil, and set out in earnest to eradicate it, and to convert the people to what they considered to be more godly pursuits. As western education was brought into these new lands, and the peoples gradually became "civilised", their use of trance as a way of life decreased. It is, however, interesting, and perhaps amusing, to note that from the turn of the century onwards, as tribal peoples became more and more westernised, spiritualism, which is very similar in principle, was becoming popular in the west. Thus, as the white man laboured self-righteously to expunge mysticism from foreign lands, it was already taking root at home!

Shamanism is currently enjoying a revival. It is becoming very popular in Britain, and even more so in America, where they have the rich background of the Native American energy upon which to draw. Of all the remaining tribal peoples, it is perhaps the

Native Americans that have the greatest connection with the spirit world. They consider their dreams to be of no psychological significance: rather, they regard them as journeys into distant worlds, or visions to warn and help their tribe. If one of the native peoples in the Americas has a dream, it is not uncommon, even today, for them to wake in the night, and drum and sing to relay the dream to others.

It is not surprising that many mediums have, as their own personal guide, a Native American, for through this connection they can access the material and knowledge of spirit communication.

Remember that full trance requires a synchronising of energies between the trance entity and the medium, and that although to some extent like attracts like, no two beings vibrate in exactly the same way. This means that there will be some depletion of the medium's physical energy, as discussed in chapter 8.

The "medicine wheels" of the Shamans are set up to make communication with a specific spirit. These are a kind of ceremonial service to spirits. Through ritual and symbols, they contact the appropriate energy, making any mismatch of energies less likely. We have not made provision for this kind of focus in the West, where communication with astral beings is a rather hit-or-miss affair.

There is a great mystique around the idea of an entity speaking through a medium, and people seem to throw caution to the winds in this situation. For the inexperienced, it can seem very glamourous to have a being from another world communicating through you. It should, however, be borne in mind that the fact of having a conversation with a third party who happens to be in the spirit world, does not automatically mean that they have a better view of the truth. Shamans, as we have seen, draw upon the knowledge of their ancestors, which is commendable, but ancestors do not have all the answers. They can only speak, as any of us do, from their own perspective. We must ever come back to the essential awareness that no-one has the right to rule us, and we must not surrender our control.

MODERN TRANCE

More recently, other uses of trance have been developed, the most common of which are hypnotism and hypnotherapy. In these instances, the practitioner takes the subject into varying degrees of trance in order to access certain difficulties, or to make positive suggestions to them in an attempt to cure their malaise. As in mediumship, the active mind is quietened, facilitating access to the subconscious, or psyche. It is as though the common consciousness steps aside, allowing an open channel to the higher mind. This state can also be obtained through chanting. It is interesting to note that a strong memorising capability arises out of learning by rote, which is a light form of chant.

Through opening up this channel, it is as though the mind opens up to greater possibilities. It is the higher, greater mind, the non-intellectual mind, the mind that communicates with God. When the channel is open, it is like a telephone connection via which we can obtain information from any chosen place, simply by dialling the correct number.

But whom or what, among the many energies in Heaven and Earth, should we call? One of the most reckless forms of mediumship is when someone opens themselves into a trance state, and waits for any entity to speak through them. This is rather like leaving your front door open or picking a telephone number at random, and expecting the person at the other end (a) to be a moral sort of person, and (b) to know all the answers. This sort of pot-luck activity is highly dangerous, and is certainly not to be recommended. Whereas mostly we are protected by our own angelic Being, some people think it fun to try a random connection, and as this is their own wish, their angel or guide will not interfere. Since no-one is without some form of darkness or negativity, this can in some cases attract a dark entity. The effect of this sort of unsuitable communication is highly disruptive, both to the physical body and to the nervous system. A bad link, formed in a trance condition, can take days, or even weeks, to sever.

Furthermore, once a connection has been made, the medium's number, as it were, is known to the entity, which can thereby easily "return the call" at any time. If one inadvertently attracts a dark force, it can indeed be the very devil to remove.

If you are determined to open up into a trance state, whether it be for mediumistic purposes or for health concerns, make sure that you know where you or your therapist are "dialling". Carelessness in this work will effectively create an unstable spiritual time-bomb, destined for unpredictable but inevitable detonation.

Be focussed at all times, and remember the golden rule that energy follows thought. Establish a good, solid connection with your angel guide over a period of time. When, and only when, that is firmly established, ask them to direct you.

Alternatively, you can follow the example of the Shamans, and create in the astral a symbol as an entry point for communication with a particular energy or Being. This is easily obtained, but it requires time and effort. Visualise a symbol or have a name as a password energy. Create the thought around it you desire and make sure you perpetuate the energy constantly, for there is nothing so dangerous as a void in energy. A void is always filled, and not always by a benevolent energy. Be very careful, however, for the more energy you give a symbol, the more you create life in it. Even if you are working one hundred per cent for the purpose of good, when you finish with your symbol, either through loss of interest or when you die, that gateway will remain open, but without an energy running through it, a vacuum will thus have been created. Since nature abhors a vacuum, she will fill it with the first energy that comes along, and this could very easily be a disruptive, negative force. So if you choose to work in this way, make sure that you put in a "safety clause", and agree with your angels or guides that when you have finished with it, they will dissolve the connection.

It is important to have some idea of the powerful and intricate workings of the energies attached to symbols, not only in the astral, but also in the third dimension. There may, for instance, be a beautiful statue in a church, that a certain person or congregation uses as a symbolic focus for their union with the higher planes. When this focal energy is withdrawn, for whatever reason, the void will be filled as described above. It is for this reason that some old churches have a very sinister feeling. In extreme cases, a church that is not properly consecrated becomes, in energy terms, rancid: it attracts dark forces, which can be harmful to all who enter the church. This situation will continue until someone knowledgeable clears the energy, and re-focuses it through proper consecration.

The use of a proper focus of the Light Forces in places of worship has largely been lost, and is only now beginning to be rediscovered. There are important reasons for consecration, which at one time was a sacred task. It becomes more and more obvious that in all psychic activities it is crucial to ask always for the greatest, highest good to work with you and through you.

Through some types of trance, a clear, open channel to higher consciousness is achieved, through which we can access many energies and much information. Indeed, there is no reason why we should not contact any energy in the cosmos: we are all inextricably linked. The inner soul being radiates a vibration which is in unison with the whole cosmos. Unfortunately we have cloaked this vibration with all sorts of other energies, not least our personality. The personality is the outer state, which, rather like a picture on a chocolate box, does not always reveal the nature of the contents. Most people communicate more with their outer image than with their real being. In fact, many people do not consciously know the reality of the inner self.

Trance has long served as a fundamental instrument for stilling the outer image and the ego self, the emotions and the mental activity. In one way or another, all religions and cultures have made use of it, through chant, dance, prayer (particularly of the repetitive type), and meditation. This, then, serves to open us to the Light Force. It is as though we take off our overcoat, and begin to reveal our true self. Used within the context of religions, it served to bring individuals into contact with the god of their faith, but the true God and Oneness of the universe has no dogma or creed.

In the past, mankind was been ill-equipped to identify God as an energy, which is why, in most religions, God has been personified, usually as a male father figure. The Universal Light Force is, however, neither male nor female. It belongs to no particular state, nation or religion. It is there for everyone, for it is the Light Revelation, the Truth which is beyond words. Of itself the process of stilling the mind and freeing the open channel will not connect you to the Light Force. An open channel can accommodate any energy, and this, as we have seen, is why it is so important to focus your call.

Fits and seizures are usually caused by some disturbance of psychic energy, although this is not widely recognised. Trouble can be caused by an involuntary opening of the channel without a focussed communication. It is as if the active mind is suddenly stilled, freeing the open channel without the individual's permission. In these cases, firstly the human mind automatically cuts of parts of the brain after which the animal earthly instinct that allows us to be alive comes into operation. The mind is appeased and connection with the fundamental functions of the mind return, and within a short period of time usually brings the person back into normal consciousness.

In some instances, however, this open, directionless channel will, as we have seen, connect with lower astral beings. They can even take over a body for short periods, but are unlikely to keep it, as the energy involved is too great. In the same way that a medium in full trance is depleted physically, so too is the person who has just had this experience of seizure. Similarly, recovery from this experience, albeit a voluntary one, can take many days or weeks.

Insufficient work has been done in this field, which contains too many controversial aspects to merit the consideration of the medical profession. However, there have been cases where an individual, with the assistance of a healer, has positively aligned their open channel whilst in the seizure, which has helped to fuse and hold the energy in a safe area until the seizure stops. This alignment to the Light Forces has great effect in decreasing the regularity of seizures, or even completely eradicating them.

Because of their loosening effect between the dimensions, any drugs are disastrous, and exacerbate the situation, for although fits and seizures set off a chemical reaction, this is not caused by a chemical imbalance. In times past, these illnesses were treated by some form of exorcism, and it is easy to see why people watching a person in the throes of a violent seizure would imagine some devil within. There is no devil, but negative energy, sometimes in the form of a discarnate soul, can take possession. Some kind of aligned healing does work, but of course those who deny the existence of anything other than the physical world would disagree.

It was once said to me that it takes as much faith to deny something as it does to believe it. No particular faith or belief is necessary in order to undertake psychic work, but it would be surprising if anyone with any experience of psychic matters were unable to acknowledge the existence of a power greater than themselves. There are, in fact, comparatively few people who would totally deny the presence of the superior force that in this book is neutrally referred to as the Universal Light Force. One can call it God, Allah, Jehovah, the Highest Mind, the Source: it really is unimportant. Blind faith is not called for, and it is ill-advised: knowledge that is more than a belief, knowledge that comes from the deep, true knowing within, is the level of conviction to which we all aspire.

The word "religion" comes from the Latin verb "to bind back," the root meaning "to select, or to choose." The Latin "religio" means, "a careful selection of fundamental beliefs and motives by the higher or spiritual intellect, a faculty of intuitional judgement and understanding."

In the opening of the channel to higher consciousness through trance, we make a selection process depending on our level of intelligence. Like attracts like. The lower worlds live out the higher. So our life and our being dictates the sort of experience we have in this aligned state. Whatever experiences are occurring below in the material world we create above, and vice versa. If we therefore see the Heart centre as the pivotal point, the dividing line of consciousness, we can understand that the astral worlds which vibrate to the frequency of the fourth dimensions are immediately contactable in the attunement to the Heart. As we have already observed, this band of energy holds many aspects, both positive and negative. People particularly in the past have spoken about the fear of God. Through trance we can if not careful connect with fear energy.

In the past, the development of mediumship has not taken into consideration whether the student is polishing the instrument that is themselves, but we are beginning to realise now the fundamental necessity for a clear instrument or channel through which spirit can work. It is no coincidence that the ancient priestesses were kept away from the masses. They were kept pure in the belief that this would bring pure information, and there is some validity in this view. However, as purity is, in essence, an energy, it cannot be falsely or mechanically achieved. Nowadays it is not necessary to be kept hidden away, although purity of motive is, as ever, essential. I strongly suggest that you read and digest the many aspects of what Alice Bailey refers to in her books as "Glamour", for until you have willingly abandoned this, you are likely to be fixed upon the negative side of the astral forces.

Possession is caused by, or through, a trance state. It is usual for this possession, to occur without the subject's conscious permission. The veils between the dimensions, when becoming thin, allow entry by a disturbed entity from the astral worlds, and it is only through realignment to the Universal Light Force that the subject will be freed from the torture of control by a foreign entity.

Sometimes, through sheer weakness of character, a person will invite a dark entity to possess them, believing that this being will have the power to make them rich overnight, or to confer upon them some un-earned status. However, nothing comes from nothing: everything that happens to you is a result of the energy that you emit. If there is no generating energy, then there will be no manifestation of wealth or power. People who appear to get rich overnight have in fact accrued this money over many years, and perhaps many lifetimes, their riches accruing within the astral bank.

The temptation to use the dark forces is clear, but what is less clear is the temptation to use bliss. Although bliss and ecstasy states are the province of saints, usually brought about by a sudden revelation of the God Force, it is very easy to engineer a situation whereby people are given a taste of them. A bliss or ecstasy state can serve the purpose of allowing a closed mind to see the higher possibilities of life, but the quest for it can become a glamour. It can become a way of abandoning life, and of relinquishing responsibility. This is not the spiritual way: we are not meant to abdicate our material responsibilities to the material worlds. We are here out of choice, and for a reason.

Some "workshop junkies" go around and around, seeking this kind of experience. It becomes like a drug to them, but after the initial burst of pleasure it teaches them nothing, for the bliss state cannot be sustained. Usually after twenty-four or forty-eight hours there is a huge anti-climax, and the individual comes down off the "drug" of bliss. Unfortunately these dependant souls then immediately crave another "bliss fix", and can fall prey to any unscrupulous, charismatic individual who can provide it. These people are merely seeking a form of entertainment, or "happening", and are probably not ready to take on full commitment to the spiritual pathway.

Mass meetings where ecstasy states occur, even in a religious context, have exactly the same effect as trance: they open the channel. This must be directed positively, or the experiences can carry people away from reality. They are dangerous, and do not serve to promote spiritual growth.

Spirituality is about balance, and this means being totally centred and aligned. If we were in a state of bliss all the time, we would do nothing. There are many beings, both on the earth plane and in the spirit world, who would tempt us for their own ends. Be careful, and try not to allow your enthusiasm to take you into areas that can deter you from your true path. Once the bliss experience finishes, it leaves a vacuum, which, as we have seen, may be filled by a negative force. If one day you do achieve a temporary bliss state, you will probably feel somewhat depressed when you come down from it, and this negative feeling can draw a negative energy into your being. After your withdrawal from bliss, you may look around you, see the imperfections of life in the material world, and not want to be part of it any more. Suicide can in a few cases seem like the only option.

Please acknowledge that the imperfections of life are there to reveal Light. It is the differences and imperfections in people that make them interesting, and from which we can learn the most. Life may not be easy, but it can be a joy. Joy is the true essence of love, and love is achieved through balance. Remember Nature's greenery - the colour of the Heart energy. It is through this energy, and only this energy, that we find harmony and peace.

When you ask for the greatest, highest good to work through you, also affirm that you are prepared to accept whatever that takes. This may lead you away from glamour, but in its place you will find the permanent richness of balance and truth.

In the past the use of full trance in mediumship was partially due to the insecurity of the medium. They were not able for whatever reason to take the responsibility of higher consciousness and therefore tried to obtain it through another entity, believing that in full trance nothing of their individual personality would remain. Like attracts like and fear attracts fear. It is possible to obtain just as much "higher knowledge," from channelling as full trance, and when one understands the possible consequences of trance it begs the question why do it? Although it is helpful for a medium to have some knowledge of trance work, all the information in trance can be brought through in other ways without the danger.

EXERCISE

Open up in the usual fashion, and concentrate for at least three to five minutes on your total connection to your breath. Purposefully draw your breath into the Heart, and expand that energy. Reach up, and ask positively for the highest, greatest good. Take your focus far beyond yourself, and see a funnel of light opening from your Crown centre to Divine Consciousness. Keep your awareness in this area for a while, and then ask for some relevant information to help you to align or adjust yourself as an instrument of Light. The focus is all-important, and you must truly desire to achieve this Divine connection, whatever it may reveal to you about yourself. The process of self-discovery is not easy, and will undoubtedly reveal things about you that are not balanced. Be prepared for this. Only when you confront your fears, which may even necessitate a different approach to life, or a change of life-style, will you be able truly to serve.

If revelation comes to you about your imbalances, never indulge in self pity. Spirit neither needs nor wants your sorrow. It needs your strength. Recognise your weakness, affirm that you will try harder, and move on.

Gradually, through enlightened observation, you will dissolve the darker side of yourself. In the meantime, embrace it with love, not sorrow.

As usual upon finishing your exercise, close in the usual way.

Books for Reference
Trance: A Natural History of Altered States of Mind, by Brian Inglis 1989.
Serving Humanity, by Alice Bailey. 1972

Chapter 11
***

CHANNELLING

Channelling is the term currently used to describe what was at one time referred to as trance mediumship. There are, however, differences between them, the principal one being that while mediumship usually refers to communication with discarnate spirits, that is, the souls of those who have "died", channelling implies communication either with entities that have completed their round of incarnations on the Earth plane, the higher impersonal guides, or those souls that have expanded beyond the individual soul unit, often referred to as Ascended Masters. Many channellers assign names to such energies, but these are irrelevant. In most cases, names serve merely as a point of focus.

More recently we have begun to see channellings from entities without identity. These are from the energy of the Universal Consciousness, and are easily discernible, as communication with a higher consciousness is never emotional or personal, being beyond the influence of the emotions and the lower mind.

If one is to be pedantic, one must say that channelling is a form of trance. A major difference is that no separate entity is controlling the channeller's energy, but from the channeller's point of view the feeling is remarkably similar to that of a strong trance state, in that, as with most forms of highly-connected mediumship, they do not remember the content of the material. It is a bit like having a dream: one can remember it if one discusses it, or writes it down, immediately on waking. If not, then within a very few minutes all recollections disappear.

Historically, the principal use of trance has been to connect people to God via a human medium, but from the beginning of this century until very recently, emphasis has been placed upon the type of trance that involves communication with discarnate spirits. This use of full trance was said to eradicate the individual personality of the medium, and there is some truth in this. There are many accounts of mediums bringing through information of which they had no prior knowledge, and displaying talents that they themselves did not possess. There was, for instance, the case of the well known medium Pearl Curran, who channelled Patience Worth. Having had little education, Pearl was virtually illiterate, and yet her mediumship produced poetry, novels, and other literary compositions; works that were way beyond the skills of such a simple woman, as was her use of obscure Anglo-Saxon words whilst in trance. That she was in trance was not in doubt: the question was, where did these skills come from? This aspect of trance mediumship and channelling is still very much open to discussion.

Whether even a full trance state completely eradicates the personality of the individual medium is unclear. To some extent, a simple, uncomplicated person, with neither aspirations nor cares, can, in certain circumstances, make a better natural medium than a more sophisticated individual. An uncomplicated soul, is often free from the intellectual reason that pervades our true minds. These people are able to open freely without "hang ups" and hence receive clearer guidance. However, the times call for all of us to take responsibility for everything that we are and everything that we do, and it must be said that to become an instrument in any aspect of psychic work, especially channelling or trance, purity of intent is of paramount importance. The more intelligent and clearer you are, the clearer and more focused will be the information that you relay.

Pure motive is not the same as good intentions, which very

often come from the ego self. Pure motive implies the desire that only good should come through you; the desire continuously to polish yourself; the desire for full revelation of any aspect of yourself that impedes your alignment with light. This means being prepared for anything, and it may necessitate a completely different way of living. It may mean abandoning familiar things and people. You must even be prepared for the possibility that channelling is not the best way for you to progress spiritually, and be ready to let it go, if that is the case. There are all sorts of possibilities for spiritual growth, but the main ingredient of all of them is surrender to the greatest, highest good. This is not submission. It is not servility. It is the all-knowing state of Divine Consciousness, to which, within our true note of desire, we are all aspiring.

Even if you have no intention of being a medium, the use of channelling in spiritual awareness is an excellent tool. The very word "channelling" is descriptive: the word "channel" means, amongst other things, "a means of access". It conjures up images of opening to a flow, and this is indeed what we endeavour to do: to open up to the flow of the greater or Divine energies. The process of communication starts when the channeller's active mind, their little mind, steps aside, thus opening an access-way to the greater, higher mind. You can connect on a higher level at many different frequencies: communication could be made with a discarnate spirit, or with a greater consciousness. Always endeavour to reach for the highest.

If you psychically watch mediums at work, you can detect exactly which frequency they use by noting the shift in energy within their aura. But from whatever place they are working, mediums very often give this link a name (as mentioned earlier in this chapter). Through constant communication with a name, some kind of personality can be formed, and if this connection is maintained and continued over a long period, a separate entity can be created. This means that a medium has literally given life to the higher, or different, consciousness.

In a way this is immaterial. Our human minds fail to grasp anything without shape, colour or form, and in giving the energy a name, one creates a form. However, if a medium develops a dependency on that form and personality, the true value of the contact is lost. My own attitude is clear in regard to channelled information: listen to the messages, then ask yourself if they resonate with your heart. If they do not, then drop them, regardless of whence, or from whom, they purport to come.

Messages from discarnate souls have been with us throughout history, and throughout the world. Even during the Dark Ages, monks and nuns were channelling. However, within Europe, or Christendom, as it was then known, channelled information had to be validated by the Church as being from God, or it fell under great suspicion, and was often banned as the work of a negative force. It is only in comparatively recent times that communication with individual entities has re-surfaced.

As far as one can ascertain, all the major religions were started, or at least influenced, by channelled material. It seems that many of the Christian prophets were channellers, starting with Moses. In about 1000 B.C. came Solomon, followed, over a period, by Samuel, Daniel, Elijah, Elisha, Ezekiel, Jeremiah, Isaiah, and, much later, John the Baptist. Their channellings were often preceded by words such as "the word of the Lord came unto me, saying.....". It is perhaps in the New testament that we find the most descriptive messages of channelling... "Hereafter ye shall see the heaven open, and the angels of God ascending and descending upon the Son of Man...The words that I speak unto you, they are spirit...ye are from beneath; I am from above; ye are of this world : and I am not of this world...I do nothing of myself; but as my Father hath taught me, I speak these things. And he that sent me is with me...He that is of God heareth God's words, The Father is in me, and I in him...Whosoever I speak therefore, even as the Father said unto me, so I speak...In my father's house are many mansions... the words that I speak unto you I speak not of myself, but the Father that dwelleth in me, he doeth the works.. for I have given unto them the word which the father gavest me".

In the twelfth century, Merlin, the semi-legendary Welsh-British bard and seer associated with King Arthur's court, was reputed to be capable of many feats of channelling. Further north, the Scottish channeller, Thoman the Rhymer was well known. Also in the twelfth century, the Abbess Hildegard of Bingen channelled a wealth of material, including the most wonderful songs, which have recently been resurrected and re-recorded. The Pope of that time, Eugene II, pronounced her channelling to be the voice of God. However, she was also known to have "fallen into possession", the contemporary expression for speaking in tongues, at which times she was obviously in contact with individual entities.

In the fourteenth century, Richard Rolle became known as the father of English mysticism through his channelling, which included transcendental music. Joseph Karo was one of a number of Jewish mystics: he channelled the celebrated spirit of Mishnah. More recent years have produced Edgar Cayce, Madame Blavatsky, Alice Bailey, and many more.

Madame Blavatsky (1831-91), who telepathically channelled the Master Koot Humi (he was said to be living in India), gave us the concept of a hierarchy of adepts, initiates, and Masters, the energies of creation, forces of evolution, and the workings of universal consciousness. In her now classic work "The Secret Doctrine", Madame Blavatsky shows us how every level of attainment allows us knowledge, and more experience, of the Cosmic Mind, as we move upwards from ordinary person to initiate, to Master and onwards, up to the planes of planetary and cosmic realities. This progression, she said, necessitates the corresponding development of power and responsibility. It was upon these doctrines that Madame Blavatsky and her friends founded what became the metaphysically orientated, and highly influential, Theosophical Society.

Another most inspiring channeller was Alice Bailey, (died

1949) who channelled the entity known as "The Tibetan", and who set down the fundamentals of modern spiritual and psychic development. One of her greatest works is "The Rays and the Initiations", in which, alongside Blavatsky, she added several important concepts to Western metaphysics. The most significant of these concerned the body's energy centres, the chakras, which were previously little known in the West, but which nowadays we take for granted when considering such matters as healing and psychic unfoldment. Bailey also brought us knowledge of the Kundalini energy, and the astral, etheric and causal planes. Although there had been some earlier contact with the concept of Eastern metaphysics, through translation of Oriental literature and individual visits to the East, there is no doubt that over the years these ideas have been popularised through Alice Bailey's efforts. Her writings have great influence these days, and in them we may glimpse some of the deep spirituality common to all great mystics and their works.

The seven rays to which Bailey referred are embodiments of seven types of energy, which demonstrate to us the seven qualities of the Universal Light Force, or Deity. According to Bailey these seven qualities have a seven-fold effect upon matter and form, and are to be found in all parts of the universe. They also have a seven-fold interrelationship amongst themselves. We can perhaps grasp this concept if we remember that Light pours down through the many layers of matter. Just as light shining through water, or a prism, can then be seen as the seven rainbow colours, so the seven rays equate to the many "builders, lords, rulers and deities."

The deeper implications of these cannot be investigated here, but other channellers have explored the idea, including Oscar Ichazo, originator of the Arica Institute training. This typology bears a remarkable resemblance to the ray qualities, using the Sufi symbol of a nine-point diagram. Much of this was introduced to the West through the teachings of G.I. Gurdjieff.

Such systems are very interesting and useful, but remember

that they are only intended as a format for the "little mind", and that study of them can never substitute for living integration with the God Force. To a true mystic, communication with different entities and spirits is not deemed to be the highest level of spiritual experience. The path of most traditional mystics is to reach higher within the levels of spiritual consciousness, moving towards loss of attachment to the material worlds, and unity with the Godhead.

The mystical path towards Ultimate Being involves many lifetimes, and is usually assumed to come at a very much later stage; one which would almost certainly entail the loss of the physical state altogether. Although we are all aspiring to progress along this pathway, it is best to deal with what is in the present, because only by doing so will we dissolve our negativities, and come into full integration.

Within the writings of channellers, there is very little to help the student towards the dissolution of the personality level. In many works, while it is made abundantly clear that the student must have control over desires and thoughts, there is very little advice on how to achieve this, and to rid ourselves of our negative emotions, obstacles, or physical desires.

Maybe it was out of need for this type of assistance that work such as Transpersonal Psychology, and a system called Psychosynthesis, were developed. Transpersonal Psychology suggests that spiritual work is likely to be handicapped by inner conflicts, negative emotional states, and repressions, and those who study it are advised to address emotional and psychological issues before, not during their psychic development. On this matter most people would agree, but there are discrepancies concerning how it might be achieved. The combination of imbalanced emotions and psychic work is equivalent to a bomb waiting to explode. All kinds of difficulties, including illusions, are prevalent where the two combine. These range from depletion of energy to a full blown possession.

Opening ourselves to the higher universal forces connects us with the core of our being, and through this connection, the outer layers are gradually revealed. These will include all the, aforementioned in the last paragraph, issues, as well as every aspect of ourselves that is out of balance. By connecting with our inner light, and allowing it to shine forth, we automatically illuminate all areas, and any problems will surface. Any matters outstanding, on whatever level, will be revealed, for in this light there is nowhere to hide.

Because we are the sum total of all of our experiences, we actually do not need to "pick over" past times. Like attracts like: if working with the energy is bringing old issues to the surface, that energy will naturally draw to us the necessary situations, which will emerge in the present. Therefore the most effective way of transmuting your fears and your negative emotions, whatever their origin, is by dealing honesty and openly with yourself today. Whatever work you do on a psychological level, you will, sooner or later, be obliged to take sole control of your life.

The danger of any kind of psychological work is that you can, if you are not very careful, perpetuate your anxieties. This will not take you forward, and what can happen is that someone can "do the rounds" of self-analysis for years, with little or no progress. One does not need to know from whence a difficulty arose. It might have been ten life-times ago. If you continue always to, lovingly, observe yourself, and to work with the Light, you will eradicate the past, clarify the present, and enable yourself finally to move on.

Roberto Assagioli, who developed Psychosynthesis, suggests that one transforms the negative elements in the personality, and synthesise them into an integrated, purposeful personality, also allowing connection between the personality and the higher self. To Assagioli, along with many others, the higher self is the true self, and is experienced in mystical or cosmic states. Assagioli does not, however, present the higher self as a means of connection with advanced Beings, but rather as the transpersonal potential for opening into the wider spiritual realities.

In all the therapies one can be beguiled by the seemingly professional aspects of the training. Certainly any form of self awareness healing can and does help, but any method is only as good as the individuals who teach them: as we have seen, in this kind of work it is all too easy for people to take themselves seriously, and to assert control over others.

If your intuition tells you that some kind of counselling or psychological work is required, look around for a good group or healer, and let your choice be an intuitive one. Experience is always of value in a teacher or therapist, but no qualification, however long it took to obtain, guarantees a pure heart. When you find the teacher or therapist of your choice, do not allow things to drag on and on. Unfortunately these kinds of practice sometimes give our little mind the perfect excuse to prevaricate on our true mission. A good practitioner will exert no control over you, and will not allow dependency to develop.

If you are genuinely seeking truth, it will be revealed to you within your environment, so if you are in any doubt, ask the highest greatest good to help. Do this by sending up a positive call for guidance for whatever you need, and affirm that you want the answer, whatever it entails. Wait and watch: the answer will come, probably when you least expect it. It is likely to be within your vicinity, under your nose, and you need look no further than your present situation for clues as to your clearance and awakening.

Nowadays we are seeing a shift away from communication with single entities into a broader vista, and several mediums have recently become aware of communication from a group of Beings. They do not present themselves in terms of personality, indeed there is a common feeling that they are beyond the personality state. The group has been variously labelled as "The White Brotherhood," "The Teachers," "The Planetary Logos,""The Spiritual Hierarchy" or as "The Professors" - my own affectionate term. It comprises a combination of entities, including some wise old discarnate souls, most of which will not reincarnate, hence the "Ascended Masters" title given by some. Also present in this group are Archangel master souls, and most recently it has included a connection with Light Beings beyond our solar system, which go mainly under the heading of "Space Brothers," or, less formally "E.Ts." This group seems to be very active at this time, largely because of the enormous shift of consciousness occurring within humanity. Without exception, when this "Gestalt" type of energy is contacted, it gives an overview for the individual and the planet.

For those who have worked at some time with an individual guide, the difference is marked, for these energies are not as soft and sweet and nurturing as our own individual communicators. They are compassionate, but their compassion is beyond emotion, and they can be quite stern, answering all our questions without fuss or frills. Strictly speaking, these Beings can be contacted on the upper astral levels, but they exist beyond the astral state. They make themselves available at this level so that they can communicate personal information when, and only when, it is relevant to a particular person's soul growth. Many teachers, including myself, feel their presence in group activities, most particularly in development classes. They never stay for longer than is necessary, and they always come straight to the point. In energy terms, they resonate somewhere between the Heart and the Throat frequency. This is interesting in itself, as this frequency is very much the "spirit level" of humanity as we enter the fifth ray state. It seems that this group is perfect for our needs at this time.

Up to this point, anyone can, with practice, attune themselves to spiritual forces. However, the next stage demands that the student attune their whole being, for above this frequency we go beyond any personal connection. The sort of channelling that occurs then is a communication with the Universal Light Force, and this can only be made by a pure instrument.

There are, of course, many different frequency layers and attunements within the universal consciousness, indeed the possibilities for any medium are endless. The higher the vibration the more intense the connection, and it is not unusual, when first making a particular link, for the channeller to speak in an automaton-like way. If the medium spends any time with that particular connection, their speech will normalise as they adjust to the frequency. As in any other area of psychic work, there is no set experience. Mediums will find their attunement in different ways, and the experience will vary from individual to individual. For sensitives, however, the difference between working from the spiritual astral planes and the universal levels would be clear. Being a pure instrument does not mean that you, as a being, are perfect. Mediums and channellers are ordinary human beings, with ordinary human functions and needs. However, at this stage some kind of advanced self-awareness would have taken place. Like attracts like, always and ever.

In 1989, after my own consciousness had made an important shift, my personal guides seemed to step back. This did not seem in anyway alarming, rather, it felt like a natural progression. At this time, so much information was bombarding me from all directions that I reached up and asked for guidance from the highest Light Force possible. Information immediately started coming through. It was not full trance, although technically it was some kind of trance condition. It felt as though I was held in a beam of energy, a melting of consciousness between this higher Light Force and myself. Having experienced many kinds of mediumship over the years, including full trance, I immediately knew that this was a different frequency, and on a level beyond the astral. After each session, I had no memory of what had been said, so it all had to be recorded.

Obviously I was curious, and asked to know with what or with whom I was communicating. The answer came back, "A unison of Light Forces: original thought." I had never heard this term, and did not really understand what it meant, other than that it was obviously very different from any trance mediumship that I had experienced in the past, and that this was not a connection with an individual entity. After half a dozen sessions, it suddenly announced, "we will now dictate a book!" This duly happened, and that book was called "Wind of Change." Just after finishing this work, I started reading a newly-published book on channelling, (see books for reference). Imagine my surprise to read a quote from 1977, of Carla Rueckert saying; "(Your) vibration or frequency is the only important part of your being, since it is an index of your consciousness with respect to the "original thought." When an individual is aware of life in its infinite sense, he is also aware of the benefits of matching this vibration with the vibration of the "original thought" (of the creator)".

With this form of channelling, the whole energy of the individual has to have expanded in order to accommodate this connection with a higher consciousness. One of the most frequent questions I am asked is, "what or whom are you channelling?" In pondering on how best to answer, and endeavouring to be completely honest, my reply now has to be: "It is me". It is a blending and alignment of consciousness between the "I" of self and the highest self which ultimately becomes the Universal Light Force; the Godhead; All That Is.

Anyone who bothers to work on their own attunement can channel this energy. The little self and the little mind have to be set aside, but because the instrument, the channeller, has integrated themselves to the higher universal forces, they can instantaneously communicate with the higher mind, the greater consciousness, the God Force. This may all sound incredible, but in fact anyone can channel, and the whole process of learning how to do so is an important one, not just to bring through information, but to set aside the petty details of the material worlds, and, primarily, to awaken the God within. By so doing, the expansion of consciousness is assured. In one of my many channellings, the information was given that "the greatest desire of anything in the whole cosmos is the desire to expand."

The need to channel at this time is very much part of the ever-present thirst for greater possibilities. It is not the highest type of psychic attunement, nor is it indicative of one who has reached the end of their journey, but it definitely reaches beyond the astral levels, and therefore beyond the main aspects of illusion and glamour: individuals who channel on this level may not be wholly Divine Beings, but they have allowed the Divine in them to speak. For the purpose of giving sittings, however, this kind of work is not appropriate, for it is too far removed from the personal state: The higher the frequency, the less personal the content, and most people who come for a sitting are seeking information about themselves personally.

All the way through our psychic development, we have seen how new opportunities present themselves at every turn. The view is different with every step, and with it our frequency changes. Our first and only desire must be to serve Spirit and Truth, for without this there is no real expansion. As we relinquish the veils that cloak the true self, our energies become lighter, with the result that their frequency changes; like, as always, attracting like. Therefore our psychic radius expands, and we can contact finer vibrations, moving nearer and nearer to God.

During the process of channelling we have to let go of the little self. Inspirational speaking is a lower form of channelling. If one is inspired, or in any way given, to look beyond the little self and be enlightened in any way, perhaps it becomes less important to know where the inspiration came. Again we can only really judge by the fruits of the experience. Channelling is a finer vibration than inspirational speaking, and the process of expanding the range becomes an amazing and joyous experience of attunement to the higher self.

What, then, is the highest self? Some people equate it with the inner guiding teacher, or even with the conscience, and both views are probably valid. As in life, it is always preferable to go to the top, so let us aspire to the highest self. But what is the highest self? It surely must be the spark of God within, and this spark is within everyone, without exception. In unfastening the outer protective garments of our personality, which is part of the process of channelling, we have allowed ourselves a glimpse that spark, and when someone has caught such a glimpse, even if it was only for a moment, the spiritual progress of that individual is assured. This flash of insight has very often already occurred by the time a student comes into a psychic development group. If it has not, then it will occur within a very short space of time, for the whole process of opening up is about letting go of the overcoat of the personality, and listening to the stillness within.

This is why in this book I have been at pains to emphasise this aspect, for it is without doubt crucial to the refinement of information on whatever level you are concentrating. In surrendering yourself to a channelled state, you automatically abandon the little self, and when one does this, one can speak only the truth: as above, so below. This speaking of truth will then echo within your everyday life, because having experienced alignment to the Light Forces, albeit for brief periods during channelling, you will desire this purity of intent in all matters. Self-discovery of an unparalleled kind will emerge, and you will be set firmly on the spiritual pathway. Expansion of consciousness is then inevitable.

Where does inspirational speaking end and channelling begin? Is perhaps the inspiration from that spark of god anyway? The further down the line we go, the more aligned our state and the higher the teaching. How do we ever know where it comes from because for so very long we have depended only on structures, and the higher the channelling the less the structure. We may be given a name, but as we have seen a name does not validate the message. Perhaps from Jesus's disciple John we receive the best advise. "Beloved believe not every spirit, but try the spirits whether they are of God, because many false prophets have gone out into the world."

EXERCISE

To begin to receive a flow for channelling, start by inspirationally speaking. Open up in the usual way, and begin to speak about whatever comes into your mind. It will help you to use a "headline", or to choose a word. Pick one of the "angel cards" perhaps, or even open the dictionary at random. Start speaking about whatever word or sentence your eye falls upon. Surprisingly, you will find that words do seem to come from nowhere. Later, when you are receiving a little flow, try thinking of a question to which you would like an answer. When you do this, you may be tempted to apply your own connotations, but be honest: let go, and see what comes.

Even on the inspirational level you will find it easier to abandon yourself completely. Take all your thoughts above your head. This may sound strange, but having opened up the Crown centre, and perhaps even completed the diamond crystal exercise in the previous chapter, you can throw all your thoughts into the air above your Crown. In this way, your thought processes are lifted beyond the levels of the little mind and the personality.

Another helpful visualisation is that of a funnel of light going up from your Crown centre to the highest possible Light Force energy. Take all your thoughts and energy as high as you can, affirming strongly that you wish to join with the highest possible Light Force energy. You are advised to affirm this at all times and mean it.

Do not labour over this exercise: start by working over very short periods of time. Concentration will at first be difficult, and during your channelling you may find your energy slipping. This loss of focus is easily recognised: you will become aware of your surroundings, and mundane thoughts may enter your head. You may even begin to listen to yourself, and to think about what you are saying. If this happens, be purposeful and disciplined, focus your energy above yourself again, and keep going.

Forging this link requires concentration and focus. For most people it will not come easily, and it may take many days, weeks, or even years, to achieve. At first you may only receive one word, but this is a start: the cork will have been released, as it were, and it is better to receive one word that is truly aligned than none at all. Later it will progress to a sentence, and very soon a flow will start.

This work is better practised in a group, or failing that, with a friend. Tape the channelling, and listen to it afterwards. Ask yourself the question, "does it speak to my heart?" If the channelling energy tells you that it is a particular person or entity, be careful. Validate it only by the purity of message, and the resonance within your heart. If at any time your channelling tells you to do something, particularly if it is something you are unsure of, you can guarantee that this is not a high Being. There is no benevolent being in the whole of the cosmos that would tell you to do anything against your will.

Some people find that they can channel by writing. However, this method is less effective in obtaining a high vibration, because the writing process involves some of the thinking brain, which can disturb the balance of frequencies necessary for a pure vibration. Unless you feel particularly drawn to this way of working, it is probably best to leave it, for it is very easy to slip into "automatic writing", and then any communication with astral beings, particularly from those of the lower astral, can come through. The lower astral energies particularly like this form of work, because through it they can feed off your energy.

Do not be too anxious about the words or the information that you may receive. Remember that the finest aspect of channelling lies not in the information received, but in the opening-up to the higher rays, creating greater possibilites, greater truth and greater wisdom. In channelling you will raise your own vibration, which will create a greater energy within, allowing you to emanate a finer, better vibration, for yourself and for those around you. You will eventually become a true natural healer, for your own vibration will affect and heal all those with whom you have contact, and even those about whom you think.

After channelling, close in the usual way. After this kind of exercise, it is advisable to connect strongly with the Earth. You can easily do this by visualising a tap-root leading from your Base centre, down past the soles of your feet, and into the centre of the Earth. Draw up energy through that root, and let it feed into the Base centre - and other centres, if you feel that to be necessary. Some kind of physical work is also helpful: gardening, washing the floor, anything that puts you in touch with your body. All channellers must seek to balance themselves. As above, so below.

Books for Reference
Channelling, by Jon Klimo 1988
With the Tongues of Men and Angels: A study of Channelling,
by Arthur Hastings 1991
The Rays and the Initiations by Alice Bailey 1960
The Secret Doctrine by Madam Blavatsky 1888.

Chapter 12

DEATH

The main function of spiritualism has always been to prove the continuation of life after what we refer to as death. Unfortunately, people whose minds are "not yet open" can never be persuaded of survival, even when presented with the clearest evidence. This book does not seek to convert or persuade, simply to present some consensus ideas on the process of death and what comes directly after it, when we find ourselves in the spirit worlds. The only incontrovertible evidence lies in the inner knowledge of our continued state beyond the physical, the knowledge that is implanted within every being. When the personality and the ego self loosen, access to this knowledge occurs naturally.

Death, for most people, is their greatest fear. Like any other fear, it must, of necessity, be fully explored, understood and overcome. This is not just about proof of survival: it involves the release of the old "baggage" that impedes our gaining of true knowledge. Many people now have the opportunity to move on beyond the karmic round, but this can only be achieved through total freedom from fear in all its aspects.

As mankind moves towards a different consciousness, he is transmuting his lower vessel, his body. A major part of this transformation is taking place within the cells of the physical state (we shall examine the implications of this in subsequent chapters), and this necessitates the relinquishing of all fears. If we can overcome the fear of death, we shall have travelled a long way down the road to full and permanent release.

Eradicating the fear of death is extremely difficult, for it is not simply a question of emotion. This fear is actually embedded within our cells, and for the best of reasons: that of survival. Because of it, we flee from danger, instinctively clinging to life. If we had always had full and confident knowledge of eternal life, we may not have bothered to protect and maintain our lives on the Earth plane, and we would therefore not have had the many karmic experiences necessary for our spiritual growth. The innate fear of death has thus been essential to life.

Many of our seemingly minor fears are connected to this instinct for self-preservation: fear of rejection, fear of loss, and psychological fears, such as fears of heights and spiders, all are related to our fear of death. Our cells have been so strongly imprinted with it, that its release needs to take place on a higher mental vibration, in alignment to the Light forces, so that we may recognise our immortality.

Because global communications have grown to the extent where none of us can close our eyes to world affairs, we are confronted with tragedies, some of which are connected with mass deaths: through war, famine, flood, and other disasters. Mass deaths do not only occur in far-away places: we are also seeing them closer at hand, through illnesses such as Cancer and Aids. The need for workers in the field of dying is essential at this time, and many old Atlantians are currently incarnate, along with experienced healers from other eras, working to eradicate fear from the dying. The value of this is beyond reckoning.

Any healer must come to terms with death on a personal level, and be able to cope with terminally-ill patients. When a soul is relieved of the anxiety of death, it will pass over into spirit in quite a different state from those who are in fear. Its passage into spirit will be smooth, and the fact of having eradicated once and for all its fear of dying, will endow it with enormous potential for higher consciousness, taking it into new and more expansive experiences, and even possibly taking it out of the karmic state altogether.

Many people state that they are not afraid of dying, only of the pain that might come beforehand. However, since fear is imprinted on our cells, even knowledgeable souls may find that they are fighting death as it approaches. As in all things, we must "remould" by living our truth, so that during this lifetime, many may transcend their fears once and for all. Obviously one cannot guarantee total lack of pain prior to death, but it certainly decreases sharply when the fighting ceases. It is ironic that while we have a whole array of helpers for the birthing process, in the West we have virtually none for the only certain event in life: death.

Birth and death are not dissimilar, although actually birth is the more traumatic procedure for the soul, which finds itself in strange new surroundings, seemingly trapped in a vehicle over which it has little or no control. Given time and a loving environment, the new baby is made safe, just as someone recently passed over is loved, and made welcome in the spirit world.

Fortunately, the common attitude towards death is gradually changing. To assist in this process, the first thing we must do is to realise the need to bring it into the open, and to talk about it, particularly with friends and relatives. Do not leave it to the last moment. If you have brought up the subject in the past, you will more easily communicate with your friends and loved ones when the time comes.

We must train ourselves, and help others to do likewise, to direct our energy into the higher mind, where fear of death , in all its forms can be eradicated. Since, as we have seen, this fear is not wholly emotional, it cannot be dealt with through the usual methods of transformation, and the use of the intellect, although helpful, will not, on its own, be fully effective. We must dig into our soul being, for it is that part of us alone that knows its immortality. In aligning it with all the other human energies, including the body, we will help ourselves finally to dissolve the fear of death. If you have worked upon yourself in the past, you are already travelling down this road, and will therefore be able to reassure and help others in their dying process. This is where healing is particularly beneficial. Spiritual healing communicates with the spirit, the core of the being, which is, as death approaches, preparing to shed its outer garment. Talk to your patients about death, give pure spiritual healing, and ask for the doorkeeper angels to help the individual on their journey when the time comes.

In one sense we all have a near-death experience every night, for in sleep we astral-travel out of the body, although we remain joined to it by the "silver cord", as described earlier in this book, the equivalent of the umbilical cord, which physically binds the unborn child to its mother. This is a cord formed of etheric matter, which loosens and finally separates at the time of death. Many people who have had genuine near-death experiences have seen their own cord. Sensitives often see the astral/etheric body of a dying person who is asleep, or in a comatose state, just prior to death. They are then floating above the physical body, attached by the cord. At the moment of death the cord separates, and the astral soul body moves over into the spiritual realms.

The death process is an interesting one, especially to students of spiritual matters. When a soul is ready to pass into spirit, it emits a withdrawal signal, to which the physical body responds. Firstly, various physiological changes occur within the heart, affecting the blood stream and the nervous and endocrine systems. These changes set off a vibration along the entire nervous system, and its etheric counterpart, sometimes referred to as the "nadis." In its turn, this vibration triggers the correct frequency impulses in the etheric counterpart of the brain. These impulses then activate the magnetic pull of the soul. A wave of energy is released, loosening and breaking the ties between the nadis and the nervous system. The etheric body is then finally detached from the physical vehicle.

In the early stages of the process, the person is withdrawing their consciousness into the astral and mental vehicles. This can be noticed in the elderly, when the body sleeps more often, and they withdraw their attention from the physical state. Initially, the loosening process is gradual. When it starts, it is immediately discernible in the eyes, as the individual begins to show signs of peacefulness, and a willingness to slip away. At this point any fighting stops, and there is a marked lack of mental effort. This is followed by the aligned etheric body, having already loosened, beginning to gather itself for the final departure. It withdraws the life force from the extremities towards what is described as the "door of exit", and waits for the final magnetic pull of the soul, as described above. At this point the soul is ready for departure, and the physical body releases its hold, and prepares for dissolution.

Sometimes at this stage, however, the physical elemental, what could also be described as the thought body, can regain its hold, and a fight may ensue that can last for many weeks. This can be clearly observed when a person struggles in their last days, and this is often connected to the pain of death. When the physical body has lost its hold, the soul gives its final directive, and physical death is complete.

When the etheric and astral bodies are released the energy or vital body continues to hold its pattern, (i.e. that which is left) usually assuming the outline of the physical form, under the influence of the thought form of that individual, and how they perceived themselves in their lifetime. This remaining body, as we shall see, will gradually dissolve when ready. In an individual who is in an advanced, highly magnetised soul state, the dissolution of this body will be very quick. However, whatever the vibration of a soul, the imprint of that life will exist for ever within the mental planes.

What then happens to the discarnate being varies enormously. It is solely dependant upon the state of that soul's consciousness, and does not represent any kind of judgement, being entirely connected with the vibratory state of the soul's substance. In accordance with the cosmic laws of attraction, the soul is magnetically drawn to its rightful place. When people speak of "the soul's choice", what they really mean is the nature and direction of this attraction.

Some discarnate spirits, unaware of having departed this material world, try to continue the state of existence that they understand. A mother, setting her table for tea, with a couple of children around, welcomes her teenage son home from work, and gives him his meal. The 'phone rings, and she is told that her son has been involved in a fatal accident. She replies that this cannot be so, as he is at home, eating his supper. Then she looks around, and finds that he is gone. This type of experience is quite common: the spirit, unaware of its death, came home as usual. It is for this reason that we have the beautiful intermediary of the angels to help people over to the other side.

One of the initial surprises awaiting a soul reaching spirit in the afterlife is the ease with which it has made this journey, and the lack of pain in that last step, for the process of actual death has no pain. In fact, to many souls there is very little experience to account for their sudden arrival in a completely different world. As can be seen from the above example, those who are unprepared for their death, as in cases of accident, can spend some time in confusion. We often assume that the person who has had a heart attack, or some other very swift form of departure, is the luckiest, but this is not the case from the spiritual point of view. Apparently the best form of death is one that gives the person time to adjust. For instance, someone who sleeps a lot, or even someone who drifts in and out of a coma, has the chance to dip their toes into the water, so to speak. There are many, many accounts of people in this last state who speak of seeing a loved one in spirit waiting for them, and indeed this is what happens, for no-one journeys into the spirit world without finding a familiar face there to greet them.

Some souls initially find their own death impossible to accept, particularly as they feel so very little difference from their normal, living state. Such people continue to do the things that absorbed them during their mortal existence. Two experiences that I had whilst training in a development circle illustrate this. Both took place on what I now know to be the lower astral levels. On the first occasion, I encountered a spirit who was totally absorbed in his task - counting his money! He had in this life been a miser, whose only preoccupation was money, and death had not altered him. He had been in spirit for thirty years, and was still counting. Who said you can't take it with you! The other experience was when I opened a door in the lower astral world, only to find myself back in time, during the period of World War Two. I was in a bar, where many pilots were busy drinking, and making merry, seemingly oblivious to their condition, or, indeed, to the passing of time. Afterwards I was told by my guides that these very young men had lived the last part of their short lives in a state of high intensity, great stress and tension, and that this carousing was their way of forgetting their woes. Upon death, they had chosen to continue to do the same. It was explained to me that this was their choice, and that in time they would move onwards.

These souls on the lower astral are not in any discomfort, and despite many attempts to enlighten them as to their true state, they continue to opt for those activities with which they are familiar. In time they will get bored with their experiences, and the guides and helpers will then be able to draw them into the expansive higher realms. It is not uncommon for a confused soul to try to carry on living, and although this can be very distressing, it is a way, at least, for most of them to realise that they are dead. For instance in a haunting of a house, the ghost or discarnate spirit gets very angry that his house is being filled by strange people, but rapidly becomes aware from this experience that they are the intruders. Most rescue work is for this reason. Obviously those souls who already have knowledge of the afterlife are more prepared, although judging by the numerous comments made through mediumistic communications over the years, nearly everyone is surprised by some aspect of the discarnate state.

In exploring the afterlife, we can make direct connections with the different stages of consciousness relayed to us by mystics throughout the ages. It seems that the spirit world is a direct copy of the earth planes in terms of levels of consciousness, or even vice verser. By studying the different stages of consciousness on the "other side", we may receive more ideas on our own state of consciousness. In spirit there are indeed "many mansions", and in recognising this we can begin to see why there are so many different descriptions of the hereafter. These stages of extra-terrestrial existence can be loosely drawn into seven categories, which may connect with the seven rays.

Most faiths supply some description of the afterlife, and of the beings that one is likely to encounter. Numerous sources teach that when a soul goes into spirit, it levitates towards different frequencies, or "mansions", depending not just upon its earthly faith, but largely upon its own frequency rate, which will literally draw it to its rightful home. The Buddhists are adamant that upon death you must head straight for the Light, and not be delayed upon the way by any devas or demons, which they believe to be merely thought forms. For many reasons there is much to be said for taking this attitude, but my information is that the stage or level at which a soul finds itself is largely dependant upon the individual's own magnetic force or vibration. We know, for instance, that some people are unable to be reached by a medium because they have abandoned their personality state and have "moved on." Once or twice I have even been told that the soul with whom the sitter wishes to communicate is already back in incarnation. Some traditions state we come back within fifteen days!

There is a stage through which every soul must pass, a place that could be directly equated with the idea of Purgatory, or Hades. In this place the soul must relive its life, seeing both the good and bad aspects of itself. This is rather like watching a film, but it is not a passive experience, for the individual actually feels how their actions have affected others, and in this way they automatically judge themselves. This stage is not as terrible as it sounds, and is certainly not the stuff of judgement that has so often been preached to us. Judgement does occur, but only by and for yourself. It is my understanding that most souls are agreeably surprised by this experience. Far from being alarmed or mortified by the number of misdeeds that they have committed, they are often amazed by how much good they have done in their lives: what we may consider to be the worst things that we have inflicted on others can sometimes, when viewed from this perspective, be revealed as something quite different.

This intermediate stage is where souls are purged, or purified, of their misdemeanours, before finding a more comfortable state. It is a stage of self love that must be willingly experienced: no soul is forced into it, although many, knowing that they will have to go through it sooner or later to advance, opt to go almost as soon as they have recovered from the shock of being in spirit. While a soul is experiencing this stage, contact via a medium is rare. It has often been explained to me that at this time the soul is in effect in some kind of convalescent home. It is impossible to say how long in earthly terms this phase takes, but it seems to be on average anything from six months to two years. After this time, the soul can go wherever it chooses.

This "judgement" stage can be encountered at any time after the earthly matter state of the lower astral and before the state which is often referred to as "Summerland". It is to this area that most mediums attune, for two reasons. Firstly, most students with just a little training in focussing can access this vibration, which is available to any living person. Secondly, the majority of spirits that communicate will not have risen higher than this level in their own vibratory note. When they ascend from this stage, they become less identifiable as they cast off their image and personality. Even at this point, the soul has already shed most of its astral body during the intermediate judgement state. In going through "Hades" or "Purgatory", they have cast off, by enlightened observation, the outer garment of their being, which is largely astral. The astral body is the intermediary between spirit and matter, and is used by most souls upon death as a vehicle to carry them onwards, but it is gradually replaced by finer and finer etheric energies, until the total abandonment of the body. The astral and etheric substances then grow even finer, until the soul completely disappears as a separate entity, probably at the level of the sixth ray.

Summerland, or as some have labelled it, Illusionland, is a place that is hard for sceptics to accept, for it appears that in this area one can literally create one's own reality: as you think, so you experience. This is the area where you might see your loved ones walking in magnificent gardens, living in an idyllic cottage, or enjoying a sweeping and beautiful landscape; indeed, whatever that person yearned for in life can now be theirs. Here the individual's mind controls everything. Upon this plane of existence, experiences are extra-sensory, and larger than life. It is the place of dreams and illusions, and the possibilities are endless. We can thus begin to understand why it is termed an illusory state: souls very often need a sojourn here to shake off their own illusions, and they do this by living them. In this state, the spirit can literally think itself into being where it wants, or changing anything around it, as long as this only affects the individual. One person cannot alter the larger scenario, because this also belongs to many other spirits.

The spirit's surroundings are limited only by its own mental and spiritual development. During its sojourn in Summerland, the soul comes to recognise itself in a much more objective fashion, at the same time realising how it could live more fully if it used its untapped potential.

Summerland is not exclusively for those who are "dead", for it is most likely to be the main area to which people go when they astral-travel during sleep. Upon waking, they feel that their experience was a very real one. Indeed, many people have reported having a dream in which they met their "dead" loved ones, either in a garden or some other beautiful place.

Summerland is probably therefore a meeting place between the Earth plane and the higher levels. It is also likely to be the place where those under the influence of drink and drugs find themselves, a place where dreams are enacted. It is from this place that astral energy can be drawn back down around the earthly soul, creating what amounts to a band of sponge-like substance that attracts thought forms. Unfortunately these can sometimes be used as a negative force which can cause possessions, hauntings and illness. On this level, every experience is super-sensitive. People report that they can literally feel the presence of a blade of grass. Natural things come alive, and the individual responds to the spirit of the natural worlds.

Obviously in spirit there is no physical body, and so, if it feels the need, the spirit creates its own. Usually at this point it is very similar to the earthly body, although in my experience, a spirit will project its body as being younger than when it departed this life, as discussed in previous chapters. In general a medium can add ten to twenty years when judging the age of death, unless the soul is deliberately projecting its body as it was at the time of death, either because it is still very much emotionally connected to it, or for identification purposes. The astral etheric body that is "manufactured" is not of a dense nature, and is experienced as a feeling state, the creation of which is directly to do with their state and how the spirit views itself, hence the chronological discrepancies in physical appearance.

Creating one's own illusions can also apply to bigotry and religious fervour: in Summerland, even those souls who think they have reached their "Nirvana" re-create the illusory environment, and perpetuate the belief. Having created an imaginary state of bliss on Earth, they continue to imagine themselves to be in a state of bliss and they simply continue to live within their own illusion. They are, of course, nowhere of the kind, but are merely clinging on to their idealised aspirations. Sadly, their state of ecstasy does not expand or enlighten, but rather it imprisons them within their own ego. This experience could be likened to that of a drug-taker, who becomes addicted to whatever they are taking, but there is a difference, in that on the Earth plane the physical body raises the alarm, and they may therefore seek to kick the habit.

It is an unfortunate fact that many souls believe themselves to be further along the path than they actually are, and in these illusory stages it is impossible to convince them otherwise. They are just as trapped as the poor wretches on the lowest astral plains, recreating their fantasies. The fact that they are pleasant fantasies does not elevate them.

When a soul is truly on a higher vibration, it is formless, and completely loses its individuality. This applies to genuinely enlightened souls who, during their earthly life, have drawn inspiration from God alone. When they shed their body, which they would have taken on as an instrument, in order to perform a specific task, they are not attracted to Summerland, but pass swiftly on to at least the level of the purity of the group soul.

Most souls, however, need the reassurance of a sojourn in Summerland, with its many familiar experiences, but unfortunately at this stage it is quite possible for a soul to get bound up in the illusions of the Earth plane. Many who would have been considered ordinary folk, with no great aspirations or desires beyond their every-day existence, linger within this secure space, and it is possible for a soul to be drawn into a loop of experience, from Summerland back into life, then back to Summerland again, and so on.

Eventually, though, the soul will begin to tire of this land of illusion, and it will finally glide into the next stage, where it will become progressively less connected to the physical worlds. In the state beyond illusion, you live consciously, and you become aware of your subtle body. This is the fourth plane; that of "colour and light". A soul that reaches this level has made a conscious decision to move onwards, no longer subject to illusory ideals. It is beginning to sense God, or the Source, in a defined way, and this is where attachment to the plane of images is finally broken.

As in all other areas, it is impossible to give an exact account, as the experience depends very much on the soul in question. Indeed, from this stage onwards, it becomes increasingly difficult to give any definitive details, because the energy goes beyond thought as we understand it. Memory disappears, except for a sort of emotional memory imprint. Colours are many and varied, some beyond our own spectrum. When mediumistic contact is made with these souls, they find it impossible to convey their surroundings in words. However, thoughts on this level are enormously potent.

This stage is largely given to the dissolution of the whole personality, which includes the shedding of its outer shell, that is, the body, which is by this stage no more than a remnant of the etheric form. This shedding allows the being to move towards the group soul state. In dissolving any attachment to the ego self, it melts into the sea of consciousness on this luminiferous plane. This is equivalent to the heart level, the alignment to light thus creating a prism echoing all colours of the spectrum.

When the being is ready for the next (the fifth) stage, it is like another kind of death. It now has perfect control over its etheric form, and has conception of an existence without form. Here, in a state of calm, it is aware of all experiences on previous planes. It knows that its forward motion is absolute, and that there is no turning back. All that it is will blend into the great sea of consciousness of which it is becoming a part. At this point, the soul is aware of its fellow souls, has greatly increased intellectual feelings, and catches glimpses of infinite horizons. This stage has been described as living like a flame. The flame is, of course, present within us all, for it is the eternal flame of life itself. It is the living flame that runs through all things, with which the soul is now absolutely in touch. This is perceptively described by J.B. Priestley in his "Dream Vision" (quoted later).

Gradually, through an attraction of energies, other souls are brought together, and all of them have to wait until there is a critical mass of group soul energy. This attraction of energy brings in all kinds of souls with their various experiences, including some from other worlds, for there needs to be a composite of nature for the next stage. Here the final anchor of physical existence is severed with the outer worlds and a casting away of the myriad of emotional experience they can now pass into yet another intermediary state of examination and review. The experience now is of a group soul type.

The following (sixth) stage is one of pure reason. All emotions and desires as known by man have gone, replaced by the aligned and true desire. Here we have the white Light of pure thought, sometimes briefly glimpsed in meditations and groups. Beings here are capable of living as white Light without form, and have joined the immortals. This is a giant meeting-place of illumined souls before they fufil their ultimate purpose.

The seventh and final stage is impossible to sum up in human language, the concept of timelessness being beyond our reality. It is a stage of oneness with God, of which we are granted brief glimpses at various stages of existence, both on Earth as flashes of enlightenment and in spirit. This is beyond doubt the greatest leap: at this final stage, individualisation, even of the group soul, completely disappears. The soul is one with the Universal Light Force. Indeed, it is the Universal Life Force, melted in the magnificent crucible of unblemished consciousness. There is a totality of realisation that cannot be obtained within any kind of vehicle or form, physical or otherwise. This is the pure Thought, the pure Light and the absolute Truth to which we are all aspiring: sooner or later we will all make this momentous leap into the state of all Being.

As we have seen, everything can be equated with energy, and death is no exception. No individual dies without the "permission" or "choice" of the soul, which by its vibration is attracted into death, knowing that it has experienced all that it can within that particular life. This is a difficult concept to acknowledge, particularly when we see mass deaths, or the deaths of youngsters, and others who have not reached the average span of life. When a soul is ready to die, it will find a physical release: illness, a heart attack, or one of a whole array of other possibilities. Many people who die young have a premonition about it. In fact, it has been given to me that everyone is prepared, usually during sleep, when either their own or a loved one's death is imminent. Unfortunately we rarely consciously remember it.

Every person has their own individual experience of passing, even in the case of suicide. Obviously most people who take their own lives are deeply depressed, and for that reason they will probably have a long spell on the lower planes, some even becoming Earth-bound spirits. Alternatively, they can literally do an "about-turn" after "Purgatory", and come straight back into incarnation. Sometimes, however, in some rare instances when a particular soul is close to a higher vibratory state, these very sensitive souls, realising that their life has nothing more to offer, and that for some reason they cannot realise any more potential, courageously elect to end their own life. This is a mainly unnecessary, but nonetheless brave task. These souls do not hang around on the lower planes, but journey immediately beyond the illusions. For various reasons, suicides are not easy to contact via a medium, and usually if a message needs to be relayed, it is given indirectly, through the intermediary of a guide.

It must be remembered that in life, as well as in "death", the flame of Light is eternal. Our essence is of that Light, and even though we shall experience many different colours along our path, we are all ultimately part of the vibrant, living God.

EXERCISE

In the brief glimpses given here, of the various vibrations on the other side, each energy has its guides and spirit helpers, and each layer of consciousness, as in the physical body, requires a re-assessment of the self at every stage. Each medium builds their own communication with spirit, with their own codes and individuality. Attunement to these different frequencies requires time and dedication, and, as an instrument, the medium needs constant care and tuning. The best thing for a developing medium, as well as their own constant self-awareness, is to practise and practise.

The bereaved generally derive great comfort from contact with departed loved ones, and the ability to act as "telephonist" in this process is a source of great joy to the medium. However, the underlying significance of these sittings lies not in relaying the trivial, if evidential, details of the life of the departed: the truly valuable aspect is the information that we occasionally receive regarding the process experienced by the soul as it progresses through the astral levels.

As we have already seen, within the astral planes there are "many mansions," and one medium alone is unlikely to become proficient at contacting all of them. However, the following key titles of the seven main stages, along with the descriptions given in this chapter, will give you some guidance on one of the most difficult aspects of psychic training.

1. Matter. 2. Hades, or Judgement. 3. Summerland, or Illusion. 4. Colour and Balance. 5. Flame. 6. White Light. 7. Timelessness.

In your attunement you will make discoveries beyond price, not just through contact with the departed, but through the blending of energies within the different layers of consciousness. We are constantly warned of the dangers and glamours of psychic work, and connecting with the "dead" is fraught with all of them. However, when it is properly implemented, the benefits are well worth the tireless efforts that a student will have to make in order to align and adjust to the multi-faceted diamond, with its array of colours and experiences.

Opening in the usual way, and as with previous exercises, make contact with a guiding energy with which you are comfortable. Ask it to reveal to you different aspects of the astral layers. These journeys will be many and varied. Log them in your memory and consciousness, where they will be useful in the future.

It is always preferable to be part of a good development group, where hopefully you will receive plenty of advice and practice, but also, when you feel a little confident, take time to sit with a reliable person who is willing to help you in your quest. Ask the souls in spirit if they are willing to communicate. Never pull a spirit's energy down, no matter what requests you have from your sitter. Always seek permission. If a particular spirit does not come through, do not worry, for there are many reasons for this, mediumship is an attunement and for all sorts of physical and spiritual reasons that attunement is not always possible and may not be anyone's "fault". Make sure when you have contact that you are not simply picking up the thoughts of your sitter: remember that emotionally it is easy to project an astral type of energy, that appears to be an entity in spirit. Talk directly with the communicator, and if there are any problems, ask your trusted guide. Usually they are very happy to answer your questions.

Particularly in the early stages, when you achieve contact with spirit, try not to go for the physical descriptions, because for reasons already stated they may not be the same as those remembered by the sitter. However, every soul is unique, and an image of a wooden leg would undoubtedly be evidential! The soul has no body, and the higher the vibration of the departed, the fainter the remaining image. Remember, too, that personality also diminishes as the soul advances. Perhaps the best evidence is some situation remembered by the spirit that has personal significance for the sitter.

Be open and honest. Do not be easily satisfied. Do not be nebulous. Focus, and ask again and again if necessary. Attunement to spirit takes time, so give yourself plenty. A medium once told me that it had taken him twenty years to receive his first "hit" at communication with a spirit being. Hopefully it will not take you this long, but be patient.

Always be aware that no matter how extraordinary the information and evidence, it means nothing in comparison with the advancement of you as a consciousness, which is a never-ending process. Most importantly of all, be joyous with your communication, for if there is no joy there is no positive, healing energy.

Many people will think you fantastic when you make a good communication with a loved one. Remember that it is simply your job, at which you have, through effort, become proficient. Be strong in your power, but do not forget your humility.

Books for Reference
Human Personality and its Survival of Bodily Death, by Frederic
    W.H. Myers. First published 1903. Abridged version 1992.
The Road to Immortality, by Geraldine Cummins 1955
Living On by Paul Beard 1980.

Chapter 13

REINCARNATION

In order to evaluate the subject of reincarnation, we must first understand that we are energy, and that we are therefore subject to the cosmic law which states that no energy can be destroyed. If we can accept this, we can begin to view ourselves as part of the unending life force that runs through everything. One could quote texts from many religions that subscribe to the idea of reincarnation, but it will never make perfect sense to us until we know it within our own hearts. As with my earlier comments regarding death, I am not seeking to convert, merely to present a perspective gained from my own experience. In common with all other aspects of this book, this chapter is intended primarily to give students of psychism something to grasp, in an area that can seem nebulous. No doubt when you begin this work, you will reach an understanding based wholly upon your own unique experiences.

Let us first define the term. The human body is used by the soul as a vehicle, and reincarnation is the soul's use of a succession of vehicles during its journey of self-realisation. If you have a car that is old and worn, you trade it in for a new one, and this can be taken as a simple analogy for the reincarnation process. We avail ourselves of a succession of new vehicles, thus experiencing a rich variety of opportunities for learning and growth.

The laws of cause and effect are absolute, and these are closely connected with reincarnation, as is the law of rebirth. This law in turn is implemented through the law of evolution. It is a process whereby we can progress further and further, moving from the dense physical material state to ultimate spiritual truth and perfection. This accounts for the many seemingly different types of people present on Earth at any one time, and for the vastly differing circumstances of people over the world. Although many souls incarnate within the same groups in order to achieve a proper relationship with their fellow man, which of course ultimately means to the Source, to God. Through this process, man advances his mind, and controls his lower aspects, which will then reveal to him his soul and its true nature and purpose.

The decision to reincarnate is not an intellectual one. It is engendered by the will, or in other words, the magnetic vibratory force, of the soul, and it is wholly governed by the vibration from the higher mental planes.

After a multiplicity of lifetimes, and through the evolution of the mental states creating wisdom and practical service, the soul will reach the point where it wants nothing for itself that is separate from the Source, and it will then finally renounce physical life. In so doing, it will escape the earthly laws of rebirth. At this point it becomes part of a soul group, a point of consciousness that may be affiliated to the sixth level of the afterlife, White Light, described in the previous chapter. At this point there is a realisation that we are indisputably related to all beings.

Cultures and civilisations rise and fall, but the same individuals come and go within them through countless incarnations. The undeniable will of the soul is to join with the Godhead and "all that is." The soul does not return to perfect itself, because it is a part of "all that is". It is, therefore, already perfect. However, the body presents unique experiences and possibilities that can be carried back to the Source. A simple analogy that of the Universal Light Source, or God, as the main computer, and ourselves as terminals. By accessing the main computer through knowledge and acceptance of our own inner light, we feed all our experiences back to base: to the Source.

At this time the emphasis must be on the group soul, which is making itself evident. Many old Atlantian souls are currently incarnate, their common denominator being healing. It is therefore no coincidence that we come across so many healers, for these souls have been brought together by the laws of attraction, and out of the greatest need for the human race to heal itself, enabling it to move towards greater consciousness. There will come a time when the gradual heightening of consciousness over many, perhaps hundreds, of lifetimes, will finally have peeled off the many personality layers, leaving us in permanent touch with the inner light, the soul force. At this stage we shall start to identify with God, and begin to remember we are part of God. This is already taking place, but the transference will not be easy because of past attitudes to service. We shall discuss this in the last segment of this book.

Not all lifetimes are of equal importance. Most of us have lived innumerable lives, some of which have brought us only a tiny bit further along the path. Information gleaned from many recent discarnate contacts indicates that we are now accelerating the process of our return to the Source. This means that instead of sometimes spending hundreds of years in spirit between incarnations, souls are now returning very much more quickly. Since we know that rapid consecutive incarnations are usually only for more evolved souls, it is probably safe to assume that there are very many more semi- or nearly-enlightened souls present on our planet today. If one considers that we act as a group, it becomes obvious that a critical-mass shift of consciousness is beginning. This is occurring partly because the idea of tarrying in the astral worlds holds little or no attraction for the soul that is advancing into true service: it quite simply wants to get on with the job. Seeing that there are certain aspects of itself that need sharpening or polishing, such a soul will incarnate in rapid succession in order to round off its development.

In many cases, however, we are now seeing a slightly different scenario, for, curious as it may sound, it is my understanding that some souls are opting to go through many lives in one body. This is made possible through the expansion and development of the physical health of the vehicle: in other words, we are living longer and healthier lives. Also, each consciousness is being fine-tuned, and separate existences are therefore no longer necessary. These days there are many people who would say that they feel completely different from the way they felt ten, or even five, years ago. They are, in fact, as different as if they had reincarnated, without having had to experience the usual childhood period.

Let us pick up the story of the soul from the previous chapter. In our discussion on death and the afterlife, we saw that there are several different layers of existence. These similar vibrational layers are what most of us have to go through over many incarnations. These experiences take place both on the physical and astral planes, the aim being to integrate the soul's light into the physical planes so that we can transcend the body and the cycle of re-birth.

As we have seen, no soul can reincarnate without examining its most recent life and expiating its wrong-doings, and this can take place at various stages of the afterlife. Lower forms of consciousness will probably not rise much beyond the "Summerland" areas, and, having come to terms with their previous past life experiences, they will then feel themselves drawn down to the Earth plane once again. The Tibetan book of the Dead, tells us, rather graphically, that if the deceased is requiring immediate return, as he urgently desires a body, in order to enjoy once again the physicality of Earth, he will see, just before re-awakening into earthly life, "visions of mating men and women, before finally passing out of the dream worlds into a womb of flesh, and once more into the waking state of material existence".

Many fears and anxieties have sprung up over the idea of people having to review past lives, but it must be clearly emphasised that no life is a punishment, nor is it a judgement. These tales are likely to have been perpetuated through the ages, by those in positions of authority who wanted to control the masses through fear.

All is energy. What we give out returns on all levels. A negative action will create a negative reaction, until we rise in consciousness to overcome our darker side. As we are the sum total of all our experiences, this composite energy, accumulating from lifetime to lifetime, accompanies us each time we reincarnate. If someone has a difficult early life, they will have brought this forward from the last one. Life is a continuous process. Patterns are formed throughout many lives, but patterns can be re-shaped. Energy can transmute.

The dangers of receiving past-life information before one is ready, became known to me very early on in my teaching. A member of the very first group I ever taught was a woman who was just getting over paralysis of the legs. During our second class she was talking about past-life regression, and I received a flash of insight. Upon further enquiry, I learned from her that seven years earlier, a regressionist had told her that in a previous existence she had been an Egyptian priestess, and, for some reason, had her legs chopped off. I asked her if she had experienced trouble with her legs before the regression. The answer was no, and on reflection she realised that the problem had started just two weeks after the regression. It was made perfectly clear to me that this sudden and traumatic memory had caused this lady to relive the experience.

One of the many questions I am often asked is, "What happens to a child who is aborted or miscarried?" Over the years, I have also had several clients who have tragically experienced cot deaths. The loss of a child, even one who is yet unborn, is one of the most traumatic experiences any adult could encounter, and I have asked for clear guidance on this matter.

When a baby is conceived, the energy of the appropriate soul is drawn close to the body of the parents, particularly the mother. In pregnancy it is possible to feel the presence of the light force energy, or soul of the unborn child hovering very close to the mother's body. As the pregnancy continues, the force of the unborn soul draws closer and closer. At birth, the soul enters the physical life force, the body of the baby. Only on rare occasions does the soul enter before birth, and even after birth it is "loose" within the physical framework. Some say it is not until the age of seven that the soul is fully integrated within the body of the child. What has been made clear to me is that in the case of cot deaths the soul, being "loose", sometimes just slips away from that vehicle, as the magnetic link between the body and the soul is simply not strong enough. This may be because that particular soul is an advanced, and perhaps an almost perfect, soul. It could be that not only does it realise that it need not live on; because of its enhanced spiritual vibration, it simply cannot live on.

Miscarriages are very similar, although some of these can be caused by a purely physical difficulty, which is nature throwing off a "bad apple". Deliberate abortion, however, is an emotive issue, because free will is in operation, and the parent is therefore taking responsibility for the life of a soul.

Immediately on conception, a mother makes connection with the soul of the unborn child, which is why, in a case of miscarriage, or even of abortion, there is a sense of bereavement every bit as strong as if that child had had physical life. Sometimes the mother senses that the soul will not unite with the body, but even if the decision is taken without that sense, what happens on a soul level is that the energy of that soul, upon abortion or miscarriage, finding itself without a physical vehicle, will draw away, and wait for the next appropriate vehicle. A soul's experience is timeless, and many aborted or miscarried souls subsequently incarnate through the same parent. The above represents my understanding of the spiritual "mechanics" involved in the process in question. It should not be interpreted as a comment or opinion regarding the issue of abortion.

One of the criticisms of the philosopy of reincarnation is that even mediums vary in their descriptions, both of the after-life and of the reincarnation process. It is as well to remember that individuals see only from their own perspective. Obviously, with so many different levels of soul consciousness, different mediums will interpret differently, and will make contact with varying aspects of the soul's journey. There are great differences in the myriad experiences of any soul, as well as varying points of departure, so to speak.

This diversity causes mediums great difficulty in ascertaining what is really happening. If, for instance, a soul is caught up for hundreds of years (as many are) in the loop that runs from earthly life to the planes of illusion and back again, this then will be the extent of its experience, which a medium may receive as a definitive description of the afterlife process. As we have seen, the further a soul progresses, the more difficult it becomes for a medium to obtain any image or description of its last personality, leading many mediums to believe that "Summerland" is all there is after death, simply because this is all they are able to access. We must always be cautious of interpreting only one perspective, for the permutations are endless. When one considers the infinite possibilities, both here and in the afterworlds, one might almost despair of receiving a clear focus on any given area.

As in all aspects of psychic unfoldment, our experiences bring us personally into greater contact with the universe and all its mysteries and possibilities. As we become aware of past lives, we become more and more aware of our endless possibilities.

There is a fundamental fact that must be understood, which is that when people reach a certain stage of their development, memories of past lives begin to surface. There is a school of thought that says that if this happens, it is because there is a psychological block connected with any past life that is remembered. My feeling is the opposite is true. When our past-life history presents itself naturally, it is not because of a block, but because there is nothing to veil us from the truth.

There are very good reasons why we have no conscious memory of past lives. A mother will very quickly forget the pains of childbirth, for if she did not, she would never choose to have another child. Past lives are similar, in that we forget so that we can keep producing a finer and finer quality of life and connection with the soul. Recently it has become very fashionable to go to regressionists, but unless one intuitively knows that certain past-life information is essential to one's current progress, it is much healthier to wait for the information to surface naturally. We are the sum total of all our experiences, and consequently our vibration emanates that energy. We will attract to us what we truly need within our lives today. Unfortunately, past-life regression has become one of the many glamours of psychic unfoldment. However, if a medium receives information about past lives as part of an overview of a sitter's present incarnation, this will undoubtedly shed some light on why certain character-istics have developed. It is interesting, but rarely essential, to have this information, and so it is wise not to over-emphasise this aspect of mediumship.

Finding out about past lives through trance is a very hit-or-miss process, and for a simple reason. Even in what is called a light trance, it is possible to access the lower astral regions. Apart from the mischievous lower astral entities that will simply play games with you, there is a more sinister aspect, of which it is as well be aware. Heavy, dark forces such as cruelty and domination are very earth-bound, and they hover in the lower realms. Anyone in trance, or even a light sleep, can inadvertently connect with these energies, and hook them down into their consciousness. Virulent thought forms, manifested as horrific memories, can attach themselves to us in this way. Putting it simply, someone can easily draw in information which simply does not belong to them. In this way, it is entirely possible that what you receive in trance has nothing to do with you. Because it is largely an astral energy, it will manifest itself within the opened consciousness, and be alarmingly difficult to dislodge. This is an explanation for the recently-recognised "false memory" syndrome.

There are many theories on reincarnation. Carl Jung accredited all mediumistic material concerning past lives as spin-off sub-personalities, seeing the "spirit world" as really only part of the inner world of the mind. Jung's idea of the Collective Unconscious posits the shared experiences of the whole human race, experiences to which he referred as "archetypes". This idea is similar to Hindu and Buddhist beliefs, that is, that we are all commonly united on a level beyond our bodies. To me, both philosophies are equally valid; it is merely the descriptions that vary. This provides us with yet another reminder that everyone perceives from their own view-point. Mediums inevitably interpret according to their own perspectives and their own magnetic force emanation, which will attract the relevant energies. Once again we see that we as mediums must endeavour to be clear, open instruments, so that we may reflect with clear heads and hearts the information given to us.

The type of information received is also dependent upon where we direct our energies. If we plug into one area alone, this will colour our mediumship. Bigotry, and a desire to control, can eventually stem from sticking rigidly to one single perspective. In the case of Collective Unconscious versus the spirit world, it becomes obvious that the manner of interpretation can vary. Two schools are simply using different terms to describe the same issues, for one can easily argue that if past-life memories belong to our inner world, that does not detract from their validity: the inner world is a mind energy, just as the outer spirit world belongs to the mind of God. If we accept that on the highest of levels everything is interrelated, and that we are all part of the mighty outbreath of the cosmos, both schools of thought can be accepted.

As mediums we are connecting points between individuals and, hopefully, the overviews of their worlds, our purpose being to help, heal and guide. We must never show a preference for any one piece of information received. Our business is to relay the details impartially, and in the clearest way possible, in order that the individual may understand it. It is not for us to impose our own perspective, nor to interpret the information.

If we consider that we are ultimately sharing this whole universe, we can all learn from each other's past-life impressions. We are all strands of energy let out from the Universal Light force, and each strand will move out into the cosmos, having different experiences through different vehicles. One of the most valuable aspects of any psychic work is the knowledge it brings of many different experiences far and wide, filling us as mediums with greater understanding and awareness of others, and therefore of ourselves.

As we have seen in other chapters, dreams are powerful tools of self-discovery, and from time to time they hold clues to our past experiences. If a child aged under five has a recurring dream, this almost certainly belongs to its previous existence. Often this will involve its last death, and this can be most disturbing for the child. Children of around the age of three or four often have nightmares. There are many theories about the reasons for this, one being that it is during this period that the unconscious mind is being activated. It is possible also that this is the time when integration of the child's body, mind and spirit takes place. Whatever the truth of the matter, this is clearly a time when many aspects are surfacing: children of this age are highly sensitive and intuitive. In most cases, unfortunately, this sensitivity is later dissolved by material living, or perhaps by the necessary intervention of the conscious mind.

Past lives are imprinted very strongly upon the soul's genetic memory, and will continue to be so until the individual ascends into the higher realms, beyond image and personality.

EXERCISE

There are many simple ways in which we can begin naturally to intuit our past experiences: the more naturally the better. There is no need to "open up", although, as in any exercise, it is best if you ask for protection and guidance from the greatest, highest good.

In a relaxed state, cast your mind over what you really resonate with in life, concentrating on those things that have not come from childhood conditionings. Do you, for instance, enjoy hearing a certain language spoken? Do you, for no apparent reason, long to visit a particular country? Conversely, perhaps, for no evident reason, you have a strange aversion to something: a language, an animal, a uniform, a colour, a smell. These likes and dislikes, that seem to come from nowhere, can be highly significant (be careful, though, that they are not simply the result of something read in a book, or seen on the television).

A very deep aversion could well be connected with your last death. For years I was terrified of fire, and from my early childhood into my twenties, I had a recurring dream about it. The dream, it transpired, was strongly connected with my last death. As an example of the previous statement, some people have an unnatural aversion to knives, or other sharp implements, for the same reason. Certain foods, and particularly smells, can evoke memories also.

I once gave a sitting during which the sitter was told that he had been a scribe monk. Afterwards he told me that his love of books was so great that he collected rare manuscripts in this life. If, with a free and open mind, you home in on such aspects of your personality, you will be drawn to distinctive pieces of information about how you were in those past times.

One of the most evocative things to do when you are relaxed and into the sense of the past, is to "see" your feet. This may sound odd, but if you take yourself back to an era in which you feel you have lived, and, in your mind's eye, look down at your shoes and feet, this should automatically access memories of the type of person and environment to which you once belonged, and if you allow it, it will help your memory to awaken. When you are truly remembering past lives, it will be a real experience, not just wishful thinking or illusion: there is a big difference. Initially this is not so easy to achieve on your own. If you definitely feel that you want to understand more about your previous lives, find a loving therapist: so much depends on the energy of the medium or therapist. Trust your own judgement, and if in any doubt, leave it alone.

As in all other aspects of psychic understanding, when in any doubt, ask for the appropriate energy in spirit to help you in your discovery. Most people who can meditate, and implement the various exercises given in this book, can, with a little effort, achieve consciousness of their own past. You do not need to go into deep levels of concentration or trance: indeed, it is better just to be naturally open to your memories. Never force an issue of past times. Some can be very painful, and, in these instances, not knowing your past can be a blessing. If you are honestly working as a seeker of truth, you will remember - when, and if, the time is right.

Books for Reference
Exploring Reincarnation, by Hans TenDam 1990
Other Lives, Other Selves, by Roger Woolger 1990
The Tibetan Book of the Dead by W.Y. Evans Wentz (Oxford University Press) 1927

Chapter 14
_____

PREDICTIONS
AND
POSSIBILITIES

Throughout the ages, man has sought answers for his own life, instinctively reaching out for messages from beyond. This is not so foolish when you consider we are all reflections of each other. Like attracts like. By externalising our problems we can maybe find an answer. This can remove any pressure, and often relieves us of responsibility for our own actions. However, if this externalising process is applied with understanding and awareness, it can be very effective in releasing tension, and eradicating the dark shadows that veil us from the truth. If we search properly within ourselves, we will find clues to our quest.

In the natural process of externalisation, things that we find all around us have long been, and continue to be, used as tools of prediction. For instance, water was used to look into the future, giving rise to the crystal ball. Stones or twigs were thrown into the air, and were then interpreted according to how they fell. With the invention of writing, letters and numbers were carved into stones, which became known as runes. Tea leaves, hands, cards, numbers, dreams, dice, colours and precious stones, hand-writing, and many other tools can be used as instruments of prediction. All these things serve as a focus for our own intuition, which is really the mirroring of ourselves.

According to some schools of thought, any method of mediumship that makes use of such aids is inadequate or inferior.

However, a tool is only as good as the person using it, and whereas it is certainly true that experienced mediums or psychics have no need of aids, being in effect their own instrument, an external point of focus can be enormously helpful, as we saw in an earlier chapter, with the use of the Tarot. The history of the development of these diverse focal points is fascinating and informative, and perhaps none more so than that of the I Ching, a complex and intriguing form of Chinese prediction and awareness. You can develop the use of these tools if you wish. Discount nothing. Messages can reach us via the most seemingly unlikely sources. The answers are always close at hand.

Prediction is, literally, to "tell beforehand", which implies a distortion of time, and the word "prophecy" means "a divinely inspired utterance or revelation". Both these expressions quite obviously indicate experiences outside the normal range. We know that prediction and prophecy have been used by humanity throughout history, as far back as the time when early man needed all the help he could get in obtaining food and warmth. The natural instincts which these days are derided by so many, may well, on occasion, have saved our primal ancestors from starvation. Later on, when communities developed, the Shaman, or wise one, of each village took over the role of both priest and prophet. One of the most important attributes of any seer has always been the power of observation, and in past times the wise ones would observe, and interpret, all the signs around them. This process would undoubtedly have included what Jung called "acausal synchronicity" or the law of meaningful coincidence. The Shamans also spoke with the spirits, using a form of what we would call spiritualism. These people often believed that one could appease the gods with gifts, or by performing certain rites which would ameliorate any negative situation. Ritual and magic developed out of these simple procedures.

Shamans, as we know, also predicted through dream analysis, and it seems very likely that they applied a mixture of instinctive psychological observation, knowledge of the Earth and how it moves, familiarity with their tribe (the elder of any tribe would make it his business to know all his people), and communication with the tribal spirits.

This way of living continued through the ages, and in the Old Testament we can find prophecies that were made around 1,800 B.C. Although prophets became public figures, however, they were periodically persecuted. One instance of this having taken place in 444 B.C., after the Jews returned from Babylon, when prophecy became punishable by death. Unfortunately, by the Middle Ages, prophets had assumed temporal powers, thus weakening the art which continued to the extent that it became considered as the province of witches and demons. As recently as the eighteenth century, psychics were killed in the name of the Church and of Christianity. Astonishingly, it was not until the 1950s that the Witchcraft Law was repealed, and even in the 1990s we are still having to clear away the débris of damage done during earlier more superstitious times.

Sometimes there is an occurrence of "en masse" prediction. This happens just before a global disaster, or some other event that will affect the lives of many people. It is as if a shock wave reverberates out of time, and is registered by many who can sensitively attune. It is widely known, for example, that in 1963, prior to President Kennedy's assassination, many people, some of whom had no previous experience of predictive gifts, dreamt of his death. I was eleven at the time, with no interest whatsoever in politics or world events. I did not know who President Kennedy was, nor what he looked like, yet a couple of nights before the assassination, I dreamt the terrible images, now so familiar to us all, that would shortly be shown over and over again on television news programmes.

Another form of prediction comes from communication with those in spirit. This is not infallible, for although some discarnate souls can see into the future, their vision is subject to their view point, and it has been said, with some justification, that dying does not necessarily raise one's I.Q!

Metaphysically, we are told that we can bend time, and that in pulling our minds away from the linear "track" we can see into the future. Psychics project ahead, and can look at events as though these were looking on from the outside. As energy follows thought, we may therefore ponder the possibility that perhaps we even create our own future. Is it, then, that the sensitive picks up the magnetic force of the sitter, and projects it back to him or her, knowing that by the laws of attraction an appropriate situation will occur? If so, are we seers of possibilities, rather than of certainties?

This brings us to the contentious and age-old issue of Fate: are our lives pre-determined, or do we have free will?

There are many opinions. Zeno, the Greek philosopher who in 308 B.C. founded the school of Stoicism, proposed the doctrine of uncomplaining submission to unavoidable necessity. A powerful influence in Scandinavian religion was the belief in the Norns, or Fates, usually thought of as "the three sisters". In Brahmic thought, Karma is the consequence of action, necessitating rebirth in either a lower or a higher form of existence, according to blame or merit, and Buddhism holds a modified version of this philosophy. In the Chinese Tao, we find that the Order of Heaven should be the Order of Earth also: the "as above, so below" concept. The Pharisees, while recognizing man's freedom, laid emphasis on Fate, and the Essenes insisted upon it as an absolute. Then again, in the Old Testament, according to Josephus, the Sadducees denied the influence of Fate, and placed good and evil wholly within man's choice.

There are even differing opinions within individual religions. In Islam, the orthodox theology is one of absolute predestination, and yet some teachers hold men responsible for the moral character of their acts. Meanwhile, the free-thinking Islamic school insists that the righteousness of God in rewarding or punishing men for their actions can be vindicated only by the recognition of human freedom.

Christianity also holds differing theories regarding the

relationship between Divine and human will, and this question continues to be the cause of considerable controversy, due chiefly to the fragmentation of the Church. While the Calvinist dogma - that salvation is determined only by God's inscrutable will - is largely retained within the creeds of several denominations, the doctrine of predestination is less emphasised in the public teachings of most of the others.

Wherever we look, the problem seems constantly to be the reconciliation of the idea of human freedom with the concept of Divine fore knowledge. Those who have not risen above the frequency of the mind are like leaves in the wind, and take no intelligent response to their own possibilities. However, once we understand ourselves to be part of God, then there need be no dilemma, because we are then able to acknowledge that we are co-creators of our own fate.

Nonetheless, there seem to be certain issues for all of us, issues that we as individuals have elected to conquer. Most souls have at least one or two major situations to address in each life, and sooner or later we are all confronted by situations that afford us the opportunity to address and transcend our issues. This could arguably be called predestination, but it is a pattern that seems to encompass all of us, and the major issues seem to revolve principally around unconditional love and acceptance: and the balancing of the Heart energy. This theme manifests within our lives in myriad situations; often uncomfortable, but always opportunities for transformation. If we do not grasp these opportunities they will recur, which is why certain people find the same situation repeating over and over again, albeit in different places and with different people. For example, most of us know at least one person who constantly, unfailingly, attracts the same kind of difficult relationship. It might appear to some that this is judgement from God, but it is we who are the arbiters in this game of life, which we are playing by our own choice.

Most people have at some time had "a feeling" about something, an indefinable sensation that is often associated with premonitions. They can come to anyone, often without any warning, and they can be unwanted, even frightening, to the receiver. Over the years I have observed that many untrained psychics receive this kind of random premonition, usually of the negative kind. This is because they have not trained their psychic faculties beyond the lower realms. Of course, there can be a certain glamour in making startling and unpleasant predictions, but most people who receive such precognition are very disturbed by the experience.

A great number of natural psychics are incarnate at this time. Many of them are from the Atlantian race, which once worked closely with the astral and lower psychic realms, and these souls consequently find it easy to work with the lower psychism in their current incarnation. We are led to believe that the fall of Atlantis came about partly because of the illusions of the astral worlds, and so it is crucial that these old souls should not once again succumb to the same temptations. The only way to transcend this energy is to make contact with the inner soul force. This is the reason for this book's emphasis on individual growth, without which there can be no expansion, and therefore no transcendence of the planes of illusion. When students are firmly balanced within the higher energies, have established contact with their soul force, and made affirmations of service, then, and only then, may they safely descend once more into the astral levels, in order to serve the higher good.

Few people deliberately remain connected within the lower worlds. People are generally hooked into them by good intentions, which can so easily lead us astray. Instead of asking yourself what you "should" be doing, it is preferable to recognise your true desires, and to seek to align them to the Divine. In the words of St. Augustine, "Love God, and do what you want." Aim always, and in all things, to work from a pure motive, and with a free, unconditional and open heart.

When we consider the glamourous possibilities of prediction, we can see why many have been tempted through the ages to use precognition as a form of control over others. Many religious bodies tacitly imply precognitive powers in their attempts to control. They perpetuate the concept of a vengeful God, a common theme being the dire prediction: "Be good, and toe the line, or else you will meet with hell and damnation!" Another popular control statement is "Your rewards will come in Heaven". The fact is that no-one can judge, or speak for, another soul, or say what that soul will, or will not, receive in the after-life.

There are also many individuals who try to create a personal following by uttering emotive predictions. These nefarious activities can only succeed through fear, or because people want to hand over to others their responsibility for their own lives. These folk are gullible and weak, but which of us can, hand on heart, say that they have never been taken for a ride, nor believed something that later turned out to be untrue? We must be ever mindful of the possibility of gullibility and vulnerability in others, and seek only to serve, never to control. We, as psychic healers, shall know that we have completed a task when our client says: "I don't need you any more".

It is for this reason advisable, if you are doing this work, to have some other form of income. If you are totally dependent upon the money earned from your psychic sittings, it can put an intolerable pressure on you, especially in the early stages, when the energy will fluctuate, and clients may be thin on the ground. Remember that you can serve spirit wherever you are, and whatever your work: street sweeper, shop assistant, surgeon, or merchant banker. Seek only to serve, with no expectations.

The major lesson for us all is that of recognising illusion. Very few people involved in this field of endeavour have not, at one time or another, been deceived, usually out of sheer ignorance, or perhaps lack of discrimination. No matter how intelligent they may be, people generally seem to lose all common sense when a psychic titillates their ego, or impresses them with psychic tricks. Such skills do not mark out the performer as an advanced being: quite the opposite, in fact. Untrained psychics can very easily pick up on the secret desires of their clients, who of course are dazzled when informed that this or that unspoken wish will soon be coming true. This is not meaningful work, and it is certainly not a very advanced form of psychism. Such demonstrations are merely shabby party tricks, performed by those who are either not yet sufficiently advanced to know better, or who get their kicks and feed their own egos by preying on gullible people. There is no room for these antics on the true path of service.

For students, prediction is the most difficult area of all. Within the context of psychic sittings, projections of the future are shown, but they are only projections, and the psychic, one hopes, will relay them as possibilities only, for the personal growth and well-being of the sitter. A client must never be allowed to interpret a projection as an absolute.

We are told that in order to know all that there is to know about the future, all we have to do is to access the akashic records. These are often referred to as a specific place, where all is known, and where we may find "logged" all that has happened and all that is to come. It is indeed a place of records, but most psychics discover it upon the astral levels, which in themselves are but reflections of reality. It must be remembered that since the astral planes are of an absorbent atmosphere, the records are being continuously and spontaneously created by our own thoughts and actions, and are therefore subject to constant change. We must also be aware that time is relative, and does not, as was once believed, travel in a straight line. We can, and frequently do, bend it. It is preferable, therefore, to seek an overview, which will give us an insight into alternative possibilities.

Some years ago, I was asked to send healing to the daughter of a good friend. She had been involved in a serious road accident, and was not expected to live through the night. In the course of sending healing, I communicated with her through the astral planes, where she was being given information regarding the pros and cons of maintaining this incarnation or moving into spirit. It was clear that the choice was going to be difficult, and that choosing to resume her life was the harder option, albeit the one that could build more spiritual muscle. I had no idea how she would choose, but knew that this decision was the toughest of her young life. To the amazement of the medical profession, she quickly recovered, and survived with no permanent damage. She had clearly been shown an overview of her possibilities, none of which were set in stone, and had then been able to communicate intelligently with her soul will.

There are, of course, occasions when one has a strong sense of the course of action that the sitter will follow. In these cases the decision has, in effect, already been made, but even in these instances we must present it as a possibility, not as a fait accompli.

To give an example: One of my students told me of something that had occurred many years earlier, before she had any real knowledge of psychic work, and at a time when she was experiencing great difficulty in her marriage. In her desperation, she thought that if only she could know the outcome, she would be able to deal with anything, and to this end she took herself off to a Tarot reader. This person immediately picked up on her difficulty, and told her straight that her marriage was over, and that she might as well pack her bags and leave. The student emerged from the sitting knowing only one thing, which was that more than anything else, she wanted her marriage to survive. From that moment, she set about making it work, and twenty years on she is still married and happy.

This reading proved to be technically inaccurate, in that the Tarot reader homed in on one possibility, which was undoubtedly linked to a strong emanation of fear from the sitter. However, this focussed my student's mind. She took control, manoeuvred her own life with her own will, and consequently prospered. The student's fear was mirrored to her by this psychic, but fortunately she was able to face it, make a decision, and walk on. One wonders what would have happened if, instead of taking control, she had simply followed the Tarot reader's suggestion, and abandoned her marriage.

The flame of life force energy within all of us is drawing us gently into the "parent flame", to which we shall all eventually return. Psychics who are fully conversant with this concept will be better equipped to interpret and guide. As psychic councillors our responsibility is very great. We must make our purpose abundantly clear, first of all to ourselves, and then to others. We do not seek to shock or entertain, only to serve the greater self within us all. There are several prerequisites for this, the principal one being a spirit of humility: an expression that is often misinterpreted. It does not mean that you must hide your light. On the contrary, you must allow it to shine forth. Nor does it mean that you must pay lip-service to foolishness, or keep quiet when you observe behaviour that you know is wrong. There are those who use the concept of humility as a means of control. Do not allow yourself to be controlled, even if the would-be controller's motives seem to be good: recognise in your heart whether or not you are serving Truth.

There is another kind of false humility: the inverted kind, that presents itself in those who are always doing good deeds. Sadly, these people are very often desperately attempting to fill their own emptiness, born of illusion. "Doing good" can also bloat the ego. Of course, this does not mean that one should never do a good deed, but it is important to look honestly at one's motives. True humility comes from alignment to light, infusing all aspects of life to the higher spiritual forces, with a pure heart and open loving mind.

Every student of psychic studies must acknowledge that this is not a precise science, and that it is impossible for any of us to get everything right all the time. If you find yourself to be in error, admit it. Never be fearful of the truth.

There is, unfortunately, a good deal of spiritual arrogance in the world today. If you consider yourself to be a step or two further along upon the Path than others it does not convey the right to preach, nor to feel self-satisfied. There are abroad at the moment many souls who genuinely believe that they have been chosen by God to do something special. This "Messiah complex" can be devastating for those who come within such a person's orbit, and also for the person concerned. My comment, when people speak of Masters and evolved souls, is that we are all Masters. We are all special. There are many awakened souls who are helping to teach and serve humanity. Anyone who has pure motive, and the desire to serve, is doing God's work. All teachers must acknowledge the fact that there are many other souls who are also teaching Truth. Understand that your greatest teacher next to yourself is the person next to you.

Psychics must be centred in Light, which means being balanced, and functioning above the lower emotional areas. Their vision must be beyond the illusory responses of the solar plexus, and they must be totally free of all personal emotional control. As we have seen, the lower forms of psychism are dangerous and unhelpful. Students must be ever alert to the pitfalls and illusions that can crop up at any stage.

Working as part of a group, whether it be within a large or a small organisation, can be fraught with difficulties. True servers of the Light keep their minds and hearts ever open, avoiding negativity wherever and whenever it may present itself. They encourage education of the highest order, using their extra-sensory perception as a tool to help expand human consciousness. In relaying any projection of the future, no matter how valid, we have to ask ourselves: what good are we doing? Are we encouraging someone to find their own strength within, so that they can help themselves? Illumination and clear messages are all around us if we choose to look, and what we see is only a reflection of ourselves.

Information received must be presented to the sitter in a clear and open fashion. It is becoming increasingly obvious that many people today have a great need to expand and to grow. Even if we have a strong notion of the correct path for someone, we cannot make them take it, nor do we have the right to try. We can only present the possibilities, and allow them to decide. This can be torturous to the soul that sees clearly, and must watch as others follow blind alleys, or cause themselves more pain, but remember that no benevolent being in the cosmos - and that includes you - does anything against man's free will. Never take the arrogant attitude that you must do something for someone's own good. Their good is their own responsibility, and you have no right to make it yours.

EXERCISE

Choose a very relaxed and comfortable position, either sitting with your feet firmly on the ground, or lying on the floor. Listen to your breathing for a few moments, and be in contact with your own balance. Ask yourself if there is anything about your life that is worrying or puzzling you. Fix your mind on a difficulty, objectively observing everything that has led up to it.

Project your worst fear. In your mind's eye, live through that fear, overcoming the consequences in whatever way seems appropriate. Take yourself through the situation, and out the other side, knowing that whatever happens, you are strong. When you have achieved this, put the whole image into Light, and breathe it into your heart.

Now project another possible outcome, this time a positive one, to the same situation, again taking yourself step by step through whatever will be required. The more detail you project the better. See the whole scenario unfolding, and when you have concluded, again surround the image with Light, and breath it into your heart.

You can project as many possibilities as you like. Ask yourself which of these paths serves the truth of who you are. At the same time, you may wish to ask for a short affirmation to assist you. Keep an open mind and an open heart, and the appropriate words will come. You can then speak or write this affirmation at least once a day for twenty-one days. Alongside this, send out a positive and firm affirmation that you want whatever will best serve you and humanity. The answer may not come immediately, although very often in focussing in this way it quickly becomes obvious. If it does not, leave it, trusting that you will know soon. Conscientiously continue to walk the path of Truth.

Close as usual.

Books for Reference
Glamourous Powers, by Susan Howatch 1988.(Although not a reference book, this is one that every budding student could benefit from reading. Take it away for holiday reading).
Magic and the Supernatural, by Maurice Bessy 1964

Chapter 15

MEDITATION

When we begin to work towards greater insight and intuition, it soon becomes clear that some form of meditation is going to be essential to our progress. On the whole it is advisable to meditate only when you really feel like it, but it must also be acknowledged that in the very early stages especially, one does need discipline and focus.

The purpose of meditation is twofold: firstly to focus right thinking and to be open to intuition, and secondly to align our inner soul force with the Divine Source: in other words, the individual personality is brought into line with the soul, and a bridge is built between the individual mind and the God-mind. This bridge is a channel of Light, which, given time, students can employ in every aspect of their lives as a complete form of communication with Divine Inspiration. The ensuing possibilities are endless, and extend far beyond psychic development. Indeed, meditation should never be practised for the sole purpose of psychic growth. There must be purity of motive: a genuine desire for spiritual expansion, and attunement to the Universal Light Force, both for our own benefit and for that of humanity in general.

There are some dangers involved in meditation, but these are usually born of impatience and over-enthusiasm. Unfoldment takes time. Be prepared to allow it to evolve, and do not be tempted to meditate continuously over long periods, because this is not helpful. Be discerning: balance is the prime objective. It is far better to spend five minutes of quality time than to try to meditate for long hours, which can lead to exhaustion, and may even delay progress for many years - or in some cases, perhaps a whole lifetime. Know that what is developed slowly and resolutely will last. Most importantly of all, please remember that any occurrences of psychic phenomena are incidental, and certainly not the purpose of meditation.

The effects of aligned meditation reach out far and wide, and are not often perceived in the three-dimensional world. The effect of clear, vibrant attunement is beyond words and beyond price, and it is in these that you will find real balance and peace.

Consciously or, more usually, unconsciously, everyone is trying to discover the reality behind the experiences of their daily lives. On the intellectual level, this search is displayed in the hunger for knowledge, and on the emotional level it manifests in the desire for happiness.

In the West we do not value philosophers. We tend to look upon them as self-indulgent intellectuals, who leave other members of society to perform life's more mundane tasks. In some Eastern traditions, however, the opposite view is taken, as people look to their philosophers for inspiration and guidance. As the role of the Church as counsellor diminishes, we are left bereft of outer guidance and help. Perhaps it is for this reason that meditation, in its many forms, has become so popular. In a frantic world, there is an increasing need for stillness, and not simply to assist us in psychic development: it is also important for general good health, and for sane living. The yogic schools are helpful in this regard, their main concern being an enquiry into the nature of man himself, and the discovery of a principle of unity, free from discord and contradiction.

If man tries to look directly at the sun he is dazzled, and can no longer see. Similarly, the extreme luminosity of the Supreme Consciousness repels the human intellect, and prevents it from identifying itself with the true soul self. This phenomenon is referred to as Maya, or illusion.

Meditation is a form of mind-control which is best described as alignment or integration. In meditation, the "how and why" is silenced in the balancing procedure. We are enabled to touch inner peace, and the essence of who we are; the soul, the part of us that is indisputably joined to the all-that-is. We touch the absolute, and know our own perfection. It is a direct and lasting experience of reality, and it defies description.

The old Delphic motto "Know thyself" implies that humankind does not know its own true nature. We tend to think of ourselves as the image we project, and our real, universal selves are obscured by the cocoon of false identification with the body, mind and senses, which mask our true being. We imagine ourselves to be limited individuals. We tend to describe ourselves by the work we do, or by our preferences. But it is the changeless element, the soul self, that provides the background against which all the shifts in body and mind, from infancy onwards, take place. It is the inner Light, in the sense that a lamp hanging from the centre of a room illumines whatever goes on in the room. The activities of the body and mind in the waking state, and of the mind in dreaming, as well as the absence of mental activity in dreamless sleep, all take place in the Light of the self.

The true self is not the mind or the body, nor is it the thoughts or the desires or the dreams. It is the inner Light, of which we usually only observe the refracted energies. As light splits through a prism, creating colours, so the light of the soul appears to take on certain limitations, and the characteristics of the body through which it is refracted. The personality and the body give their own colouring to the light of the spirit reflected in them.

In yogic tradition the soul is encased in three bodies: the physical body, the mental body and the causal body. The physical body is self-explanatory, but we must also be aware of working to balance the physical body.

The mental body consists of the vital force referred to by the

Hindus as Prana, and by the Chinese as Chi. The manifestations
of this force are the breath and the physical energy, together with
the mind or personality. In order to focus on the true self, which is
essential for genuine intuition, we must integrate and align all
these bodies. The mind can either be an enemy of the soul, a
means of binding it to the ephemeral world and a life of suffering,
or it can be the soul's friend, working in co-operation with the
soul force. Meditational practices are aimed at persuading the
mind to relinquish the upper hand, and to reconciling it to its
rightful position as a useful and willing servant of inner truth.

The causal body is the most subtle layer of the personality.
Whereas the physical body is at its most active in the waking
state, and the mind's activity reaches its peak in the world of
dream and fantasy, the causal body can be best described as
dreamless sleep. It is where all the mind's potentials lie in seed
form until they are allowed to germinate during times of dream
and waking. It is described as "the sheath of bliss", for the true
inner Light, which is bliss by nature, reflects more clearly within
it than within the denser aspects. In stilling the mind, one affords
the soul a glimpse of the bliss-self reflected in the causal body.
This is epitomised in the tranquility of dreamless sleep.

If we understand the concept that everything is mirrored in the
whole vast cosmos. We are all the microcosm, a universe on a
small scale, which is a tiny reflection of the macrocosm, the vast
universe itself. We can then observe that our universe has come
into manifestation and will remain in existence for a certain
period, to be withdrawn into the undifferentiated state of Maya
which could be likened to the cosmic causal body of God.

Like waves in the ocean, everything in the universe rises, has
its day, then subsides. Each soul, having emanated from the
Source, grows and develops over a period, then returns to the
Source. Following its conception, the human body grows and
develops, lives for a period, then dies. In one way or another, it
then returns to the earth. Each cell of the human body comes into
existence, remains for a limited period, then dies, and is absorbed

and disposed of by the body of which it was once an active part. In the same way, individual mental activity commences at the start of the day and continues until the evening, when it is once more absorbed into the causal body during dreamless sleep. The rise of a single thought, its retention by the mind for a short time, and its eventual return to the sub-conscious, is the same process, operating on a smaller scale.

Following the macrocosm/microcosm principle, the state of society and of global relationships can be seen as a reflection of the inner condition of humankind. Violence and wars are the externalization of our own inner conflicts, therefore the advancement of society, and lasting peace between nations, depend not upon international politics and economic structures, but upon individual men and women establishing their own inner attunement. Being in harmony with oneself radiates a corresponding energy into the world. This is then externalized, and when sufficient numbers of people have achieved inner stillness, we shall at last see the permanent peace that we all desire.

The goal of meditation, then, is a state of inner peace and harmony. It is not about melting into bliss, unable to carry on with material life. It is about bringing balance into all aspects of living. However, emphasis must be laid upon purity of motive, without which enduring balance cannot come into being. Pure motives, combined with disciplined focus, will enable us to break with the concentration on the animal side of human nature, which is continually urging us to satisfy our lower desires. This alliance of forces will enable us to transcend our irrational feelings of attachment and aversion, and to obtain balance and harmony, without which we have no hope of true inspiration.

Various creeds emphasise non-action, in a setting of seclusion, as a way to expand spirituality, but our very physical being involves change and movement, without which come stagnation and disease. Action, of itself is neither a help nor a hindrance to the attainment of true vision, and can become either, depending on the energy that goes into it. This, of course, includes thought, which is a form of action: as man thinks, so he becomes, because thought materialises the thinker's future environment and circumstances. Good actions and good thoughts are those born of selfless motives, which will cause no suffering to others. "As ye sow, so shall ye reap", is a natural law. It means, in effect, that we are all architects of our own fate. Our present situation, whatever it may be, is entirely the result of all our past actions, not only in this life but in many past lives.

We are the sum total of all our experiences. This can be seen, in various ways, in our daily lives. For instance, if we establish a harmonious atmosphere with our friends and family, we thereby create favourable conditions for ourselves, and draw towards us congenial company. The opposite effect is demonstrated by mean or miserly people, who make no contribution to the good of society. These people finally find themselves alone and unwanted, a state that is entirely of their own making. The longer this pattern exists, the more difficult it becomes to break free of it, and is very often only broken through the compassion of others.

There is a relevant story, told by yogic teachers, about a lion cub that was left alone after its parents were shot by hunters. The cub was adopted by a flock of wild sheep, and since it had no other experience, it grew up believing itself to be a sheep. Then, one day, it caught sight of its own reflection in a clear pool of water. It let out a roar, and in doing so it threw off its meekness for the very first time, and knew itself to be the king of the jungle. The analogy is that we, like the lion cub, imagine ourselves to be helpless individuals, and not the reality of the God-self. Unless we see through this illusion, we are doomed to a life of frustration and disappointment. By developing our insight and intuition, we can begin to identify ourselves as what we truly are, and for many people some form of meditation is their first glimpse of their own true majesty.

Before embarking on any meditational practice, it must be emphasised that meditation is not something aimed at helping us to run away from the material physical aspects of living. On the contrary, it is the very instrument that will help us to face our lives without fear. It must be remembered that we have, by our own soul force, chosen to incarnate: why then, should we want to abandon this marvellous vehicle in which we currently reside? Let us think more in terms of aligning that vehicle with the Light Force energy of the soul and of the Divine.

Some practitioners of yoga state that we are trapped inside our physical bodies, awaiting release from bondage, and other schools of thought go along with this attitude. The Christians, for instance, have often taken the stance that our bodies are dirty, and that we should look forward to a glorious hereafter, when we shall no longer be in the body. Acceptance of this doctrine causes a mind/body split, and denies us access to the incredible amount of information stored within the cells of our bodies. If we deny our physical selves, we can have no coherent union of consciousness. The physical world is only a "trap" if we see it as such: the real trap lies in believing that the material world is all there is, and in concentrating our efforts accordingly.

We probably start to meditate knowing instinctively that it will help us towards enlightenment, but meditation on its own is not enough: consciousness on all levels must be understood. Accessing consciousness without some sort of system can be near-impossible, and consequently most people need a teacher to help them make a start. One could align oneself with one of the various schools or teachings, but many of these are subject to their own dogma. If you are looking for a group, choose wisely. You could do far worse that to join a good development group, for here you will undoubtedly be given some structured forms of meditation. Although the cosmos, and we within it, are infinite, our minds need structure in order to focus.

As we have already linked much of our thinking with the seven rays and the seven chakras, these are perhaps appropriate initial areas of focus. Using the breath which is the very best focus to meditation, we can just focus our breathing into each chakra individually. Normal but focused breaths are the best.

It is interesting to note that the number seven constantly appears within different schools of meditation. We have already looked at the seven wheels of energy, known as chakras. In Hindu literature, there are systems involving seven levels of man. Theosophy, epitomised by the writings of Alice Bailey, posits seven cosmic rays of creation, with seven evolutionary races. Christianity propounds seven days of Creation, as well as seven seals, seven angels, seven virtues and seven deadly sins. We have noted in this book the seven levels of the afterlife. The Kabbalistic Tree of Life, a powerful form of study and meditation, has seven horizontal levels distributed among its three vertical pillars and ten sephiroth. This Tree describes a path from Earth to heaven, as does the chakra system.

Even outside myth and religion, the number seven recurs time and time again: seven colours of the rainbow, seven notes in the western musical scale, seven days in the week, and it is believed that major life cycles run in periods of seven years. Astrologically speaking, we have our first major turning point and transformation at Saturn's return, which occurs around the age of 28 years - the fourth phase of seven. Although there are other systems of consciousness, seven seems to predominate.

Although not essential, when you first start to meditate it is a good idea to set aside about half an hour each day. At first it is preferable to find a secluded and quiet room, but do not worry about this too much: many people live in noisy cities, and still manage to achieve focused meditation. In fact, in many ways, a certain amount of noise can be an advantage, for if you learn to meditate only in a silent place, later on you will find that any sort of noise or interruption prevents you from focussing. It is, however, wise to take precautionary measures against sudden noises: turn off your telephone and your doorbell, and tell anyone else in the house that you do not want to be disturbed for half an hour. Failing all else, you could lock yourself into the bathroom!

If you are honest with yourself, you will probably find that any interruptions, imagined or otherwise, are coming from within. To begin with, a certain effort is always required to bridge the normal lapses of attention, and to allow contemplation to supersede the flow of thoughts surrounding the selected symbol or object of focus. e.g. the chakras. All limitations are of the ego, and in time the object will be transcended. The Divine Consciousness will be found within, where it had been merely concealed by the false ego, just as a dense cloud obscures the sun.

Meditation on finite things will not bring release from the illusions and constant sufferings of worldly life. To be attached to any worldly success that results from the lower mental, experiences will serve only to strengthen the bonds of ignorance and illusion. It becomes increasingly difficult to throw off such attachments, and to enter the true mental/ spiritual experience. This will be achieved only when there is meditation on the infinity within the object of focus, and when the limited ego is dissolved within the ensuing illumination.

Alternatively, you can meditate on the infinity within the mind itself. This method allows the ego to expand to infinity, becoming one with the universe. The Divine Source and the inner Light become one. Achieving this alignment takes time, however, and it is important, even early on, to bring Light consciously into your waking life. In time, all action and thought will become benevolent, and as a seeker of truth you will be free from all delusion, and fear of death.

Many souls intend to be good, but find themselves rapidly falling into delusion and fear when they are given a position of power and status. How many people can truly say that their good intentions have led them into real good? Confucius said that unless there is wisdom, and freedom from fear, our benevolence is mere sentimentality. Until the Light within is recognised, there can be no wisdom, no freedom from fear.

At first the world and the body are felt to be real, the concept of meditation is only an idea, and the reality beyond the mind is just an assumption. But as the meditation goes deeper, there are flashes of experience, and then the concept of meditation becomes at least as real as the body. By the end, the body, the mind, and the universe as we know it, will be recognised as being illusory. Then, gradually, the Divine Light Force becomes fully manifest as Bliss, and the whole universe turns into Light.

EXERCISE

Different schools advocate different sitting-positions. Most of us in the West find the yogic lotus position very uncomfortable, and it is not necessary. It is important to be comfortable, as the meditation process is to still, relax, and, finally, completely to forget the body. So find a comfortable position for yourself: one in which nothing is crossed or tense.

As we have seen in earlier exercises, we must be prepared to let go, and a prayer or affirmation to the Highest Mind is enormously helpful. One that I often use in class runs as follows;

"Divine Spirit of Light, we ask you to draw close, to protect and guide us in everything. We ask that we be ever open to greater possibilities and greater truths, so that we may use these with wisdom in our own lives, for the good of ourselves and for the good of all. We ask in love."

"Divine Spark of Truth, open up, and help us to perceive new realities, and to obtain higher motives. Help us to emerge from the veils of darkness, and courageously face our conflicts with Light, helping to dissolve them with Love."

Simply to affirm that one is open to the highest, greatest good is perhaps the best call. Make your affirmation wisely, as thought is very potent in successful meditation. The object of meditation is to clear a cluttered mind, and for the majority of people this does happen immediately. We can give the mind a focus or symbol, such as one of the chakras, or a universal symbol, or sound. One of the best known is the sound OM, which can be spoken or sung. Though usually represented as a Sanskrit symbol, it is a word of no known language, and is revered in nearly all the mystical schools of the world. It is the highest Name of God, and it stands for the supreme truth of infinite consciousness and bliss. The inner meaning can be studied in the Mandukya Upanishad, and other texts. The OM sound is a particularly good one with which to end your meditation, for it acts as a powerful prayer, or call, to the Light of the Cosmos. It is the Amen of meditation.

Fixing your mind on the breath is an important starting process. There are many breathing techniques, but it must be remembered that these are only preliminary practices, and should not be over-emphasised. We merely use the breath to contact the inner stillness, and take us into a deeper peace by meditating on universal compassion. The easiest and simplest way is to listen to the natural rhythm of your own breathing, as explained in earlier chapters. Focussing on this alone is a powerful meditation, and if you practise it for two to five minutes a day, it will help to further your meditational skills.

When you become peaceful, and are breathing in a steady and balanced fashion, take your mind to the possibility of your own limitlessness, epitomised by the concept that "I and the Father are one". Taking yourself into the stillness, you can gently focus your thought on the breath of the universe, for as you breathe, as we all breathe, the universe breathes. You will then come to understand the limitless cosmos, and feel yourself to be a part of the awesome cosmic breath.

Meditation also indicates a focussing of thought, and we can obtain much insight by studying some of the great inspirational saints and sages. In addition to examining Masters such as Jesus Christ and the Prophet Mohammed, and the philosophies of, for example, Socrates and Confucius, remember that all classical works of art, books and music contain inspirational knowledge from the cosmos. The plays of William Shakespeare, if we read them carefully, contain many quite staggering insights into the true nature of mankind. Mozart claimed that his music, fully orchestrated, simply flowed into his head. He made just one copy of each work, after which, it is said, he altered not one note.

Meditate upon anything that inspires you. Many people find music to be particularly helpful in the early stages: the simple act of lying down and listening to a wonderful, tranquil piece of music will take us into the higher phases of the mind.

Meditation is aimed at securing detachment and freedom from unconscious compulsions and habits, and the hopes and fears that spring from our conviction of the reality of the material world. It must be said that the material world is not totally illusory: it does contain a certain reality, but we cannot understand it until we relinquish our hold on false appearances.

Welcome in the Light Forces. This can be done by visualising Light pouring into your crown from the Divine Source, and flowing through you in a stream of Light Force energy. The same thing can be done with sound. Concentrate your thought, and therefore your energy, above your head, and "hear" a note, which you then gently sound. Draw the vibration of that sound through your crown, and down in a straight channel through your body. The yogic schools practise something similar by pressing their forefinger between the eyebrows and then drawing it down the centre-line of the body, lightly brushing the nose, lips, throat, breast and navel, folding the hands over this point, and concentrating on this line, using the sensation caused by the pressure. Think of it as a line of Light running down the centre of the body. This will focus the energy, and align the Light Force. This practice will calm the mind.

When you are immersed in your meditation, you may find your mind wandering, but no thought can remain in the mind for very long, unless we give it our active support. Discipline yourself to meet any irrelevant thought with a gentle "not wanted" sign, and simply turn your attention away from it. These random thoughts are like hungry birds: at first they will plague us, for they are used to being fed, but if day by day we close our window to them and keep silent, they will very soon stop pestering us.

The process of stilling the mind, as well as being essential for higher intuitional states, is a marvellous advantage in life. To be able to think what we like, instead of being prey to any wandering thoughts, and the hypnotised victim of any orator who wishes to exploit us, is true freedom. Literally thinking for oneself is an essential ingredient of evolved mastery.

What you choose to meditate upon is entirely up to you. There are now many meditational tapes on the market which may help. It is advisable, however, to start simply, in the manner described above, or in some similar fashion. It is better not to set yourself goals, but do try to set aside some time. If you initially find it hard, do not despair. If you truly affirm your purity of intent, sooner or later you will feel the benefit of the expansion developed by meditation, and eventually you will be able to spend the whole of your life in meditation. This does not mean that you will be in trance; quite the opposite, in fact. You will have more focus, and more energy, and you will see life through eyes of innocence and wonder. You will move forward into love of mankind, and love of yourself.

As time goes on, you will be able to expand your mind into infinity. Then the mind, too, will be forgotten, and the true self, the reality beyond the mind, will blaze forth like the sun, as the obscuring clouds evaporate.

To finish this chapter there is a quote from one of the greatest modern minds, J. Krishnamurti:

"Meditation is one of the greatest arts of life, perhaps the greatest, and one cannot possibly learn it from anybody. That is the beauty of it. It has no technique, and therefore no authority. When you learn about yourself, watch yourself, watch the way you walk, how you eat, what you say, the gossip, the hate, the jealousy - if you are aware of all that in yourself, without any choice, that is part of meditation. So meditation can take place even when you are sitting in a bus, or walking in the woods, full of light and shadows, or listening to the singing of birds, or looking at the face of your wife or child. The flowering of love is meditation."

Books for Reference
Meditations, by J. Krishnamurti 1991
Yoga, by Hari Prasad Shastri 1957
Freedom from the Known, by J. Krishnamurti 1987

Chapter 16

HIGHER CONSCIOUSNESS

Simply by developing your psychic field, you have, in one sense, altered your awareness, thereby creating the opportunity for your growth on all levels. By allowing a shift of focus, you have literally let in the radiance of a different light. If this light is followed, it will reveal your true soul force, and higher consciousness will ultimately manifest itself in you, although, like the making of a good wine or cheese, this is a process that cannot be hurried.

Conscious awareness of spiritual truths is usually a long way down the path, but even before the early days, when you were experiencing the sparks of illumination, and the feeling of being pushed (as mentioned in chapter one), you were already undergoing the process of spiritual enlightenment.

It was once said to me that of all the people incarnate at any given time, only one in 60,000 is awake in consciousness. This echoes the words of Plato, when he spoke of all mankind being like prisoners in a cave that face away from the light. They are unable to see themselves or anyone else, because they are shackled, observing life through the shadows on the wall. When one prisoner escapes from the cave, and finds that reality bears no resemblance to the shadows, and returns to awaken and inform the shackled ones, he is met with derision, ridicule and aggression: he is trying to share his new-found knowledge with those too blind or too frightened to accept it. Does this story sound familiar?

In taking our awareness beyond the normally accepted levels, we enter an unknown territory, one with different scenery and no perimeters. This experience can initially be daunting, very often throwing the individual into a kind of shock. Things must be taken slowly at this stage. All the answers will come at their own pace.

Various schools of mysticism have assigned labels to the different experiences, and this can be helpful, but it is worth remembering that we are all individuals, and that no-one conforms totally to a set pattern.

More recently a Russian philosopher-mystic and his colleague, Ouspensky, state that there are five levels of consciousness. This frame-work is very similar to the Hindu and the Zen Buddhism schools of belief, and as we have seen, Alice Bailey speaks at length about the seven rays, which again can be helpful, but are not to be treated as a map. We are all different, and ultimately we shall all find our way along our various paths.

Right from those early days of being "pushed", one may have, what could be referred to as, peak experiences. These "bliss" moments are of the type experienced by saints and visionaries. They differ from person to person, but they are generally dramatic and explosive; full of wonder, with a breathtaking climax. These experiences, as we have already seen, must not be confused with the true balance of greater mastery and higher consciousness. They are but transitory glimpses of the transcendental way, and serve only to reveal the greater possibilities. It is imperative that they should not be seen as an end in themselves: following them for their own sake will take you down blind alleys. This will lead to deep frustration, and lure you towards the endless circle of Illusionland, because when these experiences are over, like an addictive drug they have to be sought again and again. This is not the stuff of spiritual growth. It is the stuff of the dependent devotee, the workshop groupie, and all those who long for another "happening". It becomes glamourous, and as the glamour fades it can darken into deep and utter despair, leaving the bereft student to wonder why God has deserted him or her. God of course, has done no such thing: God is always right under our noses.

Allow your transcendental glimpses to fill you with the wonder of living. Let the door be open to detached observation. Realise that our true essence and being is nothing to do with labels. We are not our jobs, our hobbies or our looks. In finding the ability for detached examination, we begin to realise the real self, the part of us that has the qualities of the Monad, which is the unmanifested seed, wherein the sum total of powers appertaining to its divine origin are latent. We then become aware of the God within, no longer prisoners of the five senses, which in the past have ruled our lives. It was these that said "I'm hungry," "I'm lonely," "I'm rich", "I'm poor." With our dawning awareness of higher consciousness, we begin to acknowledge - not with the little "I", but the real "I" - the hub of the wheel, the core of our being, the soul force, the truth. At this point comes recognition of the possibility of greater being.

Students frequently believe that if they find the right teacher, this individual will know all the answers, and will thus be able to guide them through. This could not be further from the truth. Only charlatans, or ignorant, untrained teachers will offer to sort out your difficulties. Truly advanced souls will not consider your personal specific deeds, words or conditions. Higher consciousness involves spiritual maturity, and that means taking absolute personal responsibility. A genuine teacher will be concerned with teaching his or her students to know and understand themselves, awakening their minds to their greater possibilities, and encouraging them to be self-reliant.

It must be remembered that everything echoes everything else. Higher awareness on one level leads to higher awareness on another. As we have already seen (it seems appropriate to recap at this point), from the very moment that we tentatively reach out from the fog of illusion, and begin to see the light, and from the instant when we consciously say "I want to expand, and help humanity", we send an unmistakeable vibrational message out to the higher planes, those planes upon which the beings exist for the express purpose of serving humanity. This is the group soul, variously referred to as the Master Ray, the Hierarchy, and other titles. Immediately they receive such a message, they start to watch the sender, to assure themselves that the message is genuine. It usually is, because ultimately all souls have at their core the true desire for enlightenment. When this is confirmed, they start communicating. To begin with this takes place largely during sleep.

The individual receives teachings from this body of Light souls, but since the information transmitted is conceptual, rather than intellectual in nature, conscious memories of it are rare. However, as we saw earlier, it is not uncommon for a student to have some inkling of having visited a place of learning, and of having been with a wise person. These teachers rarely have a face, for the energy is beyond the personality. They are using the astral planes as a kind of telephone wire to communicate, but their own vibrational frequency is far beyond that level. When you reach this point, you will start wanting to explore your own expansion: a need to meditate, and/or to join with like-minded people, usually becomes quite pronounced. Either consciously or unconsciously, you will begin to channel messages and information.

The teachers of the higher planes do not stay with a student for one moment longer than necessary. At this level there can be no dependency, for the soul must begin to take total responsibility for itself. One's actions and one's pure intent are recorded on the inner planes.

As you draw your energy into higher states, your vibratory frequency will expand, and you will align yourself to the Masters on the higher planes. You will, in fact, become part of the ever-increasing Brotherhood of Light, and you will act as an important connection between the dense, physical existence and the spiritual realms. This bond of energy is imperative for the coming times, and for the expansion of consciousness of the entire planet.

What must be realised is that the "all that is" is omnipresent. It is every bit as present with the prisoners in their caves as it is with the living beings we treat as god to whom we like to idolise. It is only through acknowledging this omnipresence that we can begin to fulfil our true potential. WE ARE ALL GOD. This theme is echoed in, although probably unconsciously, by the great painters and composers,all great works of art and music, and when we feel inspired by them it is because we are contacting the god within. Here, then, is the true insight that fosters true intuition, and each step of the way ahead will bring us a deepening of both.

Every pathway looks out over a different landscape, but all lead to the top of the mountain. As we climb to ever higher viewing points, we come into ever purer contact with our god-force, through which we come to know our higher intuitive forces. Then, when the cloak of shadows is finally removed, we reveal the brilliant light of our illumination. Each step takes us closer to knowing where we should be, and what we should be doing, until we finally come to the point where we have no more needs, no more desires, no more "should", and everything is perfect as it is.

When you become part of the group soul energy, which is a major step in your evolution, the real work begins. This has to be undertaken by and for yourself. You are your own guide, teacher and friend. This work is not of the "good works" variety usually ascribed to the spiritual; some "good works" can even be an excuse for students to stop seeking within.

As we accept the rays of "white light" our own pure inner light is also revealed. As each being is resonate with this we begin to work together automatically. This was probably unconsciously recognised at the turn of the century and it was responsible for the ideals of that time. These ideals manifested in the desire to enforce politically community living. But you could gather ten, or tens of thousands of people together, if they do not resonate in energy they will never be part of the true brotherhood of man. For the true group soul unity is within the connection of like frequencies, and when this happens we become as one and not before. So the "communes", the "united states" are useless unless their is unison within the soul state. However every soul with an open heart in the thousands of healing and development groups around the planet, or merely individuals going about their own business in light are automatically united in love without even knowing the names of the soul in the other groups, that could be thousands of miles apart.

At this stage, full integration begins, and intellectually this can create quite a complicated equation. On the one hand, you have never been more independent - able, at last, to think for yourself, and strong in the knowledge of your inner core peace, balance and love. On the other hand, you are now arriving at the group soul level, and it is at this point that one begins fully to realise that we are all inextricably joined, that one's soul is indeed a part of the greater soul, that each of us is but one single droplet of the limitless ocean. This knowledge serves not to dissolve us as consciousnesses, but rather to expand our range: we are, at this juncture, beginning to have access to the "main computer", with all the power and knowledge that this affords. This is the "knowing" state, in which we can, if we listen, know what to do, think, and say at any given moment. It is the path of integration. It is a state of understanding, and of pure reason. It belongs to the higher mind, the unity of the ocean, the freedom of oneness and the reality of complete and utter safety in all areas. It is true intuition.

This experience brings us to a state equivalent to the fifth and sixth regions of the afterlife, described in the chapter on death. Now we can begin to acknowledge the living, breathing flame of life that runs through everything: we can freely embrace life, and revel in the pure joy of living. This is so aptly described in J. B. Priestley's "Dream Vision". It is worth quoting here, for this piece also describes the depression into which one can sink when the sharp vision of the higher view is not fully realised:

"I dreamt I was standing at the top of a very high tower, alone, looking down upon myriads of birds, all flying in one direction: every kind of bird was there, all the birds in the world. It was a noble sight, this vast aerial river of birds. But now, in some mysterious fashion, the gear was changed, and time speeded up, so that I saw generations of birds, watched them break their shells, flutter into life, weaken, falter and die. Wings grew, only to crumble, bodies were sleek, and then, in a flash, bled and shrivelled; and death struck everywhere and at every second.

What was the use of all this blind struggle towards life, this eager trying of wings, all this gigantic, meaningless, biological effort? As I stared down, seeming to see every creature's ignoble little history almost at a glance, I felt sick at heart. It would be better if not one of them, not one of us all, had been born, if the struggle ceased for ever.

I stood on my tower, still, alone, desperately unhappy, but now the gear was changed again, and time went faster still, and it was rushing by at such a rate that the birds could not show any movement, but were like an enormous plain, sown with feathers. But along this plain, flickering through the bodies themselves, there now passed a sort of white flame, trembling, dancing, then hurrying on; and as soon as I saw it I knew this flame was life itself, the very quintessence of being: and then it came to me, in a rocket burst of ecstasy, that nothing mattered, nothing could ever matter, because nothing else was real, but this quivering, hurrying lambency of being. Birds, men, or creatures not yet shaped and coloured, all were of no account, except so far as this flame of life travelled through them. It left nothing to mourn over behind it; what I had thought of as tragedy was mere emptiness of a shadow show, for now all real feeling was caught and purified, and danced on ecstatically with the white flame of life. I had never felt before such deep happiness as I knew at the end of my dream of the tower and the birds."

This inspirational piece reveals to us the despair that is a common initial reaction to the realisation gained from the "overview." This stage is well documented in all major mystical works, and has often been described as "the dark night of the soul". It is indeed the darkest hour before the dawn. It is lonely, and great courage is required if one is to keep one's head, and move through it. If, however, we are able to discern the all-encompassing nature of the living flame that is within everything, we can begin to relate it to everything and everyone; and when we relate to others in this way we will not only see the best in them, but we will, through our inner connection, help them to expand their own inner Light. We shall then become true healers, using our finer intuition to understand our fellow man and, of course, ourselves. No longer shall we need to seek out "good works" in order to fufil our spiritual intent, for we shall understand that we can implement goodness wherever we are, and whomever we are with, simply by living, and by being connected to the inner flame of truth. It is then that we shall at last begin to see, uncloaked, the truth, in all its brilliance, its inexpressible glory. It is here that absolute responsibility begins, and it is here that we shall start to lose the personality self, melting into the living flame.

After this stage, when total integration has transpired, we shall take the giant leap of consciousness which is the total melting of the self into the pure Timeless Light of the Source. This, perhaps, is the real resurrection spoken of by all religions. Here, from the unity of the group soul, and the communication of higher mastery, the energy of the individual expands and rarefies. The quality of its light at this stage becomes intense, until finally the individual is not seen at all. They are enlightened, and they literally melt into Light. This is a totally transcendental state, the closest stage to absolute consciousness. It is beyond human powers of description, although from time to time it is possible to receive conceptual glimpses of it. In the crucible of white light, all facets of the body dissolve, and are no more. This perhaps is the completion of the cosmic in-breath, and in this moment the out-breath begins again. Sparks of the enlightened consciousness will once again travel outwards to physical existence. These are very likely to transpire in different places, including the possibility of different planets, or even in different universes. Once again, the eternal flame of existence is externalised.

Probably, however, we are not quite there yet! We must address the immediate issues. The vibration of the majority of the Earth's current population is of the third or fourth ray. Most of these souls are the mass of the population, waiting and experiencing the journey until, through the fourth (unconditional love) ray, they will emerge, like the men from the caves referred to in Plato's analogy. Thus the immense value of developing your true psychic awareness becomes apparent, since with each stage you are removing the veils that stand between you and your soul.

When you, as a practising healer or psychic, are working from this overview level, the type of reading you give will change. You will find that fewer and fewer of the sitter's personal aspects are revealed, unless it be to illustrate the higher ideas. Contact with discarnate astral entities will specifically only be for the greater good. The only connection with the astral being when the teachers use it to communicate, and even then that energy is unlikely to give much in the way of proof in the normal sense. Any proof will be in the hearts of both the psychic and the sitter. Let the law of attraction come into operation: by this stage you have committed yourself to service, therefore trust the process. Everything that happens, happens appropriately.

As each veil is removed, you will see the picture a little differently, and more clearly. However, each step holds pitfalls and glamours, which it is essential to acknowledge. They are often insidious, and cloak themselves in the name of "good intentions". Alice Bailey listed some of the many guises of glamour, paraphrased below:

The Glamour of Destiny: The idea that one has a "special" task. We are all special. Watch your pride.

The Glamour of Aspiration: Such total absorption in the idea of following the Light, that one becomes blinkered, and may ignore the truth that lies at one's feet.

The Glamour of Self-assurance: This is the over enthusiastic student who believes that he or she is always right. It is the stuff of fundamentalism and bigotry.

The Glamour of Duty: Over-emphasis of the sense of reponsibility. We are all in this together.

The Glamour of the Mind: The idea that through linking with spirit one has the capacity to deal with every problem. Recognise that you cannot be all things to all people.

The Glamour of Devotion: This is the glamour of the dying age. It has no part to play in the New Age. Everyone has access to truth.

The Glamour of Desire: Ask yourself what your true needs are, and align your desire to the will of God.

The Glamour of Personal Ambition: Self explanatory.

Because the very nature of this work is observation, including one's own, many students become prone to the negative aspect, which is self-pity. This is a powerful and deluding force, which exaggerates every condition, and isolates people within the centre of their own lives, and the dramas of their own thoughts. Some years ago, I spoke in a hurtful way to someone. Realising immediately that this was wrong, and that I had certainly failed to practise harmlessness, I pondered much on it, and was consequently extremely miserable. After moping around all day, I decided to seek illumination on the matter, and went into meditation, expecting criticism and a lecture regarding my disgraceful behaviour. To my utter astonishment, the message I received from spirit boomed loud and clear: "We do not want your sorrow, we want your strength". Clearly I was being told to set aside my self-pity. "Walk on" was the clear message, and it is one that I have never forgotten.

There is a often a long struggle involved in developing the wisdom to know when to speak and when to keep silent. All we can do is to keep trying our best. We will not always get things right, and if you fear failure, it would be as well to give up the journey now. Ultimately there is no such thing as failure, and in the words of my own channelling, "there is no such thing as right and wrong, only flow and blockage of that flow." My mention of "getting things right" does not imply a moral, ethical, or any other sort of measure. I am talking about flow. When you are in the flow, it feels right, and when you are not, it feels uncomfortable. The clearer your contact with the Light forces, the more uncomfortable you will feel if something in your life is off-balance. Clear the obstruction, and flow onwards. Each time you slip, learn from the fall, however serious or minor it may be, get up, and walk on. Try to practice harmlessness, but never allow that to stop you speaking your truth if someone asks you a question. If they do not ask, button up and keep silent.

Along the path there will be upsets, many of which are caused by our having expectations of others. Try to expect nothing, for giving unconditionally will spare you from disappointment. An extension of this theme is that it is possible to be continually miserable over world conditions, which seem to play the record of disharmony over and over again. Fight this always with non-recognition, and by being completely absorbed in your own work. In other words: just get on with it.

There is unfortunately often an appalling kind of spiritual snobbery. This can be born out of working or having contact with a "master." It is of the playground level of "I know something you don't." Or a feeling of superiority because you may think you are further down the road. This is dangerous and absurd. We are all on the same road. The fact that some are slightly further down the path means nothing. What matters how long it takes, we will all arrive sooner or later. Remember your greatest teacher apart from yourself is the person next to you. We can learn from the daisy under our feet, from the wonder of a child, and often we learn from the fool. Observe without criticism.

We must leave everyone free to live their own lives. It is so easy to slip into "control mode", comfortingly disguised as the offering of what we view as good advice, but other people's journeys are really none of our business. If you are specifically asked, then -

and only then - is it correct to give advice, and to impart seed thoughts. In a group environment, or as part of a society, this is often a hard rule to follow.

We like to think that if an establishment is spiritually based, everyone involved there is automatically spiritual, but actually there is often a distressing amount of pettiness and gossip in these places. Part of your journey is to lift yourself beyond these lower vibrations. Gossip is very harmful to those who start it, as well as being hurtful to those at whom it is aimed. If you hear something said which is detrimental to others, approach the offending party directly, and make a positive attempt to clear the matter up quickly, and without creating further harm. Never start a rumour, and keep well clear of those who do. Disturbance in these situations often comes about by trying to be "nice". If by being nice you are not truthful, it is not spiritual. Wrong messages are received and anger and confusion reigns. You might disagree with a family member, but you do not stop loving them. Discussion is healthy. Exchange of ideas, even different ones, are valuable. Always remember that in the polishing of stones, an abundance of grit is necessary. Spiritual polishing works in much the same way. Remember also that it is the irritant of the grain of sand that stimulates the oyster to produce the pearl.

One of the things most often misinterpreted is materiality. The inclusion of this subject in a chapter entitled "Higher Consciousness" may seem incongruous, but, as we have seen, everything is a mirror, an echo, of everything else. In our quest for higher consciousness, a balanced perspective on money, and an ability to integrate that perspective fully and comfortably with our spiritual endeavours, are essential if we are to break free of the illusion that surrounds this aspect of life in the material world. In each lifetime, everyone receives what they need for their progress. For some people that may mean that they become very wealthy, and learn lessons from having riches, whilst others can learn from being poor, and having to struggle.

The fashionable foregone conclusion that "you can't possibly be spiritual if you have money" is total nonsense, however, the old adage of "money can't buy happiness" is very true. Happiness is a by-product of right living: seek it for itself and you will never find it. Happiness, or rather, contentment, is within. Money in any case is only a form of exchange and energy. Money is subject to the same laws as everything else in the cosmos, therefore what you give out will return to you. In spiritual terms, money has become the modern "devil". This is a distorted view, and one that quite possibly has its origins in the envy of those who do not have it in abundance. Like any other form of energy, it is potentially dangerous. If one is greedy, or uses money to exert power over others, this obviously goes against the spiritual flow. But it is the obsession with, and the worshipping of, money that is evil, not the money itself. A flow of electricity must be channelled in order to create light and warmth. As an energy, money must also be allowed free flow.

A very troublesome aspect of psychic work is the question of how much should be charged (if anything at all) for a sitting or a healing session. Every person must judge this for themselves. Living as we do in a material world, we need money in order to live. If you are a person of means, and in all honesty would not resent doing the work for nothing, then by all means do so, but these days this is an unrealistic scenario for most of us. It must be remembered, also, that through such "good deeds" one runs the risk of creating undesirable perspectives (on both sides) on relationships between oneself and one's clients, and some exchange is therefore advisable.

The angels and guides that help us in our work are totally disinterested in what we charge. All they care about is the opportunity to help and heal. My advice is to set a fair and reasonable rate, one that feels comfortable, and charge it to the able-bodied adult. If there are people who genuinely cannot afford to pay, then accept a donation, no matter how small.

One of the hardest things to understand is what constitutes harmlessness. No true student of Light would want to act in an injurious way, and we all realise the need for harmony and peace.

However, this stance is often confused with weakness, and can even be used as an excuse. I met a woman once who was married, but who secretly had a lover and several "friends". When I made a comment on this situation, she retorted "I thought that was what unconditional love meant"! The need for total self honesty is imperative. Sometimes we believe that we must keep the peace at all costs, but if this means deceiving someone, either with words or through lack of them, this clearly cannot be harmless.

Deception and lies, even "white" ones, emanate an unharmonious vibration. Often what follows is confusion, and total communication breakdown. Truth has a clear resonance, because it is a healing force. It is often very hard to speak the truth, but this must be done, on every occasion. On this there can be no compromise.

Within each field of awareness, the creation of structures and boundaries, and therefore prisons, is a temptation, and in each case they must be forged through, for if we are not careful we can find ourselves trapped at each and every stage, by the limitations of structures. We belong to a limitless universe: boundaries are superfluous to our needs. The idea of limitlessness is impossible to grasp, for the little mind can only work with structures, which are man-made. The object of any spiritual work is to liberate and release the consciosuness, and to expand its field of contact. The greatest and truest desire is the desire to expand.

Please be aware that although I have described some of the many pitfalls and types of energy that may be encountered on the journey to greater awareness and higher consciousness, there are no limits, no absolutes. If we really look and listen, we shall instinctively know the right path for us. Although many of us have so far only caught glimpses of it, the beacon of Light is ever within. We know that one day all will be revealed; and when it is we shall no longer be attached to the outcome. We shall have ceased to care, not through selfishness, but rather, through the knowledge that all is well: knowing that we are part of the all-that-is is the greatest security and the only truth.

EXERCISE

There are no exercises or meditations, however elevated, that will of themselves expand your consciousness. Expanding consciousness has to be lived. We can, however, focus our light through quiet and constant dedication.

Take deep, purposeful breaths. Be aware of the flow of breath coursing through your whole body. This is the life force. Allow your whole body to absorb it, and with each inhalation feel the force of the breath move higher and higher, until it joins with the highest Light Force. Feel your breath connecting, becoming part of that Force. Feel and know the unison of energies between the highest Light Force and your own breath. Recognise them as one. Feel and know the oneness. Feel and know the peace.

As you begin to return from this unity of Light, purposefully bring it into physical reality. Do not lose the connection. Through the Heart centre, feel and know the balance of all things. If you wish for a particular focus, meditate on unconditional love. Ask yourself in what ways you have exercised unconditional love in your life today. We think we understand the principal, but it is a constantly-unfolding inspiration, a meditation that will always be relevant. The bridge of higher consciousness that you must cross is the bridge of the Heart. Only by experiencing the energy of unconditional love can our bodies, minds and souls vibrate to the higher range. We shall cross it eventually, and after this there can be no return. The view alters radically from here on.

Books for Reference
Serving Humanity, by Alice A. Bailey 1972
In the Steps of the Master, by Dr. Douglas Baker 1977
Cosmic Dance, channelled by Julie Soskin 1991

Chapter 17

THE NEW
AGE

We live in exciting times, of that there can be no doubt. Simply from an historical point of view, one would would have to be both blind and deaf not to realise that extraordinary things are happening. The last century has seen so many changes, on so many levels, that our whole way of life has altered. It is already almost thirty years since men landed on the moon, and yet only one hundred years ago, the aeroplane was still a thing of the future. The motor car was in its infancy, there was no electricity in homes, and the telephone and the radio had yet to be invented. In the course of their whole lifetime, most ordinary folk rarely travelled beyond a radius of five miles from their homes.

We, their late-twentieth-century descendants, have comparatively limitless horizons. At the press of a few buttons, we can instantly speak to people anywhere in the world. We have no excuse for ignoring the plight of the many for the sake of a few, and we have, en masse, changed our perspective: we are beginning fully to comprehend the brotherhood of man. Wars still rage, and fear and starvation are still with us, but they are now viewed with a global sense of shame, and therefore afford us the opportunity to help and to heal. These changes have fired our imaginations, and they are felt at a very deep level by those who are sensitive.

As we know, everything mirrors everything else. What

transpires on the physical level is always a reflection of occurrences on the higher levels, and vice versa; and in the physical, the acceleration of change is high. As we approach the end of the millennium, the excitement seems to be rising to fever-pitch, sometimes causing unfortunate lapses in our common sense. Similar excitement was felt around the time of the last millennium, when it was predicted, among other things, that there would be a new Messiah, and that the end of the world was at hand. Christianity was largely a persecuted creed, and time was running out for the fulfilment of the prediction, indicated in the Book of Revelation, that there would be salvation in the year 1000 A.D. Faithful Christians were therefore expectantly awaiting the second coming of Christ. These predictions were very effective as recruiting devices, and belief in the millennium prophecies became a central point of Christianity, although there were a few, such as the Gnostics, the neo-Platonists, and the Augustinians, who rejected the concept.

During this time, zealots took extreme measures to prepare for the end of the world. In the year 971, such was the expectancy of armageddon that leases were made only for exactly twenty-nine years! There were donations and conversions a-plenty. With bated breath, the known world awaited the end. When it did not arrive, true believers moved the date forward by 33 years, averring that it must be timed from the crucifixion, not the birth, of Christ. The predictions obviously turned out to be non-events, and the movement had all but vanished by AD 1055. Other apocalyptic movements have since arisen, for reasons mainly based upon a combination of blind faith in some, and the need to control in others.

What, then, are we to make of the predictions that abound today? The widely-known prophet Nostradamus (1503-66), certainly gave us plenty to think about in his "Centuries", a series of 942 enigmatic, predictive quatrains, published in 1555. From these we can deduce that he is indicating the occurrence of a series of cataclysms towards the year 2000. Echoing the Book of

Revelation, he foretells that "the sword of death is on its way to us now, in the shape of pestilence, war and famine". Although his predictions up to that date are prolific, he offers none subsequently, with the exception of marking AD 3797 as the date of the planet's death. Of course, since Nostradamus's predictions are cryptically written, no-one can be entirely sure of the dates, but the late 1990's is one of the few specific periods mentioned. Among many political and sociological statements, the major quatrain refers to a shifting of the Earth's axis in 1999.

This event is reflected in the writings of other psychics, notably Edgar Cayce, "The Sleeping Prophet" who predicts that with the shifting of the poles, frigid or semi-tropical climates will become more tropical. He, too, mentions the occurrence of a series of cataclysmic events over the sixty-year span leading up to the year 2000, most particularly from 1958 to 1998. He states, amongst other things, that the Earth will be broken up in the western portion of North America, that most of Japan will fall into the sea, and that the upper portion of Europe will be changed "in the twinkling of an eye". Land will, he says, appear off the east coast of America, open water will appear in Greenland, and upheavals in the Arctic and in the Antarctic will "make volcanoes erupt in the torrid areas".

More recently, Hideo Itokawa, an eminent Japanese professor, has discovered that on 18th August, 1999, the sun and the planets will take up the shape of the Cross, creating a phenomenon which would, he says, coincide with the destruction of human society on Earth. This grand cross of planets is in the fixed sign related to the four beasts of the Apocalypse: the bull - Taurus, the lion - Leo, the eagle - Scorpio, and man - Aquarius. This, in astrological terms, is believed to stir up extreme unrest, violence, and natural catastrophes such as earthquakes and tidal waves.

A consensus of other psychic material includes the shifting of the polar axis, together with other phenomena: new climates and ancient cities emerging when the seas subside; major disturbances on both coasts of the U.S.A., with major sections falling into the sea, and a coast-line finally being established in Nebraska; major subsidence from Florida to Texas; earthquakes in Turkey and Yugoslavia; the Gulf Stream undergoing a complete shift; some parts of the British Isles being submerged while others rise; London as a coastal town; land rising in various places, including Norway, Sweden, Denmark and Finland; most of Hawaii and Japan crumbling into the sea.

All this does, of course, sound very alarming, but what actually lies behind it? Will some or all of it come to pass, or will it, like the first millennium prophecies, come to nothing? Moreover, what does it all have to do with the New Age?

There are two ways of viewing such predictions. It is wise to be wary of those who make them, and to remember that, as at the time of the first millennium, they may be seeking to control others. We have seen charismatic figures jumping on the band-wagon, creating a following, and feathering their own nests. Many so-called New Age leaders have told their followers that evil still has a chance, and that if they do not do this or that thing, they, and/or the world, will perish. Anyone who uses these blackmail tactics is certainly not an advanced soul, for, as we have seen, the law of free will is immutable, and we should not be tempted to hand ours over, however persuasive the speaker.

On the other hand, the predictions themselves could serve us productively. Inasmuch as it concentrates the mind wonderfully, the prospect of imminent death is an excellent focus for life, so let us consider the worst possible physical scenario: let us for a moment assume that our planet really is about to convulse, with loss of life on a mammoth scale. Let us even envisage ourselves as being among those who are to die, and let us briefly examine that process in the light of what we know.

Our common sense should tell us that if these things are destined to come to pass, we cannot prevent them, and that it would be futile to follow the example of those who are feverishly creating bunkers, which they are filling with supplies of water and tinned food, in order to "survive" the upheavals. They are alarmists, and they are emanating fear, which as we know, must be eradicated for the times ahead.

We know that we are not our bodies, which are mere vehicles for our indestructible souls, and that when we discard our current vehicles we shall, without a shadow of doubt, move on to different experiences. If these are to be acquired on a planet other than Earth, then so be it. Whatever may lie ahead, we know that for us it will be no more than the latest in a long series of transitions, and that we, as our true selves, shall survive it.

One of Cayce's intriguing statements is that buried beneath the Sphinx in Egypt are the secrets of the lost civilisation of Atlantis. He also asserted that the Sphinx contains information regarding the destruction of the world before the forthcoming millennium. Cayce made thousands of projections for the future, including the coming of the "fifth root race." This terminology originated in the East, and we can loosely link it with the seven rays and the seven chakras. As we saw earlier in this book, humanity is at present fluctuating between the third and fourth rays. The pivotal fourth energy is currently upon us, epitomised by the Christ Consciousness: the Heart centre, the bridge between the lower and higher worlds, the golden Heart of Love. The fifth will take us beyond that level, to the level of the Flame. As we saw in the last chapter, it is only through unconditional Love that we can move into the higher spheres, and moving to these higher vibrations does require a kind of death, for it involves the fading of the personality state, uniting the little mind with the highest mind, and the integration of the ego, or "little I," into the higher Ego,"I" of God.

There has in recent years been a definite shift in human consciousness: would you, for example, say that you are the same as you were ten, or even five, years ago? This boundless movement of soul force must have its effect on the whole. It has been said that the movement of a butterfly's wings in South America can trigger a change of climate in London. The movement of consciousness is as effective on other levels.

Swedenborg (1688-1772), the Swedish scientist-turned-mystic, stated that the human race is not from one Earth only, but from countless Earths. He backed these statements with his personal testimony of psychic visitations, in the etheric state, to a number of planets within our solar system. He went on to say that "the entire heaven resembles one man", which echoes the "as above, so below" concept. Paracelsus (1493-1541), the Swiss philosopher, had previously stated that "Heaven is man, and man is Heaven." In more modern terms: we are all the microcosm of the macrocosm.

Perhaps it was Swedenborg who initiated the visions and experiences, linked to other physical worlds, that are currently becoming almost commonplace. Certainly over the past ten to fifteen years there has been a plethora of reports of sightings of extra-terrestrials, and of abductions, and there are some who believe that certain of our planet's current inhabitants are in fact aliens!

It is becoming impossible to distinguish fact from fiction, but if we are able to believe that everything echoes everything else, we can perhaps begin to make some sense of it all. A channelled message clearly stated that the fight between good and evil on this planet had come to an end during World War II. It also clearly stated that from that point onwards, the survival of the Light Force was assured, as was its prosperity. This decision was taken by the consensus group consciousness of the world. In other words, the world en masse wanted, either consciously or unconsciously, to move into the Light.

Alice Bailey equated the momentous breakthrough from darkness to Light with the splitting of the atom, which involved breaking through a structure that had previously been classified as impenetrable. This is mirrored on the inner level, where we break through and are altering the structure of our own cells, once believed to be immutable. The splitting of the atom released energy on a scale hitherto unknown on this planet. On the deepest of levels, humanity as a whole , utterly sick of the countless centuries of pain and violence, realised that it had had enough, and so the group soul of the world gave an emphatic "No", and "when the sun moved northward in the year 1942, the Great White Lodge knew the battle had been won".

It is no coincidence that around the time of this major release of atomic energy, work had also begun in the area of genetics, and so the very concept of changing man was started on the physical levels, as above so below again. No one can doubt that the souls born after that time were of a different "rain": a different quality. This gave rise to the "baby boomers" who became the flower children of the sixties, and are now at an age when they have considerable influence in the world. What science is endeavouring to achieve on a physical level, they are achieving on an inner one.

Let us look at the energetic aspect of this stupendous shift. Through thousands, maybe millions, of years, humanity has gone around and around on the karmic wheel. Civilisations have come and gone, and mankind has slowly transmuted from base cave-dweller to creative thinker to compassionate human being. The energy has risen from the first ray note - the base note - to the third and fourth ray notes. The Heart-light, the bridge, is the manifestation of the Light Force in the human condition: we understand this as unconditional Love. When we open to that bridging ray, we literally let in the Divine forces, which rush through our being like a lightning-flash, sweeping clear all aspects of self: the higher energies coming down into the lower ones.

In this century we have seen the founding and growth of psychology. After the war the work intensified, to such an extent that we now take for granted concepts of the human condition that were previously undreamt. Humanity is clearing its mental and emotional baggage, an activity that creates a clearer vibration from the inner Light source. This in its turn opens the way for even more clearance, and so on until finally the Light penetrates from the highest vibration to the lowest, which is the dense physical body. When the intensity of the Universal Source Light hits the physical state, it creates a disturbance on a cellular level. By aligning your whole being to the Light forces, you are shifting the very foundation of the physical body. All your atoms and cells are dissolved by the Light, and a breakdown in your very physical existence occurs.

When the cells are wiped clean, we are able to remould our whole being. When the Light initially hits the cells, it activates all past experiences held within them. As well as the obvious genetic history, it brings to the surface all past life experiences, and this is creating a very strong knowing within some people that they originated on other worlds. Many souls remember coming into incarnation on planet Earth during Atlantian times, or even earlier. Some people feel that within their genetic structures were implanted seed thoughts and memories, which when activated with full conscious memory of the last fall, i.e. the end of the civilisation of Atlantis, will help and heal the world. The Atlantians made many mistakes, but they possessed great knowledge of our world, and of others that we are only now acknowledging. It is no coincidence that there are so many Atlantians in incarnation today. They have knowledge, particularly of the astral worlds, that is invaluable in helping to clear the dark energies and fear that are currently registering on both an individual and a global level.

The clearing of fear is today's most important work. All negative reactions stem from fear, and if we are to be part of a brother-sister-hood of souls it must be obliterated. Fear in its various guises will surface in our conscious minds - but we must not fight it. We must embrace it, and dissolve it in the Love within our hearts.

Another reaction to the Light connection is a physical one. When the Light Force hits the cells, they initially react as though it were a foreign body, and treat it as an illness, which means that the immune system is affected. In a relatively short space of time, though, most people's bodies should adjust, for our vehicles are the most adaptable of instruments.

That we are changing immeasurably is not in doubt, though

what this means for humanity we can still only guess. Amongst those who are becoming aware, there is currently a general feeling of weightlessness, of lightness of being. Our frontiers on all levels have moved. Our range is becoming limitless, enabling us finally to perceive that there are endless possibilities.

Some prophets have said that there will be a new Messiah, but the New Age will be the age of Aquarius - which represents humankind itself. We therefore become our own gods. In order to make this connection we have to understand ourselves, and this brings us to the necessity for awareness and psychic unfoldment, the necessity for complete integration of energies: the knowing state. There will, of course, always be teachers, but the old Piscean Age need for Messiahs is coming to an end. If we did but realise it, we are all masters, all living gods.

Many are trying to actualise inspiration. But those who have only a glimpse of the transcendental way, seek to validate their experiences. What we are dealing with is an echo of the divine consciousness that manifests itself as love within the human condition. How can we possibly seek to validate love? Perhaps it is here that religions got it wrong. The initial spark of God made manifest by Christ, by Buddah by Mohammed and other deities, served to enlighten, but most who followed behind were not fully conscious and realised in love. Having therefore only the image of realisation, they tried to explain it by creating structures, through closed dogma. All religions at their heart and essence, have the light force within. People at this time of great movement and change are still having the same problem. People suspect something wonderful is happening, they find themselves trying to physically actualise the energy to prove psychic realities in matter. Unfortunately if we seek this kind of proof we are walking on very difficult ground. Illusion land remember is the most difficult stage from which to awaken. In illusions we can find solace, but we can unfortunately fool ourselves. The Atlantians once before deluded themselves, we must seek to break this pattern, and this can only be achieved through our individual alignment. In the New age therefore there can be no new religion, for the truth is within. We must now learn to listen to our own "internal guru!"

We know that over countless thousands of years, the human vibration has been gradually rising. It now resonates to a higher frequency, and the critical mass of energy has spilled over into a different note. This has been described to us as a golden ray on the inner planes, and as we join with these golden forces, the guides and teachers from those planes, we can hear their teachings. We then begin to vibrate at the same rate, therefore in effect becoming part of them.

Through this synthesis of energies we become part of what is generally referred to as the White Brotherhood, at which point we have information and access to energies previously unknown or forgotten. These are the early days of our transition, and it is impossible accurately to project exactly what this means for the future, but in any case as one blends with this golden ray, one becomes very much less attached to the physical worlds. Having caught a glimpse of the transcendental experience that goes beyond time, one recognises that what is happening to our world will unfold in its own way. It will be a joy to be a part of it, but one becomes less attached to the outcome.

The golden energy creates a grid that is raining energy on to the consciousness of our planet, an energy that is helping to raise the consciousness even further. This means, of course, that another "rain" of souls is incarnating: the babies of today are made of very different stuff from their parents. The first soul of this new vibration came into incarnation approximately twenty years ago. The energy accelerated around twelve years ago, and these days not all, but probably the majority, of babies are of this new race. If you look, you can see it in their eyes. This raining of souls is produced in the same way as physical rain. Each soul is drawn upwards to the higher spheres, has a sojourn in the heavens, and then, when the magnetic force is right, a group of similar souls is drawn back into incarnation.

At the same time, this almighty shift is allowing the end of karma, the law of cause and effect. Each new life has given us opportunities to balance and play out the experiences of the past. As the Light Force hits the cells, it reawakens memories of these lives, not because there is anything left to do, or to repay, but simply because, as in the making of cheese, substances are rising in order to be seen and drawn off. Karma is evaporating rapidly. When this happens to an individual, it is in effect giving them a clean page on which to write their own lives. A clear and perfect Light exists, and the endless possibilities begin.

Following the macrocosm-microcosm principle, these immense changes on the inner levels indicate that there will indeed be some planetary movement. Each one must judge for themselves what this means. Because the Earth is also a consciousness, she is going through the same procedure. She, too, is raising her frequency beyond that of karma, which means that shortly it simply will not be possible for those who still need karmic experiences to remain on this planet. Putting it simply, their magnetic energy will reject existence on a planet no longer of its own vibration, and there will be a mass exodus of souls.

In order for us to have our many and varied karmic experiences, it has been essential for us to live in linear time, but now, as we move beyond that stage, even time is becoming unstructured. Beyond the fourth ray, time becomes irrelevant, and will eventually become non-existent. As these breakthroughs occur, our energies will reach out beyond the stars, and communication with other worlds will become available. We shall have literally expanded our range, which will then extend far beyond our globe.

These concepts must be judged with reason and balance. We can already begin to attune to other stars, which we may find useful for healing and other purposes. Some people are even linking with energies from other planets, but the same rule applies to this as to any other form of channelling: judge for yourself the accuracy of the information. Just because someone identifies their contact as an extra-terrestrial being, that does not validate either the message or the being. It is so easy to fall prey to the "wow" factor. Evaluate for yourself any messages received, and draw your own conclusions. This whole area is merely another part of the multi-faceted energy connections that are becoming available to us within the cosmos.

This mass shift in awareness is actually not new. Every mystical journey ever undertaken by an individual has brought to him or her the experiences that are now becoming more common. In bygone times such experiences would, of necessity, have been kept secret (the word "occult" means hidden, or secret). When one considers that the content of this book is even now not generally understood, and would in some quarters even be ridiculed, one can imagine the quite literal danger of speaking about such things in the past. The difference now is that the raising of consciousness is happening to many, many souls, and what was once knowledge for the select few is there for all.

Be extremely wary of involvement with any group or teacher whose teachings are kept secret, especially if you have to pay to receive "initiation". True initiation can not be bought. It is established through the process of your own magnetic force allowing your consciousness to rise beyond the normal states. In the past, certain information was kept from the masses, on the grounds that it was potentially detrimental to them and possibly there was some sense in that, but we as a race have now spiritually come of age. Some people may not be quite mature enough to take on this responsibility, but, like young adults, they will learn on their feet, and no-one has the right to hold them back. For anyone that truly wants it, all knowledge is now available.

Under the general title of "Ascension", there are many stories currently circulating, about spaceships coming to rescue us from our crumbling planet. Some people purport to be "in the know", and will tell you where to be, and what to do. While I do not rule out any possibility, and would personally love to take a ride in a spaceship, I feel that these stories distract us from the real meaning of Ascension, which, in my opinion, refers to the ascending consciousness of the human race.

In my experience as a teacher over the past ten years, I have seen a veritable explosion of interest in spiritual matters, and have watched the growth of individuals speeding up at unbelievable rates. This spirit of enquiry is to be found in all walks of life, in all races and all creeds, and the rate of absorption of spiritual truths is truly breathtaking. What in the past took lifetimes to achieve is now being achieved within years, sometimes months, and some people feel that they are experiencing more than one lifetime in one body. The speed of change within myself, my students and everyone around me, has often left me breathless. As everything mirrors everything else, it would be logical to assume that ascension on the physical planes is also taking place. Many people, for instance, get a strong feeling that the world itself is moving, and a possible literal physical translation could be a "pick up" from a spaceship. However never lose sight of the greater aspect of these changes.

Having come across the bridge of the Heart, we are in a new state: we have a new perception of reality. Our aspirations have altered, and everything about us is more balanced. The view from the other side of the bridge is also breathtaking. The mists are clearing, and there begin to be revealed to us the greatest imaginable possibilities. We begin to see that there really are no limits. The experience could be likened to that of a chrysalis breaking out of its dark cocoon: we emerge like butterflies, our wings ready to carry us to untold places, to encounter untold experiences, and to recognise the unlimited colours of the kaleidoscopic energies that abound in the cosmos.

The age of Aquarius is about humankind. It is humankind coming into the group soul state. On its highest vibration, it is about the brother-sister-hood of man, which means that we must abandon all our selfish and separatist tendencies. Long have we yearned for peace on Earth, and many people have assumed that it could in some way be legislated for, but there are no politicians, no priests, no gurus, however genuine or powerful, that will bring it about. Peace on Earth is obtained within the heart of each and every Earth subject, for it is within our hearts that the battles must be fought.

When one person creates a good space around them, getting their own vicinity balanced through right actions and right thoughts, they create a clear resonance that vibrates out into the world. It affects· everything it touches. You can fight evil from your own living-room if you fight it in your heart. As everyone finds this true inner peace, the energy of the whole planet changes, and this is already taking place. As I travel around, giving lectures and workshops, I have sometimes been asked: Where is the safest place to be? My answer is always the same: Where you are.

So how do we begin to live in this new world? As we draw our vibrations up into - and beyond - the Heart note, we begin to find time moving at a different pace, and if there were only one piece of advice to be given to all of us who are experiencing the momentous changes, it would be this: LIVE IN THE MOMENT.

Too much time has been wasted on chewing over what has gone before, and worrying about what might happen in the future. If we get one moment flowing, we start to emanate a flowing, vibrant, life-force energy, that will help to heal the world. In the words of an old Sanskrit motto: "Look well on this day, for it is life.....For yesterday is but a dream, and tomorrow is only a vision, but today well-lived makes every yesterday a dream of happiness, and every tomorrow a vision of hope".

The true reason for psychic unfoldment is not to find the future, other than by right living in any moment. The New Age is not about the guru you have found, nor about the planetary changes, no matter how fantastic. It is not about creating a new religion, and it is not about spaceships. The true significance of the transition lies in Love. As we saw in the introduction to this book, it is unconditional Love that transforms. It is unconditional

Love that realises our immortality, and it is unconditional Love that will propel us forward into what will doubtless be the greatest journey of our lives. In this there is no pain, there is no torment; there is always truth, and one is forever free.

The ironic thing is that as we draw into the group soul unit, it has never been more important to know, and to think for, ourselves, for one can only cross the bridge in a state of independence. It must be your decision, born only of your own inner knowing. This is one step that you have to take for and by yourself. When you have taken it, you will understand unity of a kind undreamt of: you will know the completeness of the eternal Flame of life, and in that moment you will realise: WE ARE NOT ALONE.

EXERCISE

Energy follows thought, and so, if it is your wish, it is not too difficult to make contact with energies beyond our dimensions. Like attracts like, however, and so people who are still resonating with what have until now been considered normal vibrations, are unlikely to be able to make extra-terrestrial contact. This means that anything they link with is probably a lower astral entity, and, as we saw earlier, this is very difficult to ascertain. If you desire to make extra-dimensional contact, it is suggested that you first ask yourself why you feel the need to communicate with these "possible" higher forces. It is not incorrect to be curious, but please be vigilant and cautious. If you are on a true journey of enlightenment, you will know that all you need is at hand.

Whatever energy you wish to communicate with, start by being as balanced and as clear within yourself as you can be. Focus strongly towards the desired energy. You can make contact by means of thought, or even of sound. Send your thought to the desired contact, and listen. When you hear a note, sound it sharply a few times. Then listen, as always, with an open heart and mind, or if you are channelling, begin speaking. Ever affirm that you only wish contact with the highest, most benevolent energy.

These kinds of exercise are rather like looking through a kaleidoscope, which has entertained many a child. We are all part of this multi-coloured universe, and however vast and brilliant its colours, aligning with this coming age means recognising that all beings, in this world and in others, are part of the whole, whatever their colour, gender or state. Therefore it is with yourself and your own colour that you must be most concerned. Enjoy your contact with other dimensions, worlds and beings. Wonder at their diversity, and at the further possibilities within each of us.

When you finish your exercises, consciously and purposefully close in whatever is the most appropriate way for you. Then consciously draw into your daily life the best of the contact you have just made. Remember that the most wondrous energy in the universe is ever at hand.

KNOW THYSELF.

Books for Reference.
A Learning Experience, by Mary Bailey 1990
Millennium Prophecies, by A.T. Mann 1992
Story of the Soul, by Edgar Cayce 1989
Fingerprints of the Gods, by Graham Hancock 1995
Keeper of Genesis, by Robert Bauval and Graham Hancock 1996.
Wind of Change, channelled by Julie Soskin 1990.
Transformation, chanelled by Julie Soskin 1995.

Chapter 18
_____

INSIGHT AND
INTUITION -
THE WAY AHEAD

As more and more of the population awaken they will experience and acknowledge psychic, or unseen energies. But as we have seen, there are many fantasies and illusions in psychic work. As an example, when people first take up the idea of past lives, we suddenly find there are innumerous Napoleons, High Priests and Priestesses and I have known several Mary Magdalenes! Another illusion that comes later is that the power and surge of energy shifting us, make people believe they are the chosen ones, sent here by god, or by some impressive being from outer space to save the world! Saving the world becomes a great task and I have seen a few collapse with the strain! The idea that we are masters is possibly correct but this is common to all. It is Sai Baba who says that the only difference between him and us is that he knows he is god and as yet, we don't. This is a knowing state, and the awakening is about knowing that we are all units of divine consciousness.

Keep looking, observe. We now know through quantum physics that the very process of observation has an effect on the object being observed. Scientists know through what is called "the uncertainty principle," that we are signalling the end to the theory of a scientific model of the universe that would be completely deterministic. This has profound implications on the way we view the world. When you begin to work with energy you understand that even looking at someone affects them. Energy can not interact with something without affecting it energetically. People often think it is all right to have thoughts as long as they do not voice them, but thoughts are energies too. Everything is an energy and everything has some effect. A tiny ripple on a pond can, and does change the world.

This book has touched upon the tip of the iceberg, so to speak, of a subject of vast dimensions. Psychic unfoldment is a rich endeavour, and one that brings many surprises, but its true value lies in the discovery of your intuition. Part of the journey is about exploration and discovery. It is a great adventure, and one that can only be undertaken through your own efforts - and, more importantly, your mistakes. As any parent knows, no amount of good advice can prevent children from falling over from time to time. It is only when they do so that they really learn. In like fashion, it is your mistakes that will most effectively teach you discernment and observation, so acknowledge the value of getting things wrong; learn from your errors, and walk on.

When glamour no longer holds sway, your intuition will begin to make its presence felt. This generally starts with flashes of insight, which are very different from psychic predictions. As we have seen, true intuition is best described as knowing. It is not feeling, and it is certainly not thinking. Intuition is the higher power of the higher mind. It is the power of pure reason, and it involves intelligence, but not the intellect. Sometimes, in extreme crisis or shock, the doorway to the higher mind bursts open, enabling someone to know what to do. Intuition is knowing what to do all the time. When you are fully integrated you will know constant intuition, but until then you will have to make do with these intermittent flashes.

Intuition is the opposite of illusion, which can trap us on the mental planes. It is the soul-infused personality, created by the merging of the mind of the individual with the Monad, which is the mind of God. You may first experience this integration in meditation, when, if you have questions, they will be answered.

In time, by sending your question with the little mind, and training the higher mind to open to receive the response, you will receive your answers immediately. If your soul-infused mind is not open, the higher mind will wait for the earliest possible opportunity to feed the answer into your conscious awareness: as we have seen, this generally occurs when the body and/or the little mind are occupied with some simple task. When you receive the true, "knowing" answer, you will often wonder why it had not occurred to you before, so simple will it be. True intuition has little to do with the lower forms of psychism, but if viewed as a whole, psychic perception can centre the mind in a complementary fashion.

Experiment by sending up a question on a subject upon which you require illumination. Send it up to the highest good, and let this ascending transmission be tightly focussed (this exercise can be done last thing at night just before you go to sleep). Then let go of it, and open yourself to receive, with a clear, uncluttered mind, the descent of the answer. At first you may find that all sorts of chattering enters your head. Do not fight it, but gently and firmly discipline your mind to be free. With practice, you will receive inspiration. Be honest with yourself, and know the answer. If you continuously find this difficult (it is always hardest if the question has an emotional content), send up your question at night, and in the morning you will know what to do. Struggling makes things difficult: it is not until we let go that we can obtain peace, not only from a knowing answer, but from our open channel to the Light Forces.

In the early stages of development, when the initial flashes of insight occur, you will experience increased mental activity, and this may at first be confusing. It may cause you to be over-enthusiastic about new ideas, new ways of living, and new dreams for the progress of humanity. You may take up with one religion or cult after another. There may even be times when you feel that you are losing your mind, but after a while you will regain your equilibrium, though not before having some of your illusions shattered. Seek true ideas, not ideals. Ideals can rarely be lived, and are often born out of illusion rather than insight. The empty communes of the 1960's bear witness to this. If your ideas cannot be put into practice, abandon them. Advancement only comes by following the middle way, and in order to walk forward, you must have perfect balance. Seek to be a "happy medium!".

During these early days you will doubtless also experience increased sensitivity, to which you must not pander: being sensitive is not a good reason for hiding away - indeed, you can help others through your sensitivities. There is likely to be an explosion of psychic powers, with all the excitement that these engender, and you may begin to believe that by using your psychic faculties you can somehow save the world single-handed. Remember that your mission is to serve, and that students are only safe to use their psychic faculties when, through their own dedicated commitment to humanity, they are made ready.

Find a teacher whom you respect, but never become too attached, whether he or she is here on the Earth plane or somewhere beyond. Listen intently to the song of your teacher, but ignore the personality of the singer. A teacher should not get involved with a student's "personality baggage", and likewise the pupil should not become involved with the teacher's personal life. If you have a question, ask yourself first, teacher second, and yourself again last. Your version of the answer will always be the most appropriate.

No good teacher will seek to create a following, for a teacher's job is to train students to become teachers also. Never work with one who claims to have all the answers: good teachers know that they are themselves students, and that we are all on the ladder of consciousness, helping those a step behind, and being helped by those a step ahead.

One of the hardest things for teachers to get across to their students is that they must think for themselves, and that they have all the answers within. Teachers are not nurse-maids. They have very little interest in the day-to-day running of their students' lives, and will not concern themselves with it. From the outset, students must be made to realise that they alone are responsible for themselves and their energies. A teacher should guide but not hold, for how can you fly if your wings are clipped?

The methods now being used to instruct Westerners are very different from the ancient methods still used in the East. We are of a different energy, and even Eastern teachers are having to change their methods of instructing members of their own race, the main difference being the abandoning of the traditional master-pupil relationship. For reasons discussed in this book, masters are now allowing their students much more freedom, and encouraging and enabling them to think for themselves. This does not mean that the ancient methods were wrong, simply that the energy has moved on, and that some of the old ways are being updated and broadened. What is right for one age is not necessarily right for another.

It has been observed that the quality of students now coming into this work is much higher than that of their predecessors, and that they do in fact possess more innate knowledge. This is partly because, with very few exceptions, they are old souls, and have done some of the work before. They have also been devotional in one or other of their lives, which means that they are familiar with the insular and supplicatory environments of monasteries and ashrams. Since we never have to repeat a lesson learned, it would be futile for them to repeat this one, and so they must now live and work in the world.

Initially, with the dawning of understanding that there is more to life than the material world, it is easy to become confused, and to start to believe that it is necessary to abandon the body. We must, however, cherish the physical body. We are here for an important reason, and therefore we serve ourselves best by enjoying life. If you really want to do this work, you must love people, so please choose to look for the good in everyone. Generally speaking, if you relate only to the good, you will get the best out of others. See and appreciate the wonder of life and of living. Life on this planet, for all its apparent restrictions, is an incredible experience, and you are incredible also. Love yourself: when attention is given to the soul-self, physical life is more easily handled.

Remember that observation should not entail criticism. Never hide from negativities within yourself or others, but use the knowledge for eradication rather than perpetuation. Most things in life can be dealt with by using common sense. You do not have to manifest the alphabet in the sky in order to learn how to read. Everything taught and learnt must translate into the outer planes of life and living.

When you are working with discarnate entities, please acknowledge that there are just as many who are lower than you in vibration as there are who are higher. The group of soul servers, i.e. the professors and teachers on the higher plains, is a useful contact, but even their transmissions can be faulty. Check it out with your higher mind. Think for yourself.

You may require some confirmation of your progress, and this is very simple to obtain: if something flows, and it works, it is right, so do not seek to alter it. If it is blocked, and is not working, look again. You will observe that when there is flow in life there is also synchronicity, and the old adage of receiving what you need will plainly manifest. Be honest with yourself: "What do I want?" will bring you far closer to the truth than "What should I be doing?". Focus your true desires, and project them in whatever way possible. If they do not manifest shortly afterwards, accept that they are not correct for your growth.

We hear a lot about love. Love is born out of acceptance. This is not a sign of weakness, indeed it often requires major strength to implement. Acceptance is balance, and as a student of psychic unfoldment, the one thing you need more than any other is balance. Right thinking, and the middle way, are what you must seek. Be excited by your growth, and be enthusiastic about development, for this training goes far beyond psychic gifts. It is a training for life.

Intuition is Light, which manifests itself as Love, and when in contact with it you will observe everything with love. This is not the wishful thinking of the idealist, it is the reality of being. All your needs will be met because you will know what to do and how to be at any moment, in the moment. In opening the doors of the soul we gain insights and through connection with your intuition you will find wisdom, union with the Divine, and endless possibilities.......

Good luck and Bon Voyage.